ONE WEEK LOAN

Competitive Strategies

Bocconi on Management Series

Series Editor: **Robert Grant**, Eni Professor of Strategic Management, Department of Management, Università Commerciale Luigi Bocconi, Italy.

The *Bocconi on Management* series addresses a broad range of contemporary and cutting-edge issues relating to the management of organizations and the environment in which they operate. Consistent with Bocconi University's ongoing mission to link good science with practical usefulness, the series is characterized by its integration of relevance, accessibility and rigor. It showcases the work of scholars from all over the world who have produced contributions to the advancement of knowledge building on theoretical, disciplinary, cultural or methodological traditions with the potential to improve management practice.

The series is edited by the Center for Research in Organization and Management (CROMA) at Bocconi University, and is published through an agreement between Palgrave Macmillan and Bocconi University Press, an imprint of Egea.

For information about submissions of book proposals or the series in general, please contact Maurizio Zollo at maurizio.zollo@unibocconi.it or Robert Grant at grant@unibocconi.it.

Titles include:

Massimo Amato, Luigi Doria and Luca Fantacci (*editors*)
MONEY AND CALCULATION
Economic and Sociological Perspectives

Vittorio Coda
ENTREPRENEURIAL VALUES AND STRATEGIC MANAGEMENT
Essays in Management Theory

Enrico Valdani and Alessandro Arbore
COMPETITIVE STRATEGIES
Managing the Present, Imagining the Future

Steve Waddell
GLOBAL ACTION NETWORKS
Creating Our Future Together

Bocconi on Management Series
Series Standing Order ISBN 978-0-230-27766-3

You can receive future title in this series as they are published by placing a standing order. Please contact your bookseller or, in case of difficulty, write to us at the address below with your name and address, the title of the series and the ISBN quoted above.

Customer Services Department, Macmillan Distribution Ltd, Houndmills, Basingstoke, Hampshire RG21 6XS, England.

Competitive Strategies

Managing the Present, Imagining the Future

Enrico Valdani

and

Alessandro Arbore

First published 2013 by
PALGRAVE MACMILLAN

Palgrave Macmillan in the UK is an imprint of Macmillan Publishers Limited, registered in England, company number 785998, of Houndmills, Basingstoke, Hampshire RG21 6XS.

Palgrave Macmillan in the US is a division of St Martin's Press LLC, 175 Fifth Avenue, New York, NY 10010.

Palgrave Macmillan is the global academic imprint of the above companies and has companies and representatives throughout the world.

Palgrave® and Macmillan® are registered trademarks in the United States, the United Kingdom, Europe and other countries

ISBN: 978–0–230–30164–1

This book is printed on paper suitable for recycling and made from fully managed and sustained forest sources. Logging, pulping and manufacturing processes are expected to conform to the environmental regulations of the country of origin.

A catalogue record for this book is available from the British Library.

Library of Congress Cataloging-in-Publication Data

Valdani, Enrico.
    Competitive strategies: managing the present, imagining the future.
        Enrico Valdani and Alessandro Arbore.
            pages cm
    Includes bibliographical references and index.
    ISBN 978–0–230–30164–1 (hardback)
        1. Competition. 2. Strategic planning. I. Arbore, Alessandro,
    1972– II. Title.

HD41.V27 2012
658.4'012 — dc23   2011047532

10 9 8 7 6 5 4 3 2 1
22 21 20 19 18 17 16 15 14 13

Printed and bound in Great Britain by
CPI Antony Rowe, Chippenham and Eastbourne

To our families,
the gift we value the most and to whom,
paradoxically, we dedicate the least amount of time.

To the servant leader
*Sometimes, the people we meet, the experiences and the
events we have lived through would seem to confirm the
idea that bad money drives out the good. Do not
be fooled; honesty, morality, ethics, faith and
commitment always prevail and are the only
masters of a servant leader's life.*

He who knows how to place himself at the
service of others with humility, honesty and
a great deal of passion.

Contents

List of Figures

List of Tables

Preface

The greatest paradox that firms face in developing their marketing strategies is to reconcile, on the one hand, the consistency and focus of behaviors and, on the other, the autonomous development of original thoughts and actions.

A paradox is an assertion with an apparent contradiction between two mutually exclusive propositions. When a paradox is articulated, no one expects to have to choose between the two propositions expressed, as happens when faced with a dilemma. A paradox doesn't invite us to choose one option and abandon the other. A paradox invites us to accept both apparently irreconcilable propositions.

This idea is perhaps the true inspiration of a firm's strategic thinking and the unorthodox source of choices of behavior in the market. Predominating in this decision-making context is the management intuition and tacit knowledge of the firm and of the market, of the competition and customers: the use of paradoxes may represent an effective metaphor to stimulate strategic speculation. In an era in which a global perspective prevails in interpreting economic and political events, the most widespread paradox is without doubt that which requires "thinking globally and acting locally." This paradox is an effective metaphor to stimulate firms in defining how they combine and integrate their international activities while operating in compliance with the specific local conditions. A further paradox, which is probably the most important one today, requires "development without development": it is about growing in a market context with no growth.

"Managing the present and imagining the future" is the third paradox of the proactive firm and the subject of our book. Planning the future is a process associated with the creativity of strategic thinking, the capacity to break with conventions and to alter the status quo in order to pursue new games of movement. Management of the firm's "present" by contrast requires the resolution of problems relating to routine and daily life.

Living this paradox, in the hypercompetitive markets in which most firms operate, is no longer an option. Each firm must learn to face its present and, at the same time, allow strategic speculation to design its future, exploring and seeking new sources of advantages and new ways to pursue its mission. Management of daily life and breaking the routine: two apparently conflicting objectives. Opposites are often an illusion, or perhaps, as the ancients used to say, reality finds in human intellect the coincidence of opposites, *coincidentia oppositorum*.

The resolution of a paradox activates emotional tensions in a firm, which is comparable to the movements of a pendulum. The pendulum oscillates between two extremes but tends to stabilize in the center, a center where a unifying principle can emerge that summarizes and reconciles complex and chaotic opposites. The purpose of the formulation of a paradox, therefore, is not to rescind the contradictions but to emphasize them in order to direct and capitalize on those intellectual tensions that the very paradox engenders and channels. These tensions are the stimulus to develop new knowledge. When a paradox is subjected to the discussions of a working group, the process that is triggered in order to reach a common decision quickly elevates the tension of the contraposition of ideas. Such an emotive condition constitutes the best basis to exhort our creativity to seek the solution that brings together the opposites produced by the paradox. The greater the tension and emotional involvement that it nurtures, the greater the creativity and diffusion of the strategic conversation that the firm's human resources will engage in. This is how a paradox increases the generative and proactive potential of new entrepreneurial visions. What is more, the emotional tension neutralizes any reactionary attempts aimed at containing new revolutionary ideas, facilitating the breakthrough not only of strategic thinking but also of operating behavior.

This book was also written with due respect to this paradox: advocating the breaking of orthodoxies, yet promoting deterministic management models. It recalls not only that competitive confrontation is won with the creative power of ideas, but also that to develop and achieve results from each idea requires the disciplined deployment of actions, skills, and resources. These are the principles on which the competitive maneuvers that will be illustrated are structured.

The dynamic succession of the games of movement, imitation, and position is anchored to the concept of continuous evolution and the constant changing of orthodox and unorthodox maneuvers deployable by the firm in its competitive theater. Many marketing strategies are effective in some contexts, but can be the cause of failure in others. The true capability of a firm, therefore, is not attributable to the formulation of strategies but to its understanding of the context in which they can be applied and developed with success.

Victory may only be singular, but the concrete maneuvers must be manifold, and both orthodox and unorthodox. In the same way that musical notes can be arranged and rearranged in infinite variations and melodies, or that colors can be combined to give origin to a multitude of chromatisms, all strategic configurations are generated by the interaction of classic and iconoclastic maneuvers. The variety is such that the challenge for the firm is in knowing how to select the most effective changes offered by these two opposites. Unorthodox and orthodox maneuvers are thus generated and coevolve in an endless cycle. Our book proposes to guide the firm in this challenge, in this dynamic and paradoxical circle in which the future designed today must be the present to be managed and abandoned tomorrow.

Acknowledgments

At the end of our editorial journey, we would like to express our sincere gratitude and appreciation to the following, who greatly helped us in improving this book: Jill Connelly of Palgrave Macmillan and Vidhya Jayaprakash and her team at Newgen KnowledgeWorks, for their valuable contribution in editing our English writing; Tania Pozzi (jazid69@yahoo.it), for the great picture she shot for our cover; the alumni of our Executive Master in Marketing and Sales (EMMS) program, for all the insights, incidents, and experiences we shared together; all the practitioners we met during the Strategic Marketing Executive Program at Sda Bocconi, which has been a tremendous lab to test and refine our model; and all the colleagues at Bocconi University, for the precious feedback we always received.

1
The Revolution of the Competitive Games

1.1 Change and circularity of events

The "revolution" in the title of this chapter is meant in the astronomical sense, that is, the movement of a body (a competitive arena, in our case) which makes an elliptical orbit, ending its journey where it began. Revolution is also intended in the etymological sense, with the prefix "re" denoting an orientation toward a new state, along with a sense of abrupt change, severing all ties with the past.

The circularity of our destiny is a theme taken up by many throughout the ages, long before and far better than we do here: from the palingenesis of the Stoics to Giambattista Vico's historical recurrence, from Quesnay to Leontief's economic flow, from James Joyce to Don Fabrizio in *The Leopard*. If today's leaders want to be tomorrow's leaders, they have to make everything change. If today's followers want to become tomorrow's leaders, they have to make everything change too.

Proactive change is the categorical imperative of the *circular view* of competitive confrontation that we propose in this book. To be effective, this change can not be based on *contraposition* of forces, but on *the novelty of its form. This is a key message our book aims to formalize*: a strategy of continuously overturning orthodoxies, in light of the following:

- Today's iconoclasm will in turn become tomorrow's orthodoxy in an *endless competitive cycle.*
- Every revolution brings with it *new risks as well as new opportunities*: we have to know when the time is right to start a revolution, or to join someone else's, or to keep the peace.

- We have to know how to alternate orthodox and unorthodox maneuvers and include both in a *portfolio of strategic games* balancing risks and opportunities.
- Ultimately, the firm has to know how to govern the *different seasons* of its competitive cycle by using *different strategic approaches and competencies*.

1.2   Paradigms for the proactive firm

The success stories we tell in the pages that follow are accounts of organizations that have pursued proactive behavior with discipline and determination, focusing on reinventing initiatives, creating new markets, and redefining their destinies. The evidence we offer attests to the fact that firms incapable of anticipating and driving change have seen their market shares shrink dramatically. Such failures, we must remember, are as commonplace in exceptionally expanding sectors as in declining ones; a case in point is the emblematic example of the old IBM in personal computers.

The inability to face change is a classic characteristic of those organizations that are hostages of their histories, their myths, and their past triumphs. Today a firm's survival is guaranteed by its ability to drive the market and its entropy with an always dynamic, holistic approach. This is typical of a flexible, integrated, agile, and innovative firm – in other words, a special firm with unique traits that lives up to the definition of *proactive* (Valdani, 2000).

Proactive is a word we chose with an eye to etymology. The suffix *pro,* originally deriving from Sanskrit, in Greek means not only to go beyond, to advance, but also to make forecasts. The word *active* comes instead from the Latin *actus* as the past participle of the verb *agere,* meaning to act, to push ahead, to lead forward, to go beyond. So in describing a firm, the adjective *proactive* refers to the ability to do the following:

- to deal with events and consequences of events that have yet to occur, as did Toyota when it successfully launched the Prius as far back as 1997, when eco-friendly issues were still far in the future;
- to plan for the future while governing the present, as is done by the most farsighted petroleum companies that are working to reinvest today's profits from black gold to create and quickly develop new competencies in new markets;
- to define its destiny so as to redefine the destiny of the sector where it does business, as did Starbucks, which we discuss below;

- to discover new solutions by thinking beyond the short-term, beyond tradition, and beyond tradeoffs, as did Gore-Tex with fabrics that are both waterproof and "breathable" at the same time;
- to create value by nurturing entrepreneurial spirit, teamwork, and the discipline of creativity, as does 3M, by continuously launching an amazing number of new products;
- to learn the art of co-evolution, as does Apple, which owes its success to an impressive network of partners and application developers;
- to reinvent itself and its markets, as Google is striving to do by turning the online search sector into an infinite editorial and advertising market.

In the pages that follow, we show how we can identify a proactive firm by means of:

- A *metatheory*, that is a broader, more comprehensive conceptual framework;
- Three *constructs*, that is three fundamental concepts;
- Three *paradigms*, that is three theoretical models specific to the study of firms.

As regards the first point, the idea of the proactive firm is conceptually rooted in *chaos and complexity theory*, because such a firm self-organizes and behaves in ways typical of a *complex proactive system* (Kauffman, 1995; Brown and Eisenhardt, 1998; Sanders, 1999). A similar system adapts to change, overcoming internal turbulence and entropy. From this perspective, complexity theory describes how order and structure appear and grow through a process of adaptation. This process is set in motion when the system learns new information or new knowledge that alters its original state of balance, propelling it into a new state of chaos. In this context, chaos is not something that occurs in an organized world; instead it is the mechanism by which change begins and self-organizes, and in doing so it releases new energy.

The origins of a proactive firm are necessarily grounded in this metatheory. In today's competitive arena, complexity becomes the unpredictable attractor that serves to interconnect the various parts of the system (individuals, teams, departments, and any other organizational unit), driving the system as a whole toward the continual generation of new growth opportunities.

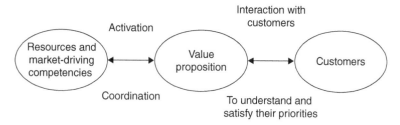

Figure 1.1 The constructs of a proactive firm

As regards the second point, a proactive firm centers on these *three constructs* (Figure 1.1):

1) the customer;
2) the value proposition;
3) the *stock* and *network* of tangible and intangible resources needed in order to offer the customer the best possible value proposition.

The central focus of the first construct defining a proactive firm is the *clientele,* a reflection of the fact that the firm exists solely and exclusively to serve the customer. Surprisingly, pages upon pages in management and economics literature are dedicated to delineating the whys and wherefores of the firm's existence while often neglecting to mention its true purpose: *to serve its customers.* It is the customer who represents the primary source of value generation for the firm, and who is indeed the only true capital asset. This is the reason why our description of a proactive firm begins from the customer's perspective, and emphasizes an ability to listen, to understand, and to predict the customer's priorities expressed in terms of the needs, desires, and benefits she or he seeks.

The second construct involves creating attractive value propositions to transfer to customers. These offerings reflect the firm's competitive ability to integrate the needs of its customers with the resources and competencies it must call into play to generate value solutions for the market.

The third construct highlights the firm's *network* of *resources* and *market driving competencies,* either stock to be tapped internally or accessed externally in the network of suppliers and complementary firms. Through *knowledge leveraging* and *knowledge building,* this stock of resources allows the firm to activate and coordinate processes that serve to generate, offer, and deliver its value propositions to customers.

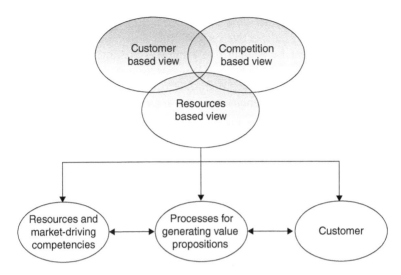

Figure 1.2 Paradigms of the proactive firm

Underpinning these three constructs, in turn, are three conceptual paradigms which we can consider as the theoretical foundations of the proactive firm (Figure 1.2).

The first is the *Customer Based View*.[1] This perspective stresses that the future value of a firm depends on its ability to do the following:

1. to acquire new customers;
2. to grow the profitability of the client portfolio;
3. to inspire customer loyalty by managing customer relationships.

The *Customer Based View* prompts the firm to focus on: 1) how customer choices and preferences can shape the possibilities of capitalizing value; 2) how the value proposition should be designed and offered to enhance customer relationships; and lastly 3) how this value should be shared by buyer and seller.

The second paradigm reflects the *Resource Based View*,[2] which holds that the value generated by the firm is contingent on the specificity, quality and variety of its stock of resources and competencies. The firm's market behavior, in turn, is conditioned by its ability to leverage and build these resources and competencies to give its maneuvers a competitive edge in current markets, or to create and enter new ones.

The *Competition Based View* is the third paradigm that we propose in this book. This perspective suggests that a firm's ability to generate value depends on the competitive game it is playing, which takes the form of three different cycles: the *Movement Game*, the *Imitation Game*, or the *Position Game*. For each one, the firm needs an appropriate stock of resources and competencies to enable it to proactively determine the most effective competitive maneuvers to guarantee market success. In the following sections we explore the theoretical rationale and practical implications of this paradigm.

To summarize, thanks to our model, we can identify the underlying constructs of the proactive firm. What is more, by integrating the three different paradigms, we can also interpret and explain firm behavior in the market from a theoretical perspective.

1.3   The *Competition Based View*: competitive games as the "seasons" of a sector

On 3 December 1994, Sony launched its first PlayStation (PS), a veritable revolution in terms of technology, performance, communication, and positioning – and all this in a sector that for years had been experiencing a dramatic decline. With the advent of the personal computer, in fact, many analysts had pronounced the sector of video game consoles dead, especially those who clearly recalled the sector life cycle graph that was drilled into their heads in business school. Against all odds, Sony took a gamble that paid off by shattering every record: 100 million PlayStations sold by the end of 2005.

Naturally, a triumph of this magnitude could not help but attract the attention of aggressive new enterprises. By Christmas 2001, Sony found itself facing a direct challenge from Microsoft's Xbox. This marked the beginning of what we call the *Imitation Game,* which over time led to a competitive escalation which could have come straight from the pages of the novel *Fight Club.* On 9 July 2007, Sony Corporation issued a press release announcing that it was slashing the PlayStation3's price tag by $100, which was 17% less than the introductory price set in November 2006. At the same time, the company publicized the launch of a model with more memory at the previous price. The same day at a press conference in Tokyo, a Microsoft executive hastened to state that the company would not lower Xbox 360 prices. Nonetheless, on 7 August 2007 the Redmond firm announced a $50 price cut on the US market, to be followed two weeks later by a €50 reduction in Europe (approximately 13%). Similar moves by both companies would replay in October, November, and December. And again in 2008, in 2009, and in 2010.

The strategic evolution in this competitive arena suggests that Sony and Microsoft are now playing what we call the *Position Game*. For PlayStation, the success of the initial version, which upended all the rules of play, is a distant memory. As later generations of consoles came on the scene, Sony reacted to competitor imitation by following the more typical and dangerous rationale of the Position Game. In other words, the company embarked on a path of continuous performance enhancements (the strategic focus of PS2 and PS3 versions) and lower prices to secure market share. Likewise, greater power and lower prices also marked Microsoft's strategy. As a result the two players became trapped in the Position Game, with shrinking or even negative margins.[3]

A reverse strategy was implemented by Nintendo. Unlike its rivals, this company started developing its consoles by following a different rationale. Using our terminology, Nintendo began playing the *Movement Game*, actually "winning the fight without fighting." And as we all know, the Nintendo Wii system, launched in late 2006, rapidly took the leadership position in the sector.

Transitioning from its earlier GameCube to the current Wii (a transition accentuated by totally different product names), the aim of the Kyoto company was to steer clear of the Position Game that Sony and Microsoft were caught up in, a game which initially kept Nintendo on the sidelines (having sold only 20 million GameCubes compared to 120 million PS2s). Rather than adhering to sector orthodoxies in a mad dash to develop unbelievably high-powered and high-priced chips and graphic processors for teenage fans, Nintendo started thinking "outside the box" in terms of the market and market demands. (For example, unlike PS3 and Xbox360, the Wii does *not* have HD resolution.) Following a new approach, the Wii no longer targeted young, expert users with dexterity in their digits to rival a virtuoso organist. Instead, the social and active side of electronic entertainment became the key concept for developing the product and related applications. The games got simpler in some respects, in order to lock in a wider audience (counter-segmentation), but they also made people actually get up and move rather than simply stay in their seats. This kind of entertainment aimed at aggregating rather than isolating, as reiterated by the choice of product name: Wii (we).

Nothing could be farther from the "bits per second" mindset. The new Nintendo positioning expanded to a more mature target as well, encompassing the whole family, parents, and groups of friends.

The unique wireless controller made new social and active gaming applications possible, in keeping with the objectives described above. Finally, by putting the predominance of power and performance into proper perspective, Nintendo realized a cost advantage over its competitors. The Wii's introductory price in 2006 was $250, compared to $599 for the PS3. Today, that translates into market leadership worth 30 billion dollars. More importantly, from a broader viewpoint, this success represents a strategic bridge for all home entertainment businesses.

This case gives us a concrete framework for the three natural states that recur over and over again in every sector: a) the Movement Game, b) the Imitation Game, and c) the Position Game. In every moment of a firm's life it is vitally important for management to be fully aware of these three seasons of competitive confrontation. In fact, behind each lies a distinctive rationale, which calls for *specific offensive and defensive ability.*

A fundamental difference with respect to climactic seasons is their timing. In fact, every firm to some extent plays the part of both follower and instigator of this cycle, which begins whenever a firm uses technological, organizational, marketing, or any other kind of innovation (as long as it has not yet been implemented by the competition) in an effort to avoid direct confrontation with its rivals. Therefore, the innovation cycle is what drives the seasons.

1.4   The innovation cycle: the driver of competitive games

Top performing companies have an ambidextrous aptitude for evolving by alternating phases of continuous improvement interrupted by phases of revolutionary innovation.[4] As a result, every competitive environment oscillates between periods of incremental change punctuated by radical transformations, or *quantum leaps.*

In the framework of the *Competition Based View*, a quantum leap is primarily a discontinuity in the line of reasoning, a break from the past, perhaps regarding management or market, but not necessarily relating to new technical or scientific paradigms. Because it is revolutionary, regardless of its nature, such an event always triggers an evolutionary cycle that takes the form of a circular succession of phases: *generation* of a new logic, *confrontation* with extant logic, *success* of the new logic, *maintenance* and *improvement* of the new (by now consolidated) logic (Figure 1.3).

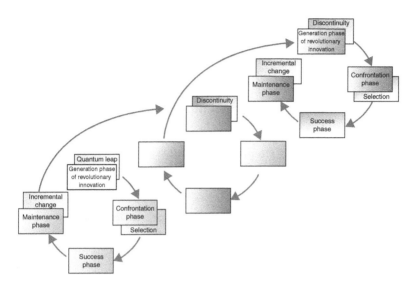

Figure 1.3 Model of the innovation cycle

When the *quantum leap* is technological, for example, the first phase marks that revolutionary moment when new technology is *generated*. The dissemination of this innovation triggers the successive phase of *confrontation* with both consolidated technologies and other emerging innovations. The outcome of this second phase is normally uncertain, and often involves costly conflicts as challengers promote their solutions over those of market leaders. If the end result is positive, the third phase of the innovation cycle coincides with the *success* and consolidation of the new technology, now recognized as a standard by all other firms. The adoption of a new standard is not only an expression of the market's natural selection process, but also reflects the ability of the innovator to compel other firms (be they potential competitors, suppliers of contents or applications, or distributors) to choose its technology as well. Along with the success phase comes general dissemination of the new technology, which emerges as the winning trajectory with respect to the other drivers of scientific progress. The fourth phase of the innovation cycle, instead, consists of a process of *maintenance* and *continuous, incremental improvement* of the innovation in question.

Figure 1.3 outlines the trajectory of the innovation development cycles that materialize through the four-phase sequence described above.

Naturally, the evolutionary speed of these cycles and the succession of quantum leaps vary from sector to sector depending on the technological and competitive specificities. This is referred to as clockspeed (Fine, 1998), and is described further in Section 3.4.

1.5   Innovation cycles and competitive cycles

The paradigm of the Competition Based View, through the model of the innovation cycle illustrated above, explains the three states of confrontation between firms, that is the Movement, Imitation, and Position Games, each with its own unique characteristics and rules of conduct (Figure 1.4).

Generating innovation is how a firm expresses the desire to avoid a direct competitive confrontation with its rivals, and the intention to satisfy new needs or create a new market. This is where the *Movement Game* begins, when a firm succeeds in moving away from the typical sector coordinates to travel in a new "orbit". In fact, we can also think of the sequence of games as a journey along a competitive orbit (Figure 1.5) that eventually takes us back to the Position Game.

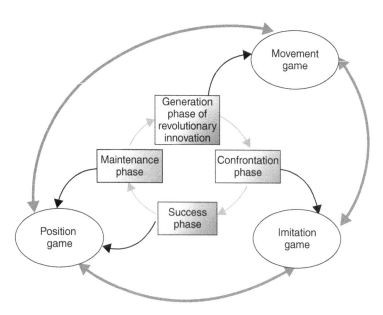

Figure 1.4   Innovation cycle and competitive games

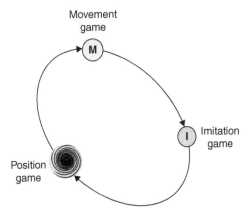

Figure 1.5 The competitive orbit: the sequence of games

How long this journey takes us depends on the magnitude of the innovation in question. At a strategy level, we find two different cases: on one end of the spectrum, *marginal or incremental innovation*, which activates low-impact Movement Games; on the other end *disruptive or radical innovation* which gives rise to a true quantum leap with respect to existing knowledge and orthodoxies, triggering high-impact Movement Games (Figure 1.6).

Low impact movement, as we can see, is nothing more than the outer edge or an extension of the Position Game. In the existing paradigm, these kinds of behaviors are positioned between maintenance and incremental improvement. A more radical break, on the other hand, clearly represents a Movement Game in the strict sense of the word.

One method for distinguishing between these maneuvers is illustrated in Figure 1.7. Referring back to our initial example, by overturning existing orthodoxies PlayStation was playing a high-impact Movement Game, marking the start of new orbital revolution. Other companies followed this same strategy with the Imitation Game, starting with Microsoft. In a few years' time, with their PS3 and Xbox 360 versions, the two rivals found themselves in the midst of a brutal position war, in other words, a direct, head-to-head battle again and again. Summing up, the duration of this *orbital revolution* does not depend solely on the scope of innovation, which determines the distance to travel, but also on other players' action and reaction times. When the succession of competitive games is fast and frequent, for instance, this is a defining trait of a hypercompetitive sector (D'Aveni, 1994).

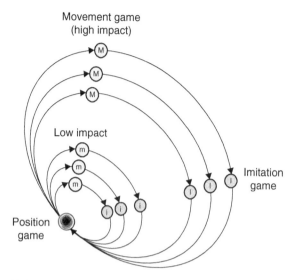

Figure 1.6   High and low impact Movement Games

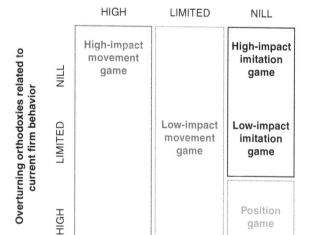

Figure 1.7   Strategic maneuvers in the competitive arena

Whether high or low impact, the Movement Game triggers the subsequent confrontation phase, in terms of both existing behaviors and possible competitor innovations. This marks the start of a new season: *the Imitation Game*. Imitation may initially be sporadic if the innovation in question is not an obvious improvement, driven by strategies that we will explore further on. As success becomes more evident, imitation rapidly infects the entire sector. Every competitor embarks on a more or less arduous journey toward the new orbital position, until the strategic coordinates of the innovator become the new frame of reference, the definitive standard of behavior acknowledged and adopted by all competitors alike.

This transition clearly signals a return to the *Position Game*, which continues until a new company (Nintendo's Wii in our case) makes a move to elude its rivals. In the Position Game, the Euclidian axes of the competitive space (that is the critical success factors) are given and well known. They are the managerial heritage embedded in the history of the sector; they are not a matter of debate. As the rivalry intensifies, maintaining control over this space equates to continually offering more for less, as we saw with the case of videogame consoles.

When this state is protracted over time, structural barriers and the profitability of the competitive arena may be part of the reason why. In fact, the combination of big profits and a high concentration of firms tends to fuel reactionary and collusive behaviors. For example, simply consider how long the Position Game lasted in the banking sector with low-level competition. But all things are in constant flux and all barriers inevitably erode over time. Sooner or later firms caught up in the Position Game are subject to the hidden dangers and costs of head-to-head confrontation, or the disruptive entry of an outsider. A new competitive cycle can be set in motion by an incumbent suffering under the profit pressures of the Position Game, or by a newcomer spurred on by new strategic opportunities that often arise from an altered economic, social, regulatory, or technological context.

1.6   The Movement Game

"Give me a place to stand on, and I will move the Earth," said Archimedes. To initiate a Movement Game, the "places to stand on" are as many as management can imagine. Indeed, disruptive levers are not exclusively or necessarily related to technology or research and development, as the widely acknowledged and accepted evidence reminds us.

For example, the distribution network can serve as a "place to stand on" for breaking with the status quo. Franchising, introduced by Singer more than a hundred years ago, vending machines and mail order sales, Amazon's website and virtual banks, the postal system delivering Netflix DVDs and peer-to-peer networks for digital music: these are just a few of the most prominent cases of Movement Games activated by reinventing the conventions of value delivery.

In other circumstances, the breakpoint with orthodoxies may be *pricing*. Here again we find Netflix, which challenged Blockbuster by debuting unlimited movie rentals at a fixed rate. In Italy, with the introduction of pre-paid phone cards, the mobile telephone market skyrocketed to success in the 1990s. Derivatives, such as futures and swaps, revolutionized the pricing of financial instruments and other goods. In this case as well, the break with orthodoxies is limited solely by the limits of management's intuition.

A new organizational format or reengineered processes are other aspects which can give rise to ample opportunities in the Movement Game. From Henry Ford's assembly lines to the Japanese industry's just-in-time, via customer-centered reengineering, these strategies have significantly impacted the trajectories of several sectors.

Equally numerous are cases in which the Movement Game leverages previously untested market positioning strategies. Examples are the famous Swatch strategy in the watch market, or Volkswagen's New Beetle, which opened the era of vintage goods with high symbolic and emotional content, later followed by the Mini and the Fiat 500.

Expanding and generalizing this dimension, we can see that a particularly profitable path for the Movement Game is creatively and completely revamping the value proposition of a sector. Success stories include Ikea, Starbucks, and the Cirque du Soleil.

We can consider as even more disruptive (though with some overlap) the strategy of companies that reinvent and reconfigure the entire business model of a sector – cases in point: Dell, Zara, and low cost airlines. Two business models, when drawn up black on white, can appear exactly the same but can differ appreciably in terms of the quality of resources and competencies implemented, or the practicability of their strategic intent.

The cases described above, which we take up again in Chapter 4, provide an overview which gives us insight into the very essence of the Movement Game. In keeping with the principles of this game, a firm's success depends primarily on how accurately it anticipates market changes and how quickly it responds to customer needs. It's not

Table 1.1   Firm specificities in the Movement Game

Behavior	Anticipating change and overturning orthodoxies.
Conviction	Innovation is the only way to avoid Position Game losses.
Value creation	By generating and co-generating new knowledge.
Management model	Deciding "how to fight", what new resources are needed, and how to develop them.
Arms	Knowledge, creativity, imagination, speed, vision.
Aim	To create or regenerate markets.
Scenario	Temporary monopoly or monopolistic competition.

enough for a firm to simply win over market share from its competitors. The Movement Game, by its very nature, calls for a particular strategic predisposition for market creation: generating value by creatively identifying new opportunities, new ideas, and new endeavors. As the circular nature of history confirms, innovation is the only way to avoid the financial stress of the Position Game, or worse still, the destabilizing effect of a competitor's Movement Game.

The specificity of this confrontation requires an array of competitive arms, based on new knowledge generation, information, creativity, and firm competency integration at various levels: inter-organization, intra-organization, and more and more often, intra-sector. This arsenal of new competitive weapons is vital for developing, applying, and disseminating technology in order to educate the market about innovation, to develop industrial infrastructure, to set new standards, and to make a quick entrance or exit from any given market.

1.7   Imitation Game

Innovation is the key to a company's ability to play the Movement Game and to create new markets, but innovation might not be the most advantageous option in every circumstance. In many cases and for various reasons, imitation may represent the most successful behavior instead, as we can see from the empirical evidence reported in the management literature. Just as the firm has to know when and how to innovate, the Competition Based View requires the firm to know when and how to imitate (Chapter 6), and how to defend its innovation from competitor imitations (Chapter 7).

Firms that follow the market pioneer or innovator play the Imitation Game, in an attempt to replicate or improve the new technology, the

Table 1.2   Firm specificities in the Imitation Game

Behavior	Following a successful business model.
Conviction	Waiting for strategic windows to open is the best way to balance market risks and opportunities.
Value Creation	By replicating and/or improving innovator know-how.
Management Model	Deciding "where and how to fight", what product/market mixes to focus on with the imitation strategy, and what new resources are needed.
Arms	Learning speed, flexibility.
Aims	To successfully establish the firm in the markets with greatest potential and contribute to developing them.
Scenario	Competition or coopetition with the first mover.

innovation sources, or more generally the business model in question. To win the Imitation Game, companies must arm themselves with the ability to quickly learn what they need to know to follow the innovator, and to tap a stock of resources that is up to the task. At one end of the spectrum, imitation can produce an exact copy (see the capsule controversy surrounding Nespresso espresso makers between Sara Lee and Nestlè). At the opposite end, imitation can be incremental, as in the Microsoft Excel worksheet, an incremental imitation of the pioneering Lotus 1,2,3. Last comes leap-frogging, a radical form of innovation with respect to the product being imitated. The world-famous iPod, for instance, was by no means the first digital audio player to come on the market. It was however an *innovative imitation* that added functionality, symbolic value, and contents available for purchase online. All this gave rise to an entirely new and successful value proposition, a case of "doing things better" rather than simply "doing things the same way".

Finally, if the aim of the first mover's Movement Game is to open a new market (and not to revitalize an existing one), imitators could actually cooperate in doing so. The astute innovator, in such cases, could in turn adopt a coopetition strategy. For example, Pfizer initially followed this rationale by not reacting directly to the attack by Viagra imitators.

1.8   The Position Game

A firm's penchant for the Position Game is a reflection of a competitive arena characterized by scripted scenarios and the usual weapons, where products have consolidated life cycles and competitors are clearly identified, and customers express structured and relatively stable needs.

As we saw with the case of video game consoles, regardless of how long it lasts, this state is the natural evolution of the Movement and Imitation Games. The competitive confrontation and the management model center on the best product/market mixes. In sectors that enjoy no protection from structural barriers (keeping in mind that no barrier stands forever), the Position Game tends to evolve toward the final frontier of value. As we will elaborate below, this scenario derives from the notion of perfect competition found in classical economic theory, where long-term profits are nil.

Position Game maneuvers cause a drastic drop in profitability that compels companies to offer more and more for less, and forces firms to constantly improve their processes, often reengineering them completely. Taking up our example once again, Microsoft launched the new version of Xbox 360 in the summer of 2010 essentially as a cost containment measure.

As we have seen, typically this state involves market sharing strategies that aim to grow market share by outperforming competitors with more effective and powerful marketing programs. These are orthodox maneuvers pitting strength against strength, high advertising investments against high advertising investments, new promotions against new promotions, and so on. Some scholars (Cook, 1983, 2006) have developed a potentially valid and useful paradigm for the Position Game. This simplifies the Differential Advantage (DA) as expressed in the following formula:

$$DA_i = X_i - M_i$$

where X_i stands for the percentage of marketing investments in the sector made by the *nth* firm, and M represents its market share. In other words, competitive advantage reflects a firm's ability to win a market share that is more than proportional to its marketing efforts. At the same time, the expression reminds us that a firm's share of the market in the Position Game is directly linked to the firm's share of marketing investments in the sector. This being the case, every additional effort made by one or more competitor has negative repercussions on the firm's market share, unless it adjusts its investments proportionally.

Conventional competitive arms, therefore, require skills and resources in order to differentiate product lines or services. Firms must effectively and efficiently manage their offerings in terms of brand, price, communication, promotion, and distribution policies, potentially to the ultimate point of market commoditization.

Table 1.3   Specificities of the Position Game

Behavior	Incremental development strategies within the framework of recognized business models.
Conviction	There is no chance and no reason for radically disrupting the status quo.
Value Creation	By leveraging the firm's current resources.
Management Model	To strive for continual improvement and/or collusion.
Arms	The ability to differentiate the offering in terms of price or value.
Aims	To increase or consolidate market share (market sharing).
Scenario (worst case)	The sector implodes toward a final frontier of value.

To sum up, since the sources of competitive advantage in the Position Game are accepted and consolidated, the formula given above is a provocation which serves to highlight the limits and risks of every possible maneuver in this scenario. What is more, the potential advantage is often a negligible one; in fact, the element of surprise is the only true differential arm in many cases. To illustrate the Position Game, the words of Alessandro Manzoni come to mind when he describes the arrival of Antonio Ferrer, High Chancellor, "And everybody, standing on tiptoe, turned towards the part where the unexpected new arrival was announced. But with everybody rising, they saw neither more nor less than if they had all remained standing as they were; yet so it was: all arose."

In the chapters that follow we offer more details on our interpretative model. Using real life examples, we discuss each game, its unique features, and related offensive and defensive strategies.

2
The Movement Game: Breaking Down Orthodoxies

2.1 Introduction

What makes a new fast-growing market? How is such a market created? The answer in many cases is almost blasphemous: it's a gift "from on high." The reality is that rapidly expanding markets are often created in mature markets by firms which successfully identify incipient, latent, or existing needs that are inadequately met by other companies. The take-away pizza or hamburger markets are examples of Movement Games initiated in the mature restaurant industry. The personal computer market was invented in the mature mainframe computer market. Couriers such as Federal Express and DHL set a Movement Game in motion by exploiting unsatisfied needs in the mature postal market. The list goes on and on, further substantiating our initial assertion. Many mature markets are primed and ready for a firm to come along and convert some part into a new rapidly developing market. This maneuver clearly represents an *indirect* attack, one that allows the aggressor to win without a fight, as in Sun Tzu words (see above). From the examples above, we can infer that new technology may represent an "enabling factor" in the Movement Game, but it is not sufficient for – and nor is it essential to – success.

The Movement Game can be activated by two types of players: *incumbent firms*, or *new players* (or *newcomers*) (see Figure 2.1 below). Incumbents already do business in a given competitive arena. To avoid the erosion inherent to the Position Game, these players implement strategies that are geared to achieving two possible objectives: 1) regenerating and revitalizing the existing market; or 2) creating as yet unexplored market opportunities, thus developing an entirely new or extended core business. We refer to the first as "concentric movements," since the core business remains the same. For example, the market for television

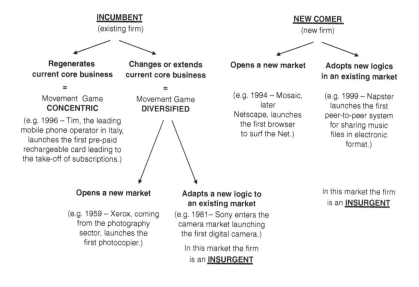

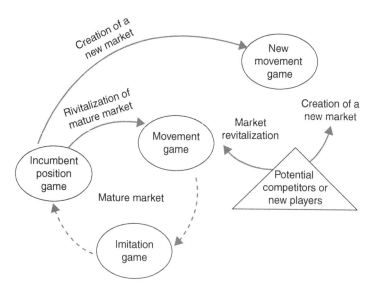

Figure 2.1   Activators of the Movement Game

sets was regenerated by incumbents who launched flat screen TVs. The second we call "differentiated movements," as was the case of Haloid, today known as Xerox. This company started out in the photography sector, and by diversifying invented the photocopy market.

When a diversified movement enables a firm to enter an existing market, the innovator will clearly be a newcomer in that arena. In this case, too, the Movement Game (which is innovative by definition) can lead to the regeneration of a pre-existing market. A firm that implements a diversified maneuver in an existing market is known as an insurgent. Think of the camera market and the then-newcomer Sony, who in 1981 made its debut by introducing digital technology with the ground-breaking Mavica CCD chip. In other cases, the newcomer who opens a Movement Game in an already existing sector is a completely new organization. An example here is Napster, which in the early 2000s revolutionized the music industry with a new file-sharing system. Lastly, there are cases where a new company is able to create an entirely new market. Netscape (formerly Mosaic Communication) did so when it invented the first web browser, as compared to other new players such as Lycos which launched the first search engines.

In the Movement Game, the challenge for the firm is to leverage its ability to deploy an unorthodox strategy, thereby confusing and disorienting the competition. Engaging a competitor in conventional and predictable maneuvers is an *orthodox strategy*, while the deployment of unexpected maneuvers and surprise tactics constitutes an *unorthodox strategy*. Whether a maneuver can be considered as one or the other depends on the assessments and assumptions of our rivals. If they expect a lateral flanking attack rather than a frontal attack, the former will be the more predictable maneuver and therefore considered orthodox. According to Sun Tzu and Sun Pin, well-known philosophers and theorists of the "art of war": "If an unorthodox tactic is applied and does not provoke a reaction, then it will succeed. Those using a large number of unorthodox tactics will attain an exceptional number of victories."

The Movement Game, through strategies of new market creation and indirect attacks on rivals, demonstrates how to "win without a fight." The subtlest competitive maneuver, one that is indirect and less visible, is the least likely to cause a rapid, violent response. Radical or unorthodox attacks are those least expected by firms in defensive positions in the market. Such moves are successful when they do not provoke immediate reactions, thereby allowing the innovator to achieve its objectives, that is creating a new market space or winning market share.[1]

Competitors are slow to react to less orthodox or indirect maneuvers for two reasons. The first involves strategic routine. This refers to a firm's behavior when it feels threatened, yet hesitates to take action for fear of having to deviate from its well-trodden path (that is its strategic routine). On occasion, this delay may have to do with timing. In other words, the threat in question arises at an inconvenient time with respect to the formal bureaucratic procedures of the firm's strategic planning process. The second reason is evident in the behavior of firms that defend their own strategies and refuse to admit that an attacker's less orthodox maneuver has any chance of success. These organizations will focus on finding objective evidence that supports their convictions instead of activating resources and capabilities to enact an effective response.

When we do not have substantial resources at our disposal and/or we do not want to provoke violent reactions from competitors, there are five different methods for avoiding head-on confrontations:

- using the element of surprise, employing unpredictable competitive weapons and adopting unexpected behavior;
- leveraging and training our strengths on our rival's weaknesses;
- transferring the confrontation into competitors' secondary markets;
- creating chaos and disorienting our opponent;
- exploiting our speed of action and innovation.

Through these actions, indirect confrontation galvanizes the search for adjacent possibilities, which we address in the next chapter. We also explore the difference between: (a) high-impact maneuvers, that is radically overtaking our opponent; and (b) low-impact maneuvers, or incrementally pushing forward.

In the next section we draw a further distinction between "anchored" and "cooperative" movements (see Figure 2.2).

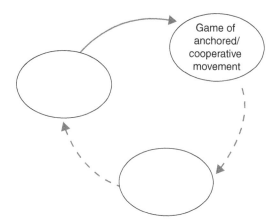

Figure 2.2   Games of anchored and cooperative movement

2.2 Games of anchored and cooperative movement

The game of anchored movement occurs when a firm first glimpses a strategic option in a conceivable market, transforming it into a new emerging market.[2] The game of cooperative movement instead is played by a group of companies that decide to integrate their resources and capabilities to create a new market.

The game of anchored movement, therefore, involves a traditional maneuver through which a first mover activates a new market by exploiting a specific competitive advantage. This is often based on some technological intuition or innovation that remains the original property of the firm and serves as the standard. The anchored game is based on the original, unique skills of the first mover (its firm-specific capabilities). However, this firm can also call into play a constellation of complementary firms or partners to accelerate the creation of the new market and the diffusion of the innovation that inspired it. In such "constellations," the innovative firm offers others its standard and, in doing so, shares the benefit of participating in the new initiative. At the same time the innovator strives to maintain the role of an anchor firm, to promote the advancement of the initiative, to define the rules of the game, and to capitalize the return on investment.

The game of cooperative movement, although always initiated by a first mover, differs from the anchored game in that the innovator firm acts on behalf of other partners rather than for itself. As a result, these partners become allies in creating and developing the new market. This game involves various forms of cooperation: alliances, federations, company associations, or joint ventures. A novel example is Visa, the credit card giant. For over thirty years Visa was a non-profit institution connecting 21,000 banks on a global level and offering its customers approximately one billion cards accepted in more than 14 million commercial establishments. Although at the end of 2006 Visa announced it was formally transforming its structure from a "membership association" to a "global public corporation", the cooperative nature of this immense network remains intact.

In the game of cooperative movement, the first mover creatively develops its intuition, generating benefits for all participants in the association who agree to support the new market creation strategy. Although in the remainder of this discussion we often refer to maneuvers of individual firms, it is useful to keep in mind that these actions can also be undertaken by groups of firms working together.

2.3 Origins of the Movement Game: the quantum leap

Some firms declare, seemingly with satisfaction, that tomorrow will be more or less the same as today. They assume that change is unlikely or unpredictable and should it occur, their organization would have plenty of time to comprehend and contend with it. These firms are doomed to fail the moment they allow such notions to infiltrate their strategic planning sessions. The most successful companies, on the contrary, believe that tomorrow's market will be very different from today's. They presume that markets can be conceived, created, and activated. These organizations are convinced that innovation is predictable and manageable and that it represents the surest way to secure their survival. According to this mindset, success is neither random nor accidental but depends on the ability to skillfully play games based on the Competition View. The key is to understand the dynamics of these games and to adopt effective behaviors and competitive maneuvers consistent with the firm's strategic intent.

The world we live in increasingly aligns itself with the principles of punctuated equilibrium. According to this theory, the environment follows an evolutionary trajectory that alternates between phases of long, gradual variation punctuated by sudden upheavals of radical change, or quantum leaps. In the competitive environment, gradual evolution is the result of low-impact Movement Games on the periphery of the Position Game, while the breaking points are where high-impact Movement Games begin.

Quantum leaps introduce deep and often dramatic discontinuities. These may result in the following situations: 1) dominating entities can quickly implode; 2) other bodies (firms) undergo profound transformations; while 3) new identities (new firms) may be generated (see Figure 2.3).

In the market, quantum leaps can be triggered by new technologies. However, we should stress that according to the Competition Based View, a quantum leap is primarily a logical discontinuity, a turning point with respect to the past that is not necessarily associated with new technological or scientific paradigms.

Such discontinuity is the result of radical innovation that can take a great variety of forms. As far as product innovation (technological in particular) goes, a common example is a killer application,[3] that is a particularly successful functionality or market application that drives the propagation of the technology, the platform, or the underlying product. For example, email was considered a fundamental "killer app"

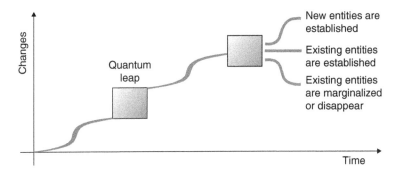

Figure 2.3   Punctuated equilibrium: quantum leaps

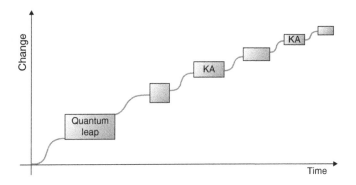

Figure 2.4   Causes of hypercompetition: a succession of quantum leaps

for the dissemination of the internet, just like the Lotus 1-2-3 spreadsheet was for the IBM personal computer, or roller coasters for many amusement parks, Tetris videogames for the Game Boy portable console, or live soccer championships for pay-TV in Italy.

It is interesting to note how the hyper competition that typifies many modern markets is validated by the unprecedented, rapid-fire succession of quantum leaps. These radical advances come with accelerated frequency, sweeping the markets along, continually reshaping their evolutionary dynamics (see Figure 2.4). Ultimately, quantum leaps are an expression of the Schumpeterian principle of creative destruction, by which firms exploit the benefits derived from their innovations, setting off Movement Games to generate and regenerate these initiatives.

2.4   Clockspeed: the speed of competitive cycles

The previous section touched on how quantum leaps – and resulting competitive games – occur at increasingly closer intervals compared to the past. What is important to emphasize is that the tempo, in absolute terms, can differ greatly from sector to sector. This is what some authors call clockspeed (Fine, 1998), or the speed of the sector's competitive dynamics and the resulting succession of competitive games in a given market context. By way of example, the IT sector is subject to an extremely fast clockspeed when compared to that of the steel industry. Software companies like to say that three months in their business is equivalent to a year in more traditional sectors.

Every arena, therefore, tends to evolve following rhythms and rates based on the clockspeed of the relative product, technology, processes, and organizational systems. This inevitably influences how long a competitive advantage can last. The implication is clear: as clockspeed accelerates, competitive advantages become more and more transitory. This means that firms must escalate their capacity to ceaselessly activate new Movement Games, identifying key resources for the imminent future every time they do so. We'll discuss this notion in the following section.

2.5   Creative destruction: how to activate
the Movement Game

Firms are aware that their initiatives cannot advance by replicating the same old rules of play, but they often rush to conform to them all the same. In striving to impose order on change, they end up warily walking down the same well-worn path.

Many management practices are effective in dealing with the present, but not in planning for the future. Outsourcing, restructuring, and reengineering processes, for example, are useful in reducing costs, but they are often less helpful in lessening the allure of conformism and the comfort of replicating familiar procedures and routines. These practices channel energy away from shaping the future, searching for new ideas, creating discontinuity, and breaking with the past. After restructuring and reengineering, after rediscovering the importance of the customer, what is missing? What needs to happen next? What stops real change – something totally different – from happening?

What is missing, and what is absolutely essential for the firm, is creative capability, or the creativity to realize change. In a hypercompetitive world, no one can afford not to change; everyone must try to design and shape the future.

In proactive firms, there are two ways of envisaging the future of an initiative. The first follows a linear projection to a future destination extrapolated from the present. In the second, the final destination is unknown. The firm advances step-by-step, day-by-day, driven by an idea and a vision. Every day, the vision is gradually refined. This process reflects the true meaning of the expression "managing the present to plan the future." Although the second method may be less reassuring than the first, it is often more logical and workable, seeing as the future rarely materializes from any extrapolation or projection of the present. This manner of planning the future requires the ability to create quantum leaps – radical discontinuities that do not lead to incremental change but rather to substantive breaks with the past and the present.

Discontinuity and change express uncertainty – not a popular word because of its connotations with doubt and anxiety – with a "disconnect" from what we know, which distances us from familiar situations and contexts. Likewise, the same discomfort arises with the idea of discontinuity, the interruption of routine. Firms are therefore reluctant to change; three different reasons explain why:

1. The first reason is a rational one, deriving from the fear of triggering a process of cannibalization and depletion of the sources of competitive advantages and thus the value of the firm.
2. The second, a more emotional reason, arises from excessive veneration of the customer. This engenders a short-term orientation focused on maximum customer satisfaction, and favors incremental improvement of the current strategy.
3. The third has organizational and financial roots. Destabilizing, revolutionary change is seen as dangerous because of its impact on the firm and the magnitude of the costs inherent in this kind of transformation.

Too often firms do what past and present numbers dictate and what past experience suggests, while checking the impetus of intuition, instinct, dreams, and the capacity to envision the future.

Firms must promote change to initiate a Movement Game. But as Steinbeck wrote in *Travels with Charley*, "It is the nature of a man as he grows older to protest against change, particularly changes for the better."[4] Activating the cycle of creative destruction[5] (Figure 2.5) is the most effective step toward embarking on a Movement Game.

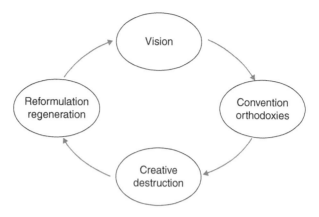

Figure 2.5 The cycle of creative destruction

The word "destruction" doubtlessly raises concern and anxiety because it is associated with chaos, turmoil, ruin, and eradication. However, the aim of creative destruction is not to destroy the firm, but to subvert conventional thinking. Destruction is the point of departure for the process of envisioning and designing the future, a process that is less orthodox and more effective because it compels us to seek out what others do not yet perceive.

As stated in the previous section, firm behavior that radically breaks with tradition can be defined as a quantum leap. Creative destruction is the process of searching for an idea, a spark of intuition that is a breach or bypassing of conventional thinking that makes a new vision accessible. This new vision can be constructed by recasting or regenerating the existing vision to initiate a Movement Game.

The first step in activating the cycle of creative destruction consists in targeting the more common and consolidated conventions. This is certainly no easy task. Although such conventions are everywhere, they are generally difficult to recognize and realize. Indeed, accepted customs and conventions are often so familiar that they often go unnoticed.

Conventions are: (a) assumptions that (b) express common wisdom, and (c) define the rules of the game in progress. Conventions are represented by all those pre-packaged ideas and norms that maintain the status quo. Examples of past popular conventions: "Competition in air transport centers on the level of service;" "Video games are for teenagers;" "Water is an undifferentiated product;" "Compact cars are not for Americans;" "Fast-food is not for Italians." The list goes on and on.

Table 2.1   Famous phrases to avoid change

	There will always be someone who will tell you: "Don't change" "It won't work" "It's impossible"
Cinema	"Silent films will never die: who on earth would want to hear actors speak?" Harry M. Warner, Warner Brothers, 1927
Cars	"The horse is here to stay, the car is simply a passing novelty." Chairman of a bank in Michigan, advising Henry Ford's lawyer against investing in his client's car industry, 1903
Computers	"There is no reason why a person should have a computer in the home." Kenneth Olsen, Chairman of Digital Equipment, 1977
Radio	"A gadget without a future." Lord Kelvin, physicist, 1897
Aircraft	"They are interesting toys but have no military value." Ferdinand Foch, French commander in World War I, 1911
TV	"In six months people will get tired of staring at a plywood box every evening." Darryl Zanuck, Head of 20th Century Fox, 1946
Beatles	"We don't want them. Their music doesn't work and now bands with guitars are out of fashion." Decca Records, 1962
Nuclear	"Nothing authorizes us to think that nuclear energy can be obtained." Albert Einstein, 1932
Moon	"Man will never land on the moon." Lee De Frost, one of the founding fathers of radio, 1967
Conclusions	"To accomplish great things, we must not only act, but also dream; not only plan, but also believe." Anatole France "Don't be afraid to take big steps. You can't cross a chasm in two small jumps." David Lloyd George

In firms, we find numerous conventions and orthodoxies; four categories are worth citing here (also see Table 2.1 above):

1. *Technological Conventions*: identifying with the immortality of established technologies and sustaining the invincibility of successful products. How many times, in the 1980s and 1990s, did we hear that nothing would ever compare to chemical photography?
2. *Product and Service Conventions*: affirming pre-packaged notions on consumption and use. How many furniture manufacturers, before IKEA, ever imagined that the customer could become an active participant in the assembly process?
3. *Marketing Conventions*: clarifying how customers think about themselves and their priorities in terms of clusters of needs. How many pasta or vegetable producers, trapped in their orthodoxies, ignored the growing importance of saving meal-preparation time? Note the growing market for pre-cooked meals and pre-washed /pre-cut vegetables.

4. *Distribution Conventions*: defending accepted behavior in terms of value delivery. How many times has it been said that people, especially in Latin countries, want to touch and feel prior to purchasing? Yet Yoox (www.yoox.com), the global Internet retailing partner for leading fashion and design brands, has successfully launched online shopping in Italy too. In the same way, long-held conventions have been overturned by the growing popularity of home banking.

Conventions are opinions, not facts, even though people find it difficult to separate facts from opinions. A convention is an accepted rule that helps us to think and act according to common custom. Conventions are therefore all those things that are accepted subconsciously, because they pertain to habits, customs, and behaviors that are so familiar to us that we no longer perceive them. In habit there is comfort, which in turn hinders change. *Recognizing conventions and orthodoxies is the first step in preparing the firm for a radical leap.* Identifying and dismantling conventions – this is the point of departure for creating a new vision and generating the intrusive strategies that can lead to extraordinary performance and instigate a Movement Game.

In athletics, Valeriy Brumel's high jump technique was the most commonly used in his day. Had Dick Fosbury not destroyed this orthodox convention with the "Fosbury Flop," he would never have surpassed the two meter mark. Until the eighteenth century, the convention in theatre was disguise and improvisation: it was Carlo Goldoni's creative destruction that relaunched stage performances in the form we know today.

Creative destruction is the attempt to put an end to tradition, to attack common wisdom. The intent of the destructive process is to stimulate the innovative thought that precedes innovation. The destruction phase is necessary because the firm is aware that its way of thinking and acting is often rooted in tradition and prejudices. Adhesion to an outdated framework drains the creative process of all energy; the search for coherence and consistency depletes creative capability.

Since change creates disorder, it causes conflict and spreads uncertainty, orchestrating an apparently anarchist context. But if change has a clear strategy, it unleashes energy and enthusiasm, thereby generating *antigravitational management* – a positive stimulus for the spirit of the firm.

The destruction phase provokes new and unexpected ideas. This phase sets the firm on a voyage unmapped and unplanned; it reveals unexplored insights into problems.

Dominant conventions and orthodoxies may be subject to either a high- or low-impact destructive process. The first involves radical maneuvers which overtake the competition. The aim is to proffer a new vision and a new business model, thereby restructuring the market and business boundaries, and even going so far as to create a new sector. A low impact destruction process, by contrast, attacks all orthodoxies and conventions relating to products, services, or processes for generating and transferring value by way of incremental maneuvers (Table 2.2).

The process of change must begin with a reflection on all prevailing orthodoxies in the firm and in the sector. It must then evolve through a period of destruction of the same, to conclude with the generation of new ideas (Table 2.3). These ideas must merge to form a new vision.

The vision concludes the process because it is a leap of imagination from the present to the future. It is the realization of the imagined scenario and points the firm in the right direction. In the late 1980s, the managing director of a large Italian publishing group invited one of the authors of this book to coordinate a two-day creative workshop with first-line management to brainstorm on possible incremental or radical improvements for the company. One manager proposed the idea of an electronic book. The hypothesis was almost immediately

Table 2.2 Low- or high-impact destruction process

Destruction	High impact/Low impact
Regeneration of the market	Regeneration of the product/service
Redefinition of the strategy	Redefinition of market behavior
Radical reconfiguration of the business model and value proposition	Incremental reconfiguration of the business model and value proposition

Table 2.3 Destroying conventions by observing reality from different perspectives

The prevalent conventions	The destruction of conventions
A locomotive with an engine tows all the railcars of a train.	Put an engine in each railcar.
The train needs a powerful engine to ensure high-speed.	The sum total of all the engines guarantees high speed.
Rails must follow the morphology of the land.	The land can be leveled or bored through (bridges, tunnels).
A train "runs" on rails.	The train levitates magnetically.

rejected, not so much for the technological difficulties, although these were extensive, but for the break with the cultural orthodoxies. However, flipping through the pages of *Business Week* ten years later, we discovered that the idea of the eBook had been realized. Today, another ten years later, the feeling that the eBook is not simply a technological extravagance is beginning to take hold. For certain segments of demand, the notion that "readers want to feel the texture and smell the pages" could prove a false convention. It is clear that *timing* is essential to launch a revolution, but waiting until the time is ripe to make a move must not become an excuse for making no move at all.

2.6 Generating the quantum leap

A widespread and common convention holds that success derives mainly from the capability of a firm to dominate the competition by staying "ahead." The most successful companies instead take a different approach: through the process of creative destruction discussed above, they work to generate a quantum leap by introducing innovations that are valuable to their customers. They pay less attention to analyzing the competition, while neutralizing competitors by avoiding the most common conventions and orthodoxies. In a declining market such as movie theaters, a widespread convention was to limit investments, in particular in capital assets, and improve other competitive areas (products, services, communication, etc.). Successful firms, by contrast, followed a different path, reinventing their business models. In this sector, in fact, the one-stop entertainment shop and multiplex represented an innovative way to reconfigure movie theaters.

This example reiterates how a quantum leap is not necessarily a technological leap: the discontinuity is first and foremost logical; it is a disrupting innovation that may be technological, financial, commercial, organizational, etc.

Starbucks gave us a further example of how to generate a quantum leap in a low-tech, high-touch sector. Unlike traditional operators, who normally promoted fast take-away consumption (as did the previous market leader, Dunkin' Donuts), Starbucks created a comfortable environment with a wide variety of drinks and snacks at premium prices. This represented a radically new way to envision the market. The intense *Imitation Game* that followed reminds us of the circularity of our destiny: an endless race.

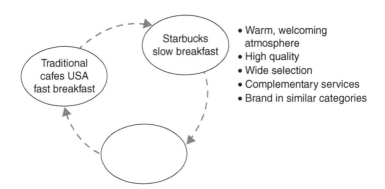

Figure 2.6 The Movement Game by Starbucks in a low-tech, high-touch sector

Successful companies, therefore, try to reason like a newcomer who wants to change the rules of the game, outflanking the principles and conventions governing the market.

In order to change the rules, players have to think and act differently. If the enterprise does not change its mindset, it will never change its behaviors. According to the most common convention, a revolutionary idea emerges in one of two ways: after endlessly mulling over a situation or problem; or as the outcome of a brainstorming session. The real key is how we see the problem, whether we can find a perspective that enables us to minimize the prejudices and preconceptions that block creative, revolutionary thinking. Evolutionary processes drive people to seek stability and safety; revolutions instead trigger the destruction of conventions. The management literature is replete with conventions and orthodoxies that take the form of paradigms, rules, and methodologies formulated to facilitate our understanding of the specific nature of a market and to guide firm behavior. The generation of a quantum leap, as we have seen, requires the company to first recognize these conventions and then bypass or destroy them (Figure 2.7).

Summing up the common conventions found in the strategic thinking literature, Table 2.4 below offers a different perspective on outflanking these orthodoxies. Many companies, for example, consider the structural aspects of their sector as defined *a priori* and formulate their strategies accordingly.

Some sectors are thus characterized by converging strategies since their boundaries are defined by conventions shared by all competitors. These common strategies are the product of a common diagnosis. Less

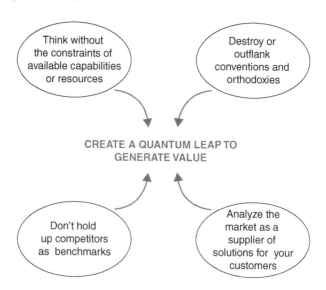

Figure 2.7 The processes to generate a quantum leap

conventional firms follow different trajectories searching for original ideas that successfully generate quantum leaps, capable of resetting the boundaries and structural conditions of relative markets.

Some firms follow converging models, comparing their strengths, weaknesses, and behaviors with those of their direct competitors. From this perspective they focus their resources to generate a competitive advantage (think of the traditional SWOT analysis). In reality, even this behavior leads firms to respect conventions, to follow the rules of the dominant game, and to pursue convergent behaviors. Compliance with conventions and orthodoxies encourages firms to confront each other with a strategy of incremental improvements. The logic of quantum leaps dictates a different perspective, motivating the company to seek new ways to generate innovations of value for itself and its customers.

The most innovative firm does not monitor competitors to formulate countermeasures in reaction to their behavior; nor does this firm use rivals as benchmarks. The innovator uses careful analysis to identify the dimensions of offerings that have the potential for generating extraordinary value for the market. Instead of creating marginal competitive advantages, this company proactively uses its resources to develop new capabilities with the aim of creating new sources of value. This will make it possible to overtake rivals and render them harmless.

Table 2.4 Generating a new perspective

Dimension of the strategy	Conventional perspective	Revolutionary perspective
Structure of the sector	The conditions of the sector are defined.	The conditions of the sector can be manipulated and reformulated.
Strategic focus	A firm can generate and develop its competitive advantages. The aim is to beat the competition.	The competition is not an *a priori* benchmark. A firm must generate a quantum leap to dominate the market.
Customers	A firm must expand its portfolio of customers by using segmentation strategies.	A firm can develop irresistible propositions for the market as a whole.
Capabilities and resources	A firm must activate a process for leveraging its resources and capabilities.	A firm must not be limited by its stock of capabilities and available resources.
Products and services offered	The conditions of the sector define the products and services that the company can offer. The objective is to maximize value for the customer.	The firm must offer the highest customer satisfaction by looking further afield, beyond the traditional offering.

Conventional firms pursue the most traditional logic of segmentation. Less conventional firms look for more original positioning criteria, striving to reach ever-increasing numbers in the market (counter-segmentation). Zara is an example from the clothing sector; this company's offerings spread across an array of market segments with varying levels of disposable income. In cases like this one, instead of focusing on the differences among customers, firms seek out unexplored convergences to promote a high perception of value for large groups of customers. This perspective, in contrast to classic segmentation paradigms, is based on the assumption that consumers are willing to give up expressed preferences in exchange for irresistible value propositions.

The proactive firm, when generating a quantum leap, does not base its behavior on available resources and capabilities when responding to the question, "What can we do with what we have?" Rather, this firm asks: "What could we do if we could begin our entrepreneurial adventure right now?"

These firms, in other words, do not permit what they have or what they know to condition their future prospects; instead they remove constraints on their capabilities and resources. This does not mean that innovative firms do not attempt to exploit their current capabilities or that they underestimate the possible reaction of the competition. They simply try to address the market while avoiding being conditioned by the common wisdom in that market. This is why the proactive firm is distinguished not only by its acumen and insight in searching out the sources of value for its customers, but also particularly by its ability to exploit this acumen and insight with passion.

2.7 Innovations that generated unorthodox maneuvers

The Post-it Note is the outcome of a highly inventive approach to innovation adopted by the American firm 3M. This company created a consolidated system of incentives that encouraged systematic experimentation, even with ideas that might not seem consistent with the target market. Post-it, in fact, began an "inconsistent" prototype: the glue on the back of these notes did not stick permanently to surfaces. Yet with this product launch, 3M successfully demonstrated that less orthodox ideas often satisfy the most implicit needs. A case in point is the need to jot down a message, make a note, leave a reminder, even in an unorganized way, and later to be able to arrange these notes as need be.

Apple successfully developed offerings with exceptional design and high emotional and social involvement, breaking away from the purely functional product features that traditionally captured the attention of the high-tech market. The company's "think different" approach expresses the less orthodox orientation of Apple, which begins with its choice of name.

A strategy of lateral thinking was also adopted by the Italian–French multinational Air Liquide with the development of Altop. This welding cylinder used in garages, and in particular in body shops, was notable for its pioneering technology. The product's closure valve, its incorporated pressure gauge, and its maneuverability (which facilitated product transportation) are all keys to this product's success, as corroborated by market research conducted following its launch. Interesting to note is the importance of Altop's bright colors and aesthetic design, which one would not expect to have a significant impact in a mechanical context. In a follow-up product launch, Liquigas introduced Twiny, a cylinder for home use with similar design characteristics.

3
The Maneuvers of the Movement Game

3.1 The search for adjacent possibilities

The idea that firms and people must change is not new. In fact, all our lives we hear from our parents, teachers, friends, colleagues – basically every thinking person – that change is necessary. So why is it that today the word "change" means something different than what it used to? It's not that we have finally embraced the meaning of change and the benefits it brings about. Instead, we are waking up and looking at a new world that is rapidly emerging around us, shaping our businesses, our institutions, and our communities. What we are looking at is not simply a world that is evolving as it always has. We are witnessing the emergence of something very new and radically different. What's changing is our paradigms, rationale, formulations, quantifications, and how we deal with probabilities and predictions.

Planning processes are no longer adequate for handling unexpected events and behaviors since such processes are based on linear rationales. In light of the characteristics of change today, we must abandon linear, orthodox perspectives, and observe the nature of things from emerging viewpoints.

But how can a complex organization such as a firm develop a capacity for "emergent" observation? One suggestion is to emulate the great thinkers and innovators, how they imagined the unimaginable and conceived the inconceivable. By virtue of their creativity and ability to question, all these people are capable of generating a quantum leap. However, the inventor does not have the freedom to make just any kind of random "leap". Innovative contribution becomes a reality in a process that is defined – in the language of complexity – as the generation of adjacent possibilities. Stuart Kauffman (1995) suggested that an adjacent possibility cannot exist until a previous possibility has been realized.

In order to simplify this notion, consider how the different organic species inhabiting our planet today would not exist if the reactions facilitating their generation had not arisen previously. Observe current molecular species and try to imagine all other species that do not yet exist today but that will be generated by the reactions of these current molecules. This observation, deriving from physics and biology, is based on the principle that nothing comes from nothing. What's more, everything that happens in the universe is the result of an unceasing process of becoming. Therefore there are no limits to that which has not been conceived until today.

In pragmatic terms, relating this principle to innovation, an adjacent possibility cannot be generated without preceding possibilities, which are not necessarily consequential or determined. Contrary to closed systems, open systems are opposed to the idea of the mechanical nature of events and exhibit the principle of emergence. Firms organized as open systems develop only as a function of that which preceded them. This means that although there is continuity, there isn't determinism in their evolutionary trajectory.

As an example, think of AT&T and Western Union at the end of 1800s. These companies were competitors in the lucrative telegraphic market. In 1876, Western Union decided not to acquire the famous Bell patent, opting not to take advantage of the adjacent possibility offered by the telephone, an innovation then in its infancy and available only for local communications. In 1879, at the end of their legal dispute, the two companies agreed to the following: until the expiry of the patent in 1894, AT&T would exit the telegraph market and, in exchange, Western Union would withdraw from the telephony market.

Like in the well-known movie *Sliding Doors* (which shows how the future changes when one path is randomly chosen over another), Western Union missed out on a simple adjacent possibility. This precluded the company from a much wider range of extraordinary growth opportunities and related competitive strategies: from long-distance telephony to the *Yellow Pages*, from mobile telephony to data connectivity, from video entertainment to all those services made possible by digital communication. Sliding Doors. One hundred years later, these two companies and their strategic opportunities are completely different. Similarly, Microsoft's first decision when faced with a new adjacent possibility called the World Wide Web was to stop it from spreading. However, demonstrating great determination, flexibility, and speed of action, the company made a rapid and vigorous turn-around. If it hadn't, we can only imagine where the Colossus of Redmond would be today.

Every firm should therefore ask itself, with honesty as well as insight, which adjacent possibilities are more favorable to generating something truly new. In competitive markets, this knowledge is strategic because when an adjacent possibility begins to appear, it will inevitably be realized. We can't say when, but we can be certain it will happen. The first mover will be the firm that sees this possibility first.

The success of the first mover derives from the ability to perceive an emerging prospect, an adjacent possibility, and to quickly give it material form. To develop this capacity, a firm must see itself from the market's perspective, not observe the market from the window of its conventions; the firm must look beyond traditions to conceive new possibilities. The expression "innovation" comes from the Latin word *novus*, which means to create something new, but it also derives from the root *nu*, which gives the idea of "now". An adjacent possibility is therefore something new and now. Innovation is something that does not exist: neither in memory nor in our expectations of the future. It is now, and therefore it is absolutely new.

Many firms lack the capacity for change due to their difficulty or inability to:

- perceive an emerging a threat;
- build on an emerging opportunity.

Cognitive failure to recognize the signs of a threat or opportunity gives rise to the need for intellectual openness of the people in charge, who could question the rules, the principles, and the creeds that generate the success of today's firm.[1] The credos of business leaders, the people who could make their firms change course, limit their ability to see adjacent possibilities, making them so short-sighted as to fail to perceive the obvious. They resist modifying the identity and mission of the firm and insist on interpreting the world from a familiar perspective, according to the paradigms with which they were educated. These people are not stupid or indifferent; they are dangerous because they are entrenched in their beliefs. If we accept that a firm is the manifestation of an idea, then we can attribute the cognitive failure of many firms to their inability to generate and develop new ideas. Cognitive failures are the expression of human fallacy and therefore often inevitable. A firm must therefore be proactive, and be able to change quickly to avoid the potential destruction of its market opportunities. In many firms, instead, the culture of defending conventions prevails over the culture of proactivity. Rather than rejecting these orthodoxies, they become the absolute truths that govern the firm. To ensure continuity and survival, firms reduce their proactivity to adapt to their interpretation of the market. By refusing to go beyond the confines of their imagination and explore the endless possibilities that lie there, these organizations deny that complexity and change are essential to all winning systems, while sanctifying orthodoxies.

Cognitive failure to recognize change and adjacent possibilities generates devastating consequences for every individual and for every firm. The reasons for this failure are implicit in the term *establishment* with which we identify organizations and firms. The word *establishment* comes from the Indo-European *sta*, referring to the concept of position, resistance, arrest, non-change. From this, all words such as stable, stasis, and static derive. Therefore, firms and institutions are born with an original sin: opposing the new, opposing change. In order to survive, firms must relearn the meaning of innovation, abandoning the search for stability. Otherwise, they will find themselves reliving their past. The winning team must change before the other teams do. The maneuvers of the Movement Game, described in the previous chapter, are based on this principle.

3.2   Adjacent possibilities for high- and low-impact Movement Games

Adjacent opportunities (or possibilities) represent the different paths along which firms can play a Movement Game. In light of this, we should reiterate that the most crucial decision for a firm is always choosing between the following: (1) initiating a Movement Game to regenerate its core business; or (2) initiating a Movement Game centered on exploiting adjacent possibilities that change its own strategic boundaries (see Figure 3.1 below).

1. The first option pertains to adjacent possibilities that are "concentric" to the core business, which essentially remains intact, sustained by innovative strategies. The change of behavior can be more radical or less radical with respect to existing orthodoxies, giving rise to a concentric movement of respectively high- or low-impact. When in the mid-1980s Starbucks completely revamped its approach to selling coffee in the US, this involved a concentric maneuver because its core business remained the same. However, it was a high-impact move in terms of novelty and had repercussions on competitive

market dynamics. Similar examples are McDonald's and Benetton, with their franchising initiatives in the 1950s and 1970s respectively. We more commonly see incremental concentric maneuvers, as with the Movement Game that LG undertook in the air conditioning market when the firm first launched the stylish Art Cool line in 2004. Other competitors quickly followed suit with imitation maneuvers, contributing to creating a new premium segment especially sensitive to aesthetics and design.

2. In the second case, we refer to diversified adjacent possibilities because they involve redefining or expanding the core business. These are often high-impact maneuvers, or rather, radical innovations. To cite some well-known examples, think of Xerox which started out in the photography sector and then invented the photocopying business; or Sony which entered the photography sector by exploiting digital technology. An additional example is the Costa cruise line. The Costa brothers, in 1924, acquired their first steamboat to transport raw materials for their core business: the production of olive oil. Over time the fleet of steamboats grew, and in 1947, also began carrying passengers. In the 1960s Costa became the first European company in this sector, and the first in the world to offer Caribbean cruises. In all these cases, the firms in question did not radically change the rules of their own sector, but those of a sector new to them, as with Sony. Or they established the rules for a completely new sector, as in the case of Xerox or Costa cruises.

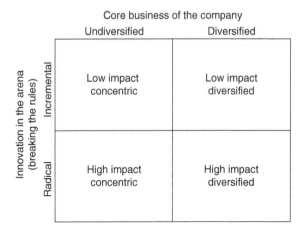

Figure 3.1 The taxonomy of Movement Games

The game of diversified movement can also be played with more incremental rather than radical innovation. For example, Findus launched its indirect attack on the Italian pasta market with high-quality pre-cooked frozen meals.

All these cases remind us that the Movement Game, whether diversified or concentric, high- or low-impact, is based on the market driving capability of the innovation and the element of surprise. We'll discuss this further in the remainder of this chapter.

We should note that the distinction between high- and low-impact is artificially dichotomous, since, in reality, the magnitude of impact with respect to existing orthodoxies can be gauged along a strategic continuum. For the same reason, classifying *ex-ante* the different adjacent opportunities as high-impact or low-impact is a complex task.

Nevertheless, for simplicity's sake, Figures 3.2 and 3.3 below position the different maneuvers *a priori* based on more common cases. Keep in mind, aside from this classification, that such moves are not mutually exclusive: they can coexist, synergistically and even co-dependently.

Adjacent possibilities that are most likely high-impact, as shown in Figure 3.2, may arise when a firm:

1. develops and adopts a radically new technology (Sections 3.3, 3.4 and 3.5);
2. discovers new markets, new segments or untapped geographical areas (Sections 3.6 to 3.12);
3. radically redefines the value proposition (Sections 3.13 and 3.14);
4. reconfigures the business model (Section 3.15).

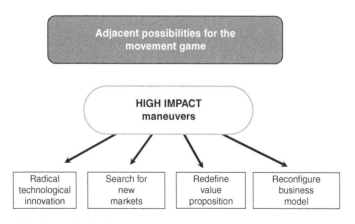

Figure 3.2   Generally high-impact Movement Games

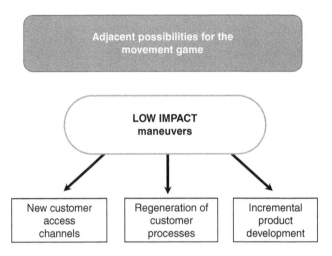

Figure 3.3　Generally low-impact Movement Games

Lower-impact maneuvers, summarized in Figure 3.3, may consist in:

1. designing new ways to access customers (Section 3.16);
2. reengineering customer processes (Sections 3.17 and 3.18);
3. incrementally developing the product (Section 3.19).

An alternative representation of adjacent possibilities (albeit not an exhaustive one) is proposed in Figure 3.4, which highlights the continuum between high and low impact, a distinction that often can only be assessed on a case-by-case basis. At the conclusion of the chapter we also suggest a model for evaluating a firm's portfolio of innovations, which should balance lower-impact competitive maneuvers (and therefore less risky) with higher-impact actions (higher growth potential, but greater risks of failure).

Before examining the most common maneuvers, we should remember that the aim of all Movement Games is to laterally or indirectly attack a rival firm, to surprise and potentially overtake it.

In competitive games, surprising the adversary is a method for achieving relative superiority. Surprise amplifies the firm's freedom to maneuver because it generates confusion, uncertainty, and doubt in rivals by reducing their determination and desire to react.

If a rival does not recognize an opportunity in the market to create a new source of competitive advantage, the element of surprise may

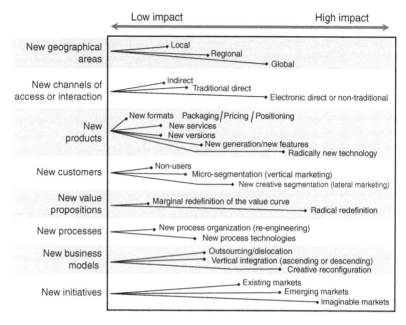

Figure 3.4   Partial summary of adjacent possibilities

contribute to reducing the perception of a threat. The firm that decides to seize the opportunity will be seen as illogical or irrational. Although the element of surprise is not a source of advantage, it does allow the firm to initiate a new innovative game to delay the reaction of opponents in preparing the resources and the maneuvers to respond to the attack.

3.3   Overtaking maneuvers via technological innovation

The scholar Peter Drucker stated that the greatest discovery of the modern era was the invention of innovation.[2] In this section, we use the term with particular reference to scientific or technological innovation. As the well-known science-fiction writer Arthur C. Clarke noted, real progress in technology cannot be distinguished from magic.

In a Movement Game based on technological innovation, a firm can commit three errors:

1. Not investing in new technologies;
2. Investing in the wrong technologies;

3. Not being able to handle incremental improvements and to develop new technologies at the same time.

The source of the most daring Movement Games is often the courage to generate and disseminate new technology. Technology is much more than a new product or a new production process. It is an attempt by human beings to control the physical world by making full use of imagination and creativity.

The insurgent firm develops "disrupting" technologies, killer applications that reduce the value of existing products and technologies by meeting the same needs or offering new functionalities, with greater benefits or lower costs. For example, earthquakes or volcanic eruptions are manifestations of complex interactions between geological forces underneath the surface of the Earth. Quantum leaps, which target the balance and evolutionary cycle of a market, are often an expression of the emergence and recognition of a killer application. As with natural phenomena, a killer application is the manifestation of the complex interaction between the forces of knowledge and competition. In the market, this application can have the same destructive effect as an earthquake.

In the previous chapter, we described a killer application as an innovation that exerts a destructive force on the balance of a market by imposing a radical change in its demand behavior. The speed and disruptive power with which this change spreads is a function of the angular coefficient of the curve of dissemination of the innovation. First the fax machine, then the cell phone, and then email exemplify innovations that generated new markets. Email was a killer application that sidelined traditional mail much more quickly than the car made horses obsolete.

Punch cards, a method for processing and storing data, were replaced in the 1980s by the floppy disk. In the 1990s, especially in the US, the floppy disk was replaced by the zip disk, which had the capacity of 100 floppy disks. At the beginning of 2000, the CD made the zip disk obsolete, offering 650 MB of storage space. Today the market is differentiated. In order to satisfy the primary need for storage capacity, DVDs, blu-ray disks, and external hard drives are some of the current solutions. At the same time, USB flash drives are the popular option for consumers who want greater convenience and need to transfer files (rather than to simply store them). In addition, flash memory cards such as the SD, miniSD, or microSD, for hand-held devices and cameras, are now widely used thanks to their portability. Finally, clouding solutions – such as

SkyDrive or similar services, allowing clients to store files in remote servers – are more recent options. All these are examples of *co-existing* new products and services that no one can do without today.

3.4   The S-returns of a technological innovation

In order to appreciate the effectiveness with which technology can activate a Movement Game and make a radical change in the market, we need to review the S-curve principle.

The S-curve correlates investments in a given innovation and the returns on these investments.[3] The principle of the curve is obvious and intuitive. The returns on the investments in question, in the initial phase of the innovation's life cycle, are low but rising. The first part of the S shows returns that rise at increasingly higher rates, while, in the second part, this increase in returns slows down. In the last stage of the life cycle of a technological innovation, any additional investments aimed at improvement do not guarantee any incremental return on performance. The quantum leap is positioned at the beginning of the S-curve (see Figure 3.5 below), and gives rise to the innovation that activates the Movement Game.

The S-curve may represent an effective tool for stimulating innovation and activating a technology-based Movement Game. By analyzing the curve, we can predict when the benefits brought about by investments in improving the technology or innovation will run out. When we've exploited the innovation as far as possible, incremental improvements and further returns on our investment become difficult. At this point, the business model underlying this innovation reaches obsolescence,

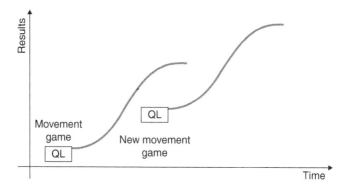

Figure 3.5   The S-curve

thus becoming even more vulnerable to attacks from other more effective and efficient innovations.

Before reaching the limits of the innovation, the firm must decide whether to accept a new Movement Game, exploiting a new quantum leap, or risk having to defend itself against a rival who may pre-empt the firm in creating a competitive discontinuity.

Figure 3.6 below represents the mature and emerging technology curves that drive Competition Based View games. The first represents a defensive strategy in a Position Game; the second shows attack positions in a Movement Game to win market share and customers.

A proactive firm knows how to generate and manage a quantum leap to activate a new Movement Game while avoiding technological discontinuity. These firms identify their position on the S-curve relative to their current and potential rivals. Their aim is to plan when to develop new technologies, new products, and new processes, anticipating their competitors' Movement Games. Observing the angular coefficients of the S-curve (Figure 3.7), we can clearly see the need to activate and manage a new Movement Game.

These coefficients measure the productivity of the innovation, the ratio between resources invested and the results achieved. In the second half of the curve, the angular coefficients show that increasing the investment does not produce an equivalent increment of results; in fact, results tend to regress. In each sector, a technological discontinuity, triggering a leap from a mature to an emerging innovation, may lead to an increase in productivity ranging from 5:1 to 30:1. Any attempt to improve a mature technology can therefore be neutralized if, through

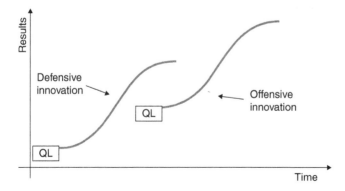

Figure 3.6 The obsolescence and emergence of innovation

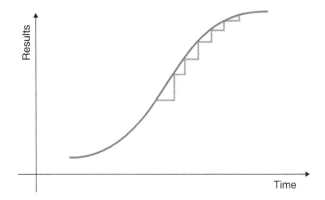

Figure 3.7   Angular coefficients of the S-curve

a Movement Game, a curve with significantly higher productivity is introduced into the market. Improving productivity of our sales force or a production plant by 10 or 15% is therefore ineffective if, with a quantum leap, we can generate a Movement Game with an innovation that enables us to achieve productivity four or five times higher.

3.5   The early stage of an innovation and the speed of replacement

An innovation's market debut and its commercial success grow sequentially over very long time horizons. Some innovations require a great deal of lab time to be generated and developed, as is the case with pharmaceuticals. Conventionally, this period is the lead time from the birth of an idea until its commercialization. The launch of the innovation marks the beginning of the introductory phase of its life cycle, the length of which varies depending on the market's acceptance of the new product or service. This period may be characterized by a "non-use" period of the product. The non-use phase measures the time between the commercial launch and the actual take-off of the innovation (sometimes called the "tipping point").

The innovator may therefore have to invest vast resources over a protracted period of time before seeing any market success. In the meantime, other rivals may take advantage the first-mover's fatigue and frustration to make an imitation maneuver.

Table 3.1 shows examples of products and the average time from market launch to customer acceptance. We can see that the time

Table 3.1 The embryonic phases of innovations

Products	Time from market launch to commercial acceptance	Comments
35 mm cameras	40 years	The product was introduced in the 1920s but remained limited until the 1960s, when the Japanese cut prices and brought the product into the mainstream.
Ballpoint pens	8 years	The idea was patented in the late 1800s. The first commercial success occurred in the late 1940s, but not until eight years later did the product overcome its "fad" status.
Credit/Charge cards	8 years	The first charge and credit cards appeared in the 1930s; Diner's Club started in 1950. It was not until the late 1950s, however, that the products gained widespread acceptance.
Diet soft drinks	10 years	It was not until Royal Crown promoted the product that it gained widespread acceptance.
Light beer	9 years	Pioneers spent nearly a decade trying to figure out how to position the product on the market.
Mainframe computers	10 years	First introduced in 1946, only slightly more than 100 computers were sold by 1956, the year IBM surpassed Univac.
Microwave ovens	20 years	Invented in 1946, the first commercial microwave was not introduced until 10 years later. After numerous false starts, it was not until the mid-1970s that microwaves gained widespread acceptance.

Continued

Table 3.1 Continued

Products	Time from market launch to commercial acceptance	Comments
Non-alcoholic beer	6 years	Imports lingered on the market for at least six years until consumers developed a taste for the new product.
Paperback books	5 years	Paperbacks have been around since the American Civil War, but appeared in their modern formats in the 1940s. A number of failed before consumers became interested.
Personal computers	6 years	The market started with selected users, but demand did not explode until IBM entered the picture.
Answering machines	15 years	The market evolved slowly, starting in the late 1950s. Demand did not explode until the mid 1980s.
VCRs	20 years	The first commercial model was introduced in 1956. It was not until 1975 that the home video market took off.
Videogames	13 years	Started in 1972, the market boomed, then went bust. Not until 1985, with Nintendo's debut, did long-term demand materialize.
Warehouse clubs	7 years	Sam's Club entered the market only seven years after the Price Club.

Source: Schmaars S.P. (1994).

horizon spanning from the introduction stage to the use of the new product or service varies on average between 5 and 40 years. The more time the innovator spends in developing the idea in the laboratory and promoting the product during the introductory phase, the greater the opportunities for competitors to develop their imitation maneuvers. When the product is not ready for the market or the market is not ready for the innovation, the innovator's maneuver is likely to be premature and non-economic. As we'll see in the following sections, barriers are raised, hindering product development and adoption. In these cases the pioneer, rather than enjoying and benefiting from typical first-mover advantages, falls into a trap, often only recognizing it as such in retrospect.

3.6   The creation of a new market

Creating a new market is a high-impact overtaking maneuver, the optimum option for avoiding frontal confrontation with the competition. With such behavior, the firm views sector boundaries and market segmentation from a radically different perspective, and attempts to impact competitive commitment by changing the rules of the game.

A Movement Game oriented to create a new market is an example of a lateral maneuver or flanking attack; the aim is to overtake adversaries in areas that are not heavily defended, if at all. In the 1980s, for example, Japanese car manufacturers mounted an indirect attack on Europe by opening the unprotected off-road market. In this way, they were able to grow without triggering the immediate reaction of incumbents, while postponing a more direct attack to the following decade.

It stands to reason that a firm should shore up those businesses where it most fears being attacked. Flanking attacks are launched to try to take advantage of one of the fundamental principles of competition: train all available firepower on your rival's weaknesses. In terms of marketing strategies, firms tend to deploy all forces where their opponent will most likely attack. This strategy does not allow for setting up the same line of defense on all fronts; in fact, fewer defenses will be allocated where threats are not foreseen.

In Movement Games, the flanking attack is mobilized against the least defended areas. This maneuver is generally undertaken by attackers with limited resources, or ones that are more perspicacious in targeting an opportunity with respect to their rivals. The game is a search for windows of opportunity, identifying favorable spaces. Here firms can demonstrate their capabilities and create a useful platform where they can subsequently consolidate their positions of dominion on a broader scale through a more direct confrontational strategy. The maneuvers in question may involve:

1. Activating an emerging market, as Skype did for VoIP telephony (see Sections 3.7 to 3.9);
2. Re-segmenting or regenerating an existing market in a creative and innovative way, as Findus did with its successful frozen pasta products in Italy (see Section 3.10).

In both cases, the likelihood of success is directly proportional to the existence of the following four conditions:

a) The company manages to develop a genuine policy of market creation by identifying strategic windows, generating markets or niches not served by competitors, and avoiding head-to-head confrontation.
b) The market in question is characterized by positive growth rates, and thus the increasing revenues of the innovator are generated by exploiting the potential for growth in primary demand without soliciting reactions from rivals.
c) The market niche, used as a Trojan horse, can ensure the future dimensional development necessary to ensure a source of profit not only to compensate the resources deployed, but also to generate cash flows to support a frontal attack strategy.
d) Competitors are led to underestimate the threat of the new entrant. This may be because they believe the new firm is unable to acquire more than marginal share positions; or this move may actually give rise to opportunities that also favor previously consolidated competitors.

Once again, for this strategy to succeed it is clear that the firm must have more than just functional technical competencies. Also critical are market driving capabilities that translate into a deep knowledge of the market, enabling the firm to meet the most elusive and specific needs and emerging benefits sought by customers and not yet perceived by rivals.

3.7   Activating emerging markets

The imagination of a firm is the expression of its ability to invent new markets. The boundaries of a market are dynamic and subject to constant expansion. Expansion is prompted by changes in priorities expressed by customers, but also by the firm's aspirations and dreams. There are three different types of markets: existing, emerging, and imaginable (Figure 3.8).

Using the health market as an example, by abandoning the traditional definition of therapeutic areas, it is easy to trace their evolutionary and creative trajectories. The market space can be divided into:

- existing market: disease management (diagnosis, prescription, and care);
- emerging market: health management (prevision, prevention, and correction);
- imaginable market: management of individual wellbeing and the search for ways to prolong life.

For companies operating in this meta-market, opportunities present themselves that stimulate firms, alone or in coevolution with other partners, to imagine the new spaces that may turn into the emerging markets of tomorrow.

Reasoning in geographic terms, firms have always designed products and services for customers and markets of more advanced and wealthier countries. Existing markets are therefore mainly those within the USA–Europe–Japan triad. Firms, by way of localization and

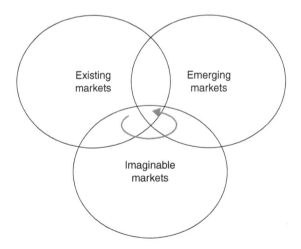

Figure 3.8 Existing, emerging, and imaginable markets

opportunities, have indeed focused their resources and their attention by serving 14% of the world population, the most privileged markets with the highest economic value. These markets have not only become more competitive, but today are the most saturated. New opportunities, therefore, may be found in the so-called "86% solution"[4]: searching for emerging markets in Asia, Africa, and South America, where 86% of the population of the planet resides. HP, for example, developed a battery and solar panel system for printers and digital cameras for the Indian market. For 9 dollars a month, these devices are rented out to local photographers who go about to villages, where even poor people are willing to buy photographic keepsakes of festivals and events.

Microsoft developed a special and more economic version of Windows for Thailand, Indonesia, and Malaysia. Companies such as Nokia, Intel, Sony, and Xerox are working in a similar direction, as are multinationals of consumer goods such as Procter & Gamble, Johnson & Johnson, Unilever, and Colgate. Dannon, for example, recently developed an extremely economic and nutritional yogurt for Bangladesh. Many firms have started studying projected world economic rankings while acknowledging the following:

- The potential customers in these markets not only have less disposable income, but they also express different needs.
- The markets in question are very fragmented.
- Infrastructure normally ranges anywhere from poor to non-existent.
- The distribution systems are local and unspecialized.
- Products and services must not simply be adapted, but instead must be designed to respond to very differentiated local resources, structures, and needs as compared to existing markets in more industrialized countries.

In order to identify emerging markets, beyond the geographical location, firms must study the consumers of the future with sophisticated ethnographic and instrumental research to learn the asymmetries that characterize and distinguish them from traditional markets.

Today's markets include traditional markets that offer products and services positioned on medium-high quality levels and offered at medium-high prices. Emerging markets, instead, are low-cost markets, a growing phenomenon that will impact all industrial and service sectors. The rise in the cheap offerings is polarizing the market structure along two extremes: high value and asymmetrically low cost. This marginalizes the entire gamut of intermediate-range offerings, those lying between high-priced and economical (but good quality).

As we've shown above, market spaces are dynamic and subject to expansive trajectories, in the sense that each imagined market today will be an emerging market tomorrow, until one day it becomes an existing market. The challenge for the firm is to know how to simultaneously manage existing markets, to develop emerging markets, and to design and activate imaginable markets. The search for emerging and imaginable markets is a fascinating Movement Game that requires the firm to come up with a shared vision that depicts and interprets the future. The ability to foresee future customer priorities and to imagine future business scenarios is the basis of this game of overtaking the competition.

To prepare for the future and create the new markets of tomorrow, firms need to respond to the following questions:

- Will we continue to serve the same customers we serve today? Who will the customers of tomorrow be? How will they be different? What will their priorities be? What solutions will they seek for their needs?
- Who will the competitors of tomorrow be? What will their sources of competitive advantage be? What game will they play? What will the new rules of this game be?
- What market driving capability must we develop to compete in the emerging and imaginary markets of tomorrow? What alliances must we join in order to develop and pursue new initiatives?
- What skills will our staff need to have? Which business model should the company use? If our firm did not exist and we could create it all over again, how would we envision it? How would we design it?

3.8 Emerging markets: the low-cost case

Many markets show a clear structural change that tends to polarize on two asymmetric aspects: trading up and trading down.[5] These expressions suggest market polarization:

- toward the top, with customers willing to pay premium prices to access a very different, highly emotional and experiential value proposition, connoted by high-quality products and services. In this perspective, for example, the Fiat Group sought to re-launch the Maserati brand.

- toward the bottom, with consumers who want to spend the least possible amount to purchase basic no frills products or services, of acceptable quality and reliability, and aligned with the design and fashion features of offerings in the trading up market. From this perspective, Renault owns Dacia as a low-cost brand.

The most critical situation arises for value propositions positioned in the middle of the market bifurcation. This intermediate position often fails to offer the emotionality of trading up or the accessibility and economy of trading down. For companies positioned at this "fork in the road," the challenge of the competitive confrontation lies in capturing the attention and meeting the priorities of customers who have become very selective, expert shoppers.

The bifurcation of the market has been accelerated by the expansion of the trading down market (often known as the low-cost or cheap market). This relatively recent phenomenon is triggering a widespread contamination process in numerous trade sectors, including some unexpected ones, resulting in the democratization of consumption. This phenomenon underscores how consumer citizens tend to always trade up in a few categories and trade down in several others, however limited their economic resources may be.

A recent topic of hot debate among firms and economists, psychologists, and sociologists who analyze purchasing patterns is why consumers are so attracted to the low-cost market. Many agree on the following reasons:

1. The evolution in purchasing behavior from economies of needs to economies of desires. In the first, there is a wide gap between supply and demand, to the detriment of the former; the second sees a stronger expression of collective priorities, galvanized by a greater availability of resources and offerings. The economy of desires is followed by an economy of instant gratification, typical of an era of abundance and prosperity, leading up to the recent phenomenon of the economy of access to goods and services. In this phase, consumers buy simply because they can, and since they are better informed of the value of things, they tend to pay lower prices or make more contained cost sacrifices.
2. The assertion that restricted availability of resources does not reduce consumption if needs can be satisfied with low-cost products and services.

3. An orientation toward cheap, which for many consumers is an expression of intelligent "cool" behavior. Customers have become experts in honing their selection criteria and purchase processes thanks to the drastic reduction of information asymmetries between supply and demand. The internet facilitates collecting information and comparing goods. But consumers also enjoy unearthing what they're looking for at the most competitive price in the "grand bazaars" of physical and virtual marketplaces. Furthermore, even the customer with greater disposable income is happy to access low-cost goods and services.

4. The low-cost market is the result of the opening of economies and the globalization of markets. In many countries, in particular in Asia, access to and availability of extremely competitive production factors are incentives for low-cost products and service provision.

5. Thanks to their consolidated knowledge, customers have difficulty acknowledging the value of goods which have come to be considered commodities. As such these items no longer justify the large price discrimination with which they are offered.

6. Low cost is no longer synonymous with perceptions of low quality; likewise, a higher level of quality is not necessarily associated with a proportionally high-cost product or level of service. Customers have started to appreciate, prosaically, that a low-cost item is not necessarily inferior to a premium-priced good.

These and other reasons have been interpreted creatively by firms who, by reconfiguring their business models, have succeeded in offering a response to market solicitations by grasping an opportunity and filling a competitive void. The phenomenon of the low-cost market is here to stay, beyond the cycles of economic trends, because it fulfills the needs of the people and responds to their aspirations.

3.9   How to confront a low-cost market: defense strategies

All firms have had to confront competitors offering value propositions at more competitive prices. But only a few companies have demonstrated the readiness and ability to face the challenge of a low-cost competitor.

Low-cost rivals do not simply offer a price reduction to their customers; they have first demolished the dominant orthodoxies and then reformulated their business models. They have done so with such originality that not only have they paralyzed competitors with the surprise factor, but they have won over customers by effectively satisfying a previously unsatisfied need. These firms have made it possible to purchase a product or access a service at an extraordinarily low price, and all this without downgrades.

Perhaps the most serious error that a traditional competitor can commit when confronting low-cost rivals is to treat them as if they were traditional competitors.[6] To ignore a low-cost competitor may indeed force a defender firm into a strategic retreat from the market, abandoning the customer segments that it can no longer serve without a radical price cut. However, the instinctive reaction, to confront these rivals, risks triggering a price war; with subsequent spiraling price cuts, this scenario would dramatically reduce profitability not only of the business but of the entire sector. A firm's low-cost strategy is often based on very clear and consistent choices as far as:

1. Selecting the customer segment to serve;
2. Offering a quality product or service, or at least an advantageous one;
3. Containing costs – constantly and even obsessively – that may facilitate corresponding price cuts.

In the literature, companies such as WalMart and Aldi (retail), Southwest and RyanAir (air transport), IKEA (furniture) or Zara (clothing) are among those mentioned most often with reference to case histories and best practices. These companies implement new strategies where cheap does not mean impoverishing the offer or being marginalized into the downgrading area of the market. Instead cheap expresses a radically new way to develop the market by reconfiguring the value proposition.

In light of this reality, waging a price war may be very risky because customers will probably prefer the lowest price, the perceived quality or service being equal. The defense and counterattack against a low-cost competitor calls for a structured process, as illustrated in Figure 3.9 below.

A firm confronting a low-cost competitor first has to assess whether the strategy is intended to cover a customer segment that the firm doesn't currently serve, or if the attack is aimed at undermining the core customers of the firm. If the low-cost rival's intent is to win customers that no other company currently serves, at least in the short term, then such a strategy may not be harmful or threatening and would not call for an immediate counterattack. By watching and

When a low-cost company enters your sector

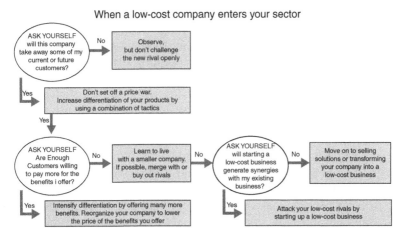

Figure 3.9 How to respond to low-cost challenges

waiting, the firm can assess the evolution of the market and customer behavior, and glean useful information in preparing a more logical defense strategy without destroying value, as would be the case with an immediate reaction.

From this perspective, some businesses share the idea that the low-cost competitor may even play an important role in developing the market and attracting new customers. Once they are familiar with the cheap product or service, these new users may subsequently migrate toward more expensive, more complex alternatives. However, this hypothesis may be contradicted by the changes underway in many markets. Low-cost competitors often educate customers by encouraging them to give up certain benefits and advantages offered by greater value propositions in exchange for a very competitive price.

When a firm foregoes a low-cost reaction, it must coexist with its price rivals by redefining, differentiating, and re-articulating its value proposition. The offering must be truly irresistible to justify a significant price increase. Firms that adopt this behavior, successfully confronting low-cost competitors, stand out for the following reasons:

1. They constantly – and rapidly – innovate their portfolio of products and services.
2. They earmark major investments for building brand identity.
3. They set up an independent retail network.

4. They persuade customers to pay for the value inherent in the tangible and intangible benefits of their offering.
5. They offer benefits with objective, measurable, exceptional quality.
6. They shore up their offering with appealing attributes that low-cost competitors cannot guarantee.
7. They pay attention to managing the entire experiential process, exploiting every touch point to serve and delight their customers.

Clearly, these considerations call on firms to explore vectors that they can use to differentiate their offerings.

In order to face a low-cost competitor while avoiding direct confrontation on the critical success factor of the far more competitive price, a firm can't simply make its value proposition irresistible. It must also strive to minimize the price differential by reengineering its processes and reducing its costs.

Firms that have differentiated their propositions and simultaneously reduced their price differentials with respect to the low-cost competition have succeeded in defending themselves. These firms have managed to slow the migration of customers to more economically competitive offers.

In other cases, when a sector begins its evolutionary trajectory toward low cost, traditional businesses find themselves having to compete for an increasingly restricted market, making an ever-decreasing number of customers pay higher prices. To avoid shrinking revenues and profits, the firm must consider opportunities for developing low-cost activities on par with their opponents, as suggested in the model in Figure 3.9 above. But this is a treacherous and strategically complex path.

Thanks to their knowledge and capabilities, which are easily and quickly adaptable to the new low-cost context, traditional firms work on the assumption that their rival's low-cost business model is simpler than theirs. This rationale is expressed in a dual sense, in that the company continues its traditional activity but constitutes a new company or brand with a low-cost positioning. We can see this strategy in action with airlines, or among financial intermediaries, with banks and insurance companies frequently founding new, no frills companies, with more basic offerings.

Traditional firms adopt this strategy to defend against flanking or even frontal attacks by emerging low-cost rivals. These incumbents aim to serve customers they do not traditionally reach, with value propositions consistent with customer expectations that reduce their cost-sacrifice. Such a dual strategy, traditional and low-cost, it is often manifested in:

- using the same brand or original brand endorsement (ING and ING Direct, in the banking sector);
- creating a new brand (Unipol and Linear, in the Italian insurance sector).

The benefit of a new brand is that it won't confuse customers, and may minimize the reactions of intermediaries (agents or distributors). A differentiated brand also allows the firm to effectively communicate the new value proposition, which must differ from that of the parent company and must consolidate the new positioning and customer perceptions. Organizing a new, separate, and independent firm facilitates the creation of a new business model, structured on different capabilities and resources; this new organization hires personnel who share these new values.

By setting up an autonomous and independent business unit and giving it responsibility for developing a low-cost operation, the risk of interference and contamination by the parent company is mitigated. But this is often not enough, as we can see from examples in the air transportation sector. Low-cost airlines that had spun off from traditional firms were subject to restrictions on their business. In addition, institutional constraints such as those imposed by trade unions made it impossible to hire staff at lower wages than those of the parent company. Real low-cost competitors, on the other hand, enjoyed greater freedom of movement.

Summing up, then, dual strategies are effective if the underlying aim is development and profitability, rather than a reaction to the threat of low-cost firms. In this situation, the far more critical option is to leave the traditional firm its freedom of movement, and to give the low-cost spinoff the autonomy to compete on the market. The goal is to generate innovations and restructure the respective business models, merging and incorporating them where appropriate.

If, however, it is not possible to pursue a dual strategy, to let low-cost activities co-exist with the original higher price activities, then firms can consider two different moves. The first is to assess the evolution of their value propositions, from the product offerings to the customer solutions. The second, more radical option is to turn into a low-cost firm, abandoning the original mission.

In the first case, building a solution does not simply mean integrating products with a variety of services, expanding the bundling of the offering. A solution must offer customers the opportunity to delegate the management of less strategic processes, to reduce costs and risks, and to develop their own revenue and profits. Becoming a solution provider reduces the transparency of the proposed price and increases the dependence of customers on the solutions offered. Instead, radically adopting the low cost strategy (and in turn restructuring the business model) is a very difficult path, because it means developing and internalizing often new and asymmetric competencies compared to those needed to manage the traditional firm.

3.10 Innovative market segmentation

Exploring the market to identify new customer segments and to win potential customers who are currently not being served: this is another Movement Game that requires exceptional creativity and imagination.

Creative market segmentation is a Movement Game that motivates firms to look for customer groups, areas of needs and benefits that are not served at all, or inadequately satisfied by the competition (Figure 3.10).

The recent segment of luxury compact cars is a case in point (e.g. the Mini), as is the creative segmentation of Swatch watches back in the 1980s (and still successful).

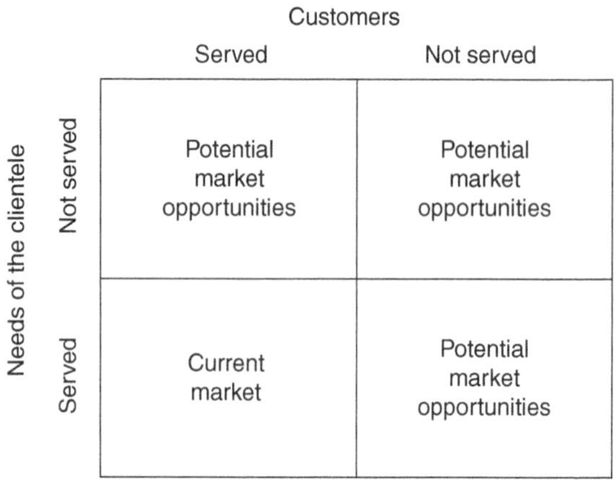

Figure 3.10 Identification of new segments

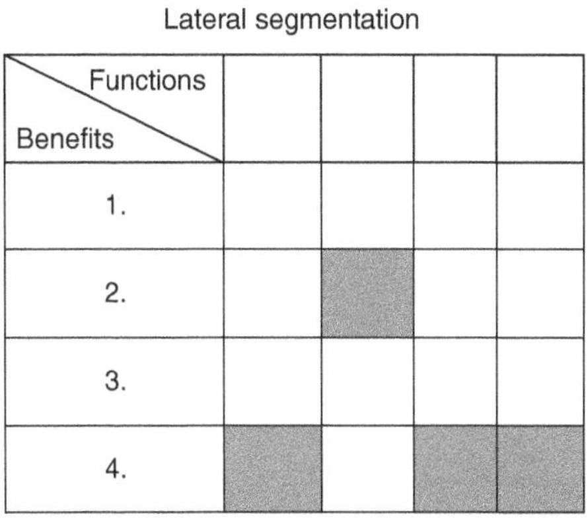

Lateral segmentation

Functions / Benefits				
1.				
2.		▓		
3.				
4.	▓		▓	▓

Figure 3.11   Lateral segmentation

De Longhi's small portable air conditioners are the key to this company's significant competitive advantage on an international level. De Longhi confronts its rivals with more substantial resources, innovatively satisfying an incipient need expressed by the market: mobile domestic air conditioning.

A new market segmentation, in order to achieve success, must respect certain principles.

1. The firm must be the first to occupy a market segment; otherwise, the confrontation would be reduced to an offensive attack against a position, albeit a weak one, already covered by the competition. Furthermore, to conquer an undefended market segment the firm may need very limited resources, while winning back a segment by a rival undoubtedly takes a more costly effort and commitment.
2. A game of lateral movement, segmenting the market, does not specifically require developing new products. Innovative behavior, adopting more original and creative competitive weapons, is necessary. The launch of pre-cut, pre-washed vegetables is an telling example. Bonduelle, though using a very mature product, has achieved excellent competitive results with these goods, leveraging the growing need of many customers to save time. How many similarly obvious solutions are hiding in our markets today?
3. To successfully re-segment a market, we need highly evolved intuition and understanding of operational, emotional, social, emergent, and future needs, be they implicit or explicit. In this case, market

segmentation by product or service does not yet exist or is still in a latent or embryonic phase.

4. The element of surprise may once again be vital for success. By its very nature, the flanking attack is a surprise attack and differs from clear-cut offense/defense battles, in which we can predict what is about to happen and where. The greater the surprise, the more time the adversary needs to prepare and deploy his defense reaction.

3.11   The search for new markets and geographical segmentation

The search for adjacent possibilities to extend the geographic range of a firm's activities is a Movement Game which, in competitive contexts without boundaries, must be explored by each firm as a strategic development opportunity.

The search for a new market requires a thorough exploration of three vectors: countries, products, and customer segments to serve, as suggested in Figure 3.12.

After analyzing the three vectors in various combinations, the firm selects one of the four strategies in Table 3.2, pertaining to what country to enter, whether to target the customer segments already being served or different ones, and whether to offer selected customers

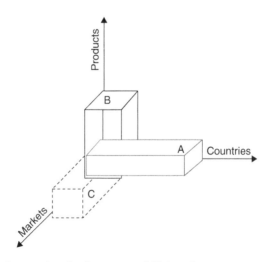

Figure 3.12 International adjacent possibilities: the country–product–market triad option

Table 3.2 Overtaking and attack maneuvers in international markets

Country market	Market and market segments served	Products	Vectors and growth option
Country 1	Current customer	Current	1
Country 2	segments or markets	New	2
...	New markets or	Current	3
Country n	customer segments	New	4

From a STRUCTURALIST view	To a RECONSTRUCTIONIST view
The conditions of the sector are given and firms are forced to compete within the pre-established limits.	The market boundaries and the structure of the sector are not defined a priori but instead can be redefined by the actions and conviction of the players.
Competing firms use the same best practices.	A new market space is generated breaking the cost-value trade-off.

Figure 3.13 From a structuralist view to a reconstructionist view

the existing value proposition or one that has been customized for them.

The Fiat Group, for example, sells its main brand only in select countries, serving customers with its city cars; elsewhere it only offers the Alfa Romeo brand, exclusively targeting customers who are more attracted to a sporting brand image; still other markets have Fiat, Lancia, and Alfa Romeo. The Ferrari and Maserati brands, instead, are managed in various countries with autonomous policies consistent with their strategic positioning in the automobile market.

With geographical segmentation a firm evaluates adjacent possibilities, exploring the national and international territory. The search centers on markets where there are no potential competitors or where rivals may be vulnerable to an attack or less inclined to react to an incursion.

3.12 The search for new markets and segments: the advantages of the first mover

Breaking ground in a market or a new segment, as discussed in the previous sections (3.6 to 3.11), may offer the first mover exclusive advantages that translate into entrance barriers for followers. The main barriers are:

- Economies of scale: The innovator has more time to achieve economies of scale before rival imitators make their entrance. These economies can guarantee cost advantages that are useful for preventive defense maneuvers or for blocking entry to competitors.
- Image and reputation: Pioneers may benefit from a major boost to their reputation thanks to the image generated by their innovative products. The innovator can shore up its reputation and customer relations, promoting brand loyalty (see the following point).
- Brand loyalty and customer conversion costs: If the first mover offers new technology with greater benefits and a competitive price, this may: (a) reduce the costs of conversion perceived by customers who already buy alternative products; (b) asymmetrically, enhance brand loyalty among its customers, increasing the costs of conversion to imitator products.
- Strategic positioning: When the first mover can anticipate the changes that will occur in the market following the innovation, this firm has the opportunity to choose the best placement for its products or services, thus reducing opportunities for imitation.
- Learning economies: Greater familiarity and experience with the technology and the market offer the innovator advantages over imitators in the processes of improving, producing, and applying the technology.
- Access and control of distribution channels: For followers and late-comers it may be difficult and expensive to penetrate the distribution channels already used by the innovator, because businesses will resist efforts to crowd their shelves and catalogues.
- Technological standards and network economies: When the first mover succeeds in consolidating its dominion in the market, it may set the bar for the technology involved. This firm may also implement innovation maneuvers, anticipating the moves of imitators and setting down the rules of the game for followers. The first-mover advantage is also amplified in the case of products or services whose value is proportional to the number of pre-existing customers. This is the case of online auction sites or instant messaging software.
- Controlling scarce resources: The innovator can also exercise the right of first refusal, or may control raw materials or other resources, or production and marketing factors that maximize the entrance barriers for imitators.

- Licenses and patents: Legal protection of the innovation is essential in order to reduce the possibility of imitation and raise the imitator's costs and reaction times.

To ensure success, the innovator needs to develop specific market driving skills, such as:

- Innovative attitude: The ability and determination to exploit R&D capability to pursue the innovation.
- Intuitive knowledge of the market and customers: Intuitive because creating and developing new markets and new products and services cannot be adequately supported by market research. Customers often have a hard time expressing their incipient or latent needs; they are often not even aware of the benefits and opportunities offered by the new technology.
- Technical production capability: To ensure the success of the innovation, it is critical that the firm develop suitable capabilities to ensure the functional physical integrity of products and services, and to guarantee production at competitive costs.
- Market penetration capability: Beyond research and technology development capabilities, a guarantee of success for an innovator involves critical marketing capabilities. For example, the firm must accelerate the process of dissemination, adoption, and use of the innovation; it must educate customers, cooperate with distribution, or (a more audacious move) create or access new distribution channels.

3.13   Overtaking the competition by redefining the value proposition

Customer-centric firms design, implement, and communicate an irresistible – and therefore extraordinary – competitive value proposition.

As we mentioned above, the biggest difference between a Movement Game and an Imitation or Position Game lies in the recognition that to win, players have to stop wanting to fight the competition. The most decontextualized example in the business world has been Le Cirque du Soleil.[7]

The lure of a traditional circus is founded on four elements: the marquee, the clowns, the acrobats, and the animal acts (the fiercer the better). To pursue the competition, Le Cirque could have attempted to enhance its attractions by acting on the four traditional success factors. Instead, this company initiated a Movement Game by developing an overtaking maneuver that reached new heights in creativity and demolished the conventions of traditional circuses.

Le Cirque du Soleil: 1) with its marquee, redesigned a space reflecting the classic symbol of the circus while strengthening the related semiotics to reflect the memory of more mythical circuses; 2) eliminated the animal stunts; 3) reduced acrobatics and the number of shows, and made them more elegant and exciting; 4) enhanced the value proposition by creating new shows, using components almost entirely alien to the circus, such as plot, music, artistic dances, and new attractions.

Instead of proposing a combination of attractions like traditional circuses do, Le Cirque du Soleil has connoted every one of its shows with a different story recalling a theatrical performance or musical, with soundtracks, lighting, timing, and the "wow" factor of the acts – all in harmony with the theme and stage design. All this shifts the spectator's attention away from the humorous and risky elements alone to a more sophisticated sense of charm and emotionality.

The strategic content of Le Cirque du Soleil's Movement Game has not only revitalized a less attractive and more mature sector, but has allowed the company to pursue success without taking customers away from direct competitors. By redefining the value proposition, on the one hand Le Cirque has recaptured the interest of their main customers, children, who today are attracted to other forms of entertainment such as new media and consoles. On the other hand, the firm has brought adult customers back to the circus, who find appeal instead in a one-of-a-kind show.

As we mentioned before, the conceptual foundations of the Movement Game are based on the generation of quantum leaps and the creative destruction of orthodoxies and conventions that dominate a firm and a sector. Redefining the value proposition emboldens the firm to overtake the competition by activating a Movement Game; this prompts the firm to abandon a structuralist view in favor of a reconstructionist view.

The structuralist approach motivates the firm to redefine its value proposition to beat the competition, either by strengthening and differentiating its most critical components or, in contrast, by reducing costs. The reconstructionist approach instead calls for a different intellectual perspective, recognizing that the market boundaries, the structure of the sector, and the value proposition are not given but can be reconfigured creatively, generating new visions and new rules in terms of best practices by reformulating the tradeoff between cost and value. In the reconstructionist view we would find it hard to judge whether or not a sector is attractive, because this attraction can be modified by the determination of a firm which is intent on entirely rebuilding the sector, as did Le Cirque du Soleil.

3.14 The value curve

A value proposition is the holistic experience that a company creates and transfers to its customers. In other words, the firm offers its customers a solution for fulfilling their expectations and priorities by bundling products and services. Therefore, the value proposition defines the magnitude and the extension of the value exchange that takes place between the buyer and seller.

Many Movement Games begin with a reformulation of the value proposition. This is a way for a firm to enhance the value provided to customers by serving increasingly larger portions of their needs more effectively and/or efficiently than rivals. This can be done by reinforcing the functional features and benefits of the offer; by bundling or unbundling products and services, or combining them in a package of more complex offerings; connecting with customers in original ways; reducing transaction costs; supporting the customer in certain stages of the value chain; or offering customers comprehensive solutions to their needs. The creative process of reformulating the value proposition may be facilitated by using the value curve.

The value curve, the graphic representation of the value proposition offered by a company to its customers,[8] is a simple but powerful tool for reconfiguring and regenerating business behavior by destroying current conventions. On the horizontal axis, the value curve shows the specific components of the proposition in question: product (defined according to the most critical indicators of customer satisfaction), price, services, channels, and information. The vertical axis illustrates the relative level of performance, measured through a comparative, objective, or perceptive evaluation of the various propositions offered by the firm and by competitors (see Figure 3.14).

The graphic representation of the value proposition that the value curve gives makes it easier for us to understand the different ways in which competitors are trying to satisfy the needs of their customers.

The more conventional structuralist approach to managing the value curve implies incrementally improving the performance of the key components of the offer, without changing or radically reshaping the curve. Instead, innovative players of the Movement Game which follow the reconstructionist approach seek to creatively and radically redraw

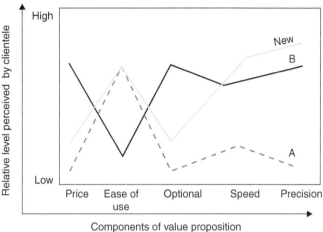

Figure 3.14   The value curve

the value curve: eliminating, reducing, improving, or significantly innovating every component of the offering.

In order to drive this process, the firm has to answer these four questions:

1. Which components of the offer could be eliminated?
2. Which components of the offer could be reduced below the standard of the competition?
3. Which components could be improved, raising the bar with respect to rivals?
4. Which new components could be created and integrated to revolutionize the value proposition, as compared to rivals?

The first question predictably prompts reflection on how much each component of the value proposition actually contributes to customer satisfaction. Firms that are too focused on competitive confrontation tend to reinforce all the components that are also offered by their rivals. Instead, companies could eliminate insignificant items, or others that may even reduce the value offered to the customer segments in question, in a changing environment.

In order to respond to the second question, instead, firms should consider reducing investments in components that are necessary but overvalued. In this case, too, routine may be the real trap. In fact, routines make firms slow to recognize changes in demand which may be substantial, but so gradual as to easily go unnoticed. By eliminating or reducing some components of the value proposition, the firm also acts on cost structures, introducing cost savings that positively reflect on customers' cost sacrifice.

With the last two questions, the reconstructionist approach urges firms to evaluate what they can increase or create in order to propose new and irresistible value for the customer. The third question encourages firms to seek out every incremental and substantial improvement that would serve to strengthen the components of value recognized as critical to customers but neglected until that moment, perhaps due to outmoded customs or simple shortsightedness. The fourth question sets the firm on a search for new sources of value for customers, more radically breaking conventions and orthodoxies, as in the case of Le Cirque du Soleil, IKEA, or Ryan Air. Innovative firms, through the answers suggested above, tend to generate new value curves or redraw existing ones.

To sum up, value innovation is not about delivering the latest technology to the market; innovation in the value curve means offering customers a memorable experience.[9] When the value curve of a firm is fundamentally different from the competition and this difference is recognized by customers for the value it guarantees, then the company should try to resist premature innovation. In such cases, the company should focus on expanding its business geographically, improving its processes to gain experience, reconfiguring its incremental business model, and growing its market share. This approach is also useful because it can discourage imitators from investing resources to pursue further innovations.

3.15   Overtaking the competition by reconfiguring the business model

In the case of overtaking maneuvers, or rather, in the high-impact Movement Game, the search for adjacent possibilities may lead to reconfiguring the business model, an area that offers various speculative opportunities. Every business is subject to a continuous and dynamic process of change. A firm may decide to restructure its business model in light of anticipated structural modifications in the market environment. A similar move may also be prompted by a variation in the financial ambitions of the firm.

Two business models, when drawn up on a sheet of paper, may look exactly the same, but can differ significantly in the quality of resources

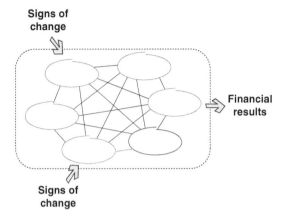

Signs of change

Financial results

Signs of change

Figure 3.15   The change

or in the implementation capability of strategic intent. Reconfiguring the business model is a way to recombine and reconnect the different components to find a solution that balances the model and delivers a sustainable advantage. The adjacent possibilities that arise from reconfiguring the business model can be classified according to the radical nature of the maneuver, which may vary as follows:

1. Outsourcing and dislocation of activities (generally lower-impact);
2. Ascending and descending vertical integration;
3. Creatively reconfiguring the entire value chain (generally high-impact).

Let us review each of these in turn.

1. Firms often opt for dislocation of a number of activities or an entire production process in order to exploit the comparative advantage of specific geographical areas for certain production factors, in particular the labor force. A well-known case is Nike. Today many other companies have followed suit; for example some American businesses have transferred their call centers to India. The race to invest and externalize in Asian countries (and India in particular) is an opportunity not only to enter new emerging markets with extraordinary internal potential, but also to access qualified labor at an extremely competitive cost. Intel, for example, has numerous research labs in these areas. Many companies have opted to delocalize the more critical phases of

their business models while centralizing the coordination of related activities. Outsourcing, instead, is an adjacent option more closely resembling integration. This alternative involves long-term contracts with certain suppliers that do not oblige the firm to commit to rigid integration. On the contrary, these agreements can provide many benefits for satisfactory and flexible new sources of supply.

2. The options of ascending or descending vertical integration are effective in ensuring firm growth or cost containment. Access and control through ascending vertical integration of key suppliers can be a critical success factor and may also give the firm a considerable advantage over its rivals. With descending vertical integration, instead, the firm seeks privileged access to demand by directly controlling retail outlets and customer relationships. We can find many examples in the high fashion or luxury sectors, as with Cartier or the Luxottica network. These maneuvers result in the disintermediation of distribution, and also serve to establish a direct relationship with the market and with end-users. This enhances market-sensing capabilities, enabling the firm to recognize signs of change in the priorities of customer needs before rivals do. Many firms have set up their own sales networks and e-commerce sites. By doing so, they have a closer connection to customers, which strengthens relations and promotes the sense of membership in a community, activating a reciprocal exchange of knowledge and value.

In order to appreciate the significance of modifying the business model, a useful illustrative example is the transformation process in the personal computer sector. By examining its evolution over time, we can discern three different eras, each characterized by a distinctive business model. The Apple era represents the early stages of development. Apple's business model was based on integrating R&D and developing company-owned hardware and operating systems. Next came the IBM era, characterized by the broad-scale use of PCs, obliging the market to accept the IBM-compatible dogma. However, the success of this company brought with it the seeds of the destruction of its future market dominion. When IBM chose to reconfigure its business model with respect to Apple, this decision was based on the correct conviction that designing, producing, and distributing PCs called for different, even asymmetric skills, as opposed to those needed for manufacturing mainframe and minicomputers. To rapidly circumvent such complex technical-functional barriers, IBM decided to turn to outsourcing. The production of microprocessors was delegated mostly to Intel, while for the implementation of its operating system, IBM opted to partner with Microsoft, then in its infancy. This courageous and innovative redefinition of the business model, in fact, brought about the establishment of strategic partners which, in time, became the real owners of the key resources for producing PCs and of the value generated by this business. In the end, IBM acknowledged that personal computers are no longer an attractive component of its portfolio. In fact, in 2005, the company sold the division to its Chinese partner Legend, establishing the joint venture Lenovo, of which IBM now holds less than 5% (2012 datum).

While we wait for the upcoming fourth era, the third we can attribute to Dell, which activated a very innovative Movement Game. (See the next point on the creative reconfiguration of the business model.) In the 1990s, Dell instigated the reconfiguration of the whole PC supply chain with: (a) an almost total recourse to various forms of outsourcing, and (b) descending vertical integration, with the disintermediation of all traditional specialized retailers. Dell sold its products directly to end users, either private or corporate, first via catalog, then via telephone, and currently by using a personalized offer configurator via the internet. This strategy, without neglecting customer assistance, generated the emerging low-cost PC market. Dell's interpretation of the business model, the basis of this strategy, differentiates it from many other rivals, as Kevin Rollins, vice chairman of Apple, highlights in his response to the following question:

> *What is it about the direct sales model and mass customization that has been difficult for competitors to replicate?*
>
> *It's not as simple as just having a direct sales force. It's not as simple as just having mass customization in plant or manufacturing methodology. It's a whole series of things in the value chain from the way we procure, the way we develop the product, the way we order and have inventory levels, and manufacturer and service support. The entire value chain has to work together to make it efficient and effective.*

3. Creatively reconfiguring the business model. Reengineering processes to double productivity can provide excellent results. But these results can quickly deteriorate if a competitor radically restructures not only its processes but also its entire business model, as evidenced in the Dell case in the 1990s.

In some cases, a possible path for regenerating the business model may be profoundly intervening on process organization in order to develop incremental competitive advantages compared with competitor performance. In other cases, however, the business model can be designed in a totally different way, to support a strategy of radically overtaking the competition and profoundly influencing customer behavior.

Many firms have regenerated their business models, seeking greater effectiveness and efficiency, in light of the first approach. In the automotive sector, an often-cited benchmark is Toyota's innovations to its business model through "Kaman", "just-in-time" and so forth. In fact, Toyota was able to achieve significant competitive advantages thanks to the competencies it developed, its effective and efficient management of the most critical supply chain and production processes, and its alignment with the priorities expressed by customers. However, in regenerating its business model, the company did not modify the traditional meaning of driving and mobility.

Other firms, instead, have designed new business models that have profoundly influenced the way in which we work and live. In other words, they have not only responded to the need for productivity or effectiveness but have also overtaken potential competitors with their Movement Game by deeply affecting their customers' behavior, culture, and expectations. These changes have also impacted customer relations and access channels to the firm, as well as the purchase, use, and consumption methods of the firms' products and services.

Companies such as IKEA, Google, Amazon, Federal Express, Southwest, Zadar, Dell, and McDonalds are only some of the convincing examples of extraordinarily innovative ways to design a radically different business model. And thanks to these original business models underpinning Movement Games, these companies have successfully activated new (and in some cases low-cost) markets.

The impetus for redesigning an organization with respect to competitors, to satisfy customer expectations in different ways, is a trend that characterizes many markets, that we can interpret in the two dimensions of Figure 3.16.[10]

On a time horizon beginning in the middle of the last century and continuing up to the present, we can identify three different stages of development for expectations expressed by the market and answers offered by firms. The first phase is controlled expectations. In the presence of economic and structural constraints, the market expressed a relatively modest demand, and the expansion of consumption was limited. The second phase, from 1970 to 2000, coincides with a cycle of extended options which saw dizzying growth in

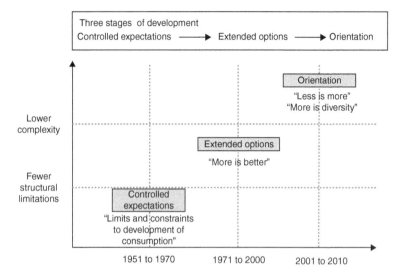

Figure 3.16   The three stages of development of market expectations

the supply and demand of goods and services. During this period, firms responded to the increasing and changing expectations by extending the variety of their offerings. As proof of the scale of products and services developed in this stage, simply look at the shelves of supermarkets, consumer electronics, and clothing stores served by big organized distribution, or television network schedules, or the long list of telecommunications, insurance, and banking services. The most surprising paradox – brought about by the exponential increase of the variety of choices – is rejection and dissatisfaction of these complex offerings by customers, the very people for whom these products and services are designed. Customer dissatisfaction is an indicator of a widespread desire for simplicity. Customers want less complexity and entropy; they want to spend less time and fewer resources on searching for information in order to evaluate and select products and services.

This new need for simplification has given rise to the third phase: orientation. Now customers express a complex and paradoxical priority, where less is more and where more is diversity. Obtaining less is valued more highly because it is the answer to questions that, implicitly or explicitly, consumers address to themselves and to firms.

For example: "What can I do without? What is it I don't need? What is it I don't need to know?" The second component of the paradox, where there is greater diversity, responds to the findings that consumers do not want to buy or consume less; instead they want to buy and consume differently.

The products and services consumers appreciate most are those that reduce "hidden costs" or involve non-monetary cost sacrifices (such as learning). This new phase of customer orientation, where less is more and more is diversity, has stimulated many companies to rethink their value propositions and to provide a response that is in line with this priority. The creation of emerging markets marked by low costs, authenticity, or simplicity, is a clear and successful response. The customer gets less, but this "less" is more highly valued because it comes with different modalities and value propositions. The emerging markets in this third phase call for completely new business models, not simply ones that are consistent with this new orientation. These models must offer complicated and sometimes even paradoxical answers, because they must strike a balance between opposite needs. Figure 3.17 exemplifies the cases of Zara and Southwest from this point of view.

3.16   The search for new customer access channels

With various low-impact maneuvers, firms can identify original adjacent possibilities by exploring distribution channels that offer customer access: company-owned retail chains, large distribution (associated, organized and specialist), franchised chains, shop in shops, corner shops, outlets, temporary shops (pop-up stores), catalog sales, vending machines, telesales, multilevel chains, work-site shops, fairs and markets, machine to machine, e-commerce, m-commerce, promoter networks, infomediaries, etc. Firms can also expand the possibilities for customer management through multichannel policies: operating in several distribution channels, developing new channels, or creating new distribution formats ranging from the indirect network to direct sales. The complex multichannels of a bank, for example, represent creativity generated in a mature industry in order to address the challenges underway in the financial intermediaries market. Equally interesting is the case of entirely automatic drugstores, already very popular in some parts of the world, especially Japan. These are innovative stores with no shop assistants; they are modeled on vending machines, and are open 24 hours a day and restocked daily with fresh goods.

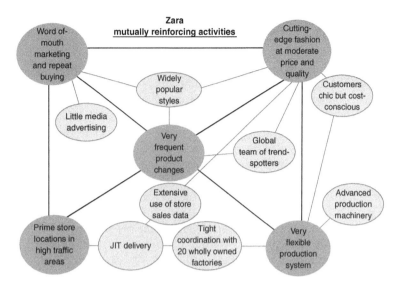

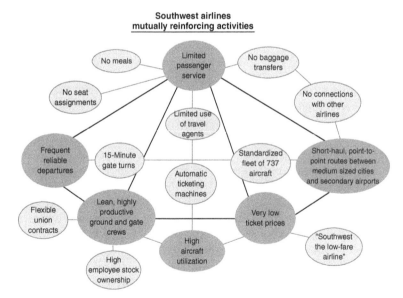

Figure 3.17   The three stages of development of market expectations: Zara and Southwest Airlines

By seeking out new distribution channels, whether they are physical or virtual, direct or indirect, firms attempt to:

1. Activate multiple possibilities of contact between customers and firms to meet specific priorities and respond to different purchasing patterns;
2. Differentiate the offering in order to limit possible channel conflicts, increasing brand equity, creating new positioning and defining alternative price policies to discriminate the value proposition;
3. Reach new customer segments.

The adjacent options that firms can select on the "channel" vector may be used in the Movement Game to support lateral overtaking maneuvers (Table 3.3).

3.17   Regenerating customer processes

The disappointing treatment that many customers are subject to is not simply the result of accidental events. It is symptomatic of firms' weaknesses, and reflects the fallacy of their insistence that they actually place the customer at the center of their attention. What is most disturbing is that, in some cases, it is not only individual firms that try the patience and exhaust the tolerance of their customers, but whole business clusters. For examples we can look to retail, insurance, banking, hospitals, transportation, public utilities, and so on.

Being a customer can be difficult and in extreme scenarios even terrifying, but this can be attenuated by the extraordinary experiences people have when passionate firms treat them like real customers, as in the examples below:

- A municipality commemorates residents' silver wedding anniversaries by sending the couples a scroll; or a city that mails out driver's license expiration reminders, or schedules children's vaccinations.
- An e-commerce site, if it mistakenly delivers the wrong book, informs the customer of the mistake and gives her the book free of charge to apologize for the inconvenience.
- A hotel gives its guests eight varieties of pillows to choose from to ensure they will sleep well; hotels can also offer customized breakfasts, letting guests chose from a wide variety of options, including a prepare-it-yourself meal.

Table 3.3 Adjacent and potential "channels"

Possible channels	Direct sales	Owned stores	Franchising	Retailers Mass retailers	Vending machines	Corners Piggy Backs Shop in shops	E-com Mobile-com TV-com	Catalog sales	Fairs and markets	Etc
Type of customers served										
Priority needs satisfied										
Experience offered										
Access mode										
Assured skills										
Necessary skills										
Costs										
Interoperability										

- Car dealers take care of customers in the same way they do their cars.
- Couriers offer satisfaction or money-back guarantees.

If some firms are extraordinary in serving their customers, establishing a consistent benchmark, then how can many others be so insensitive, and fail to give their customers a satisfactory experience? Because, beyond their public statements, these companies are unable to manage customers in the way they deserve. The reasons are twofold. First, these firms are unable to expand and develop the true culture of customer orientation, placing themselves at the service of their customers and striving to delight them. Second, the enthusiastically planned customer-centric practices fail to generate an irresistible experience every time the customer has contact with the company and its products and services.

In high-impact Movement Games, the value proposition is reconfigured by adopting the reconstructionist method. In low-impact Movement Games, the value proposition can be suitably re-evaluated to pursue an effective overtaking maneuver of the competition through:

1. the experience factor;
2. reengineering the customer process.

1. The experience factor

Designing an experience means recognizing that customers do not buy a product or service solely for its technical-functional features. In fact, customers also respond to the sense of identity that it projects on their lifestyle and for the "holistic satisfaction" they get from buying into the value proposition in question.

Therefore, in order to meet and keep its customers, the firm seeks to design, communicate, and transfer an irresistible value proposition. Achieving success means sharing with customers a mutually beneficial exchange of value. Starbucks, as we can see in Figure 3.18, does not just sell a cup of coffee. Instead, it offers customers a valuable experience that they acknowledge by their willingness to pay a considerable price premium. New entrants who are attracted by the firm's great success and margins, however, are increasingly challenging this benefit.

The experience that customers have with a firm emphasizes the differential they perceive between what the firm promises and what it actually does to meet their expectations.

Figure 3.19 above simplifies the meaning of experience. The value proposition expresses a promise that is communicated to the customer.

Figure 3.18   The experience factor

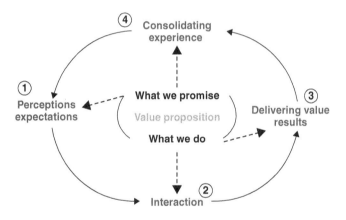

Figure 3.19   The significance of experience

This promise influences customers' expectations and perceptions, or what they presume will happen and what they will obtain. What the firm actually does to achieve and transfer the value proposition to its customers materializes in all the interrelations that the customer experiences with the firm. These coincide with the touch points set up to manage the relationship (to make everything that the firm planned actually happen). The experience gained in the process of interacting with the firm positively or negatively impacts the customers' sense that they have obtained a result: the perceived value (what is actually delivered).

An irresistible value proposition is achieved when the firm manages its customers' entire experiential process in an extraordinary way, with

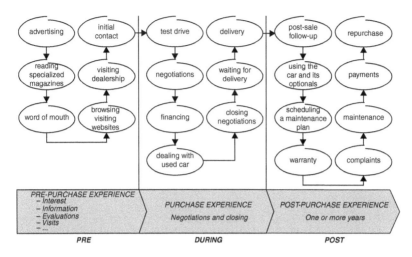

Figure 3.20   The path of experience and its touch points

respect to its rivals. This path may be denoted in different ways. The one in Figure 3.20 below, which many of us are familiar with, is a simplified reconstruction of the process of buying a car.

By analyzing Figure 3.20, we can focus on some useful considerations for improving customer experiences. The first is that this path can be subdivided into three different phases:

- First, the pre-purchase experience. This involves deciding what to do to obtain a result or benefit that satisfies the customer's priorities. In this phase the customer collects information, pays careful attention to the advertising or promotional communication, visits a point of sale, navigates online sites, converses with the sales staff, talks to friends, family etc.
- Second, the actual purchase experience. This centers on customer experiences during the purchase, payment, installation, and use of the product or service.
- Third, the post-purchase experience. This refers to the customer's experience in maintaining the expected results and benefits.

By looking at the experiential path, we can come up with two initial questions:

1. What are the critical customer activities and experiences before, during, and after the purchase process?

2. What opportunities are there to improve the value experience related to every phase of the experiential path?

In order to effectively respond to these questions, we must make a second observation that clearly emerges from our analysis of the experiential path. In each pre-, during, and post-purchase phase, the customer interacts with the firm at pre-established touch points. Touch points are all the contact points through which customers interact with the firm, where they develop their impressions which positively or negatively impact their assessment of the experience. Touch points lend themselves to different classifications and may be attributed to:

1. Products and services, connoting experiential moments in relation to their technical-functional components; performance, aesthetics, or design; sensory stimuli, etc.
2. Personal relations, considering direct interactions between customers and staff (sale and non-sale); this relates to empathy, listening skills, willingness to provide information, reassurance and solutions, the spirit of cooperation, energy, professionalism, etc.
3. Communication activities, underpinning all the campaigns, events, content and material to inform, communicate, represent and persuade customers; communications transmitted through all possible online and offline media.
4. Environment and atmosphere, describing the experience gained by the customer via all touch points relative to the environment, and atmosphere of a point of sale or any place arranged to facilitate a relationship with or access to the firm and the use of its products and services.
5. Systems and administration, covering all the touch points designed instead to facilitate and manage relations, administrative transactions, and customer support. This category also includes all invoicing processes, payment methods and systems, ATMs, call centers, toll-free numbers, assistance services, maintenance, and guarantees, etc.

All the touch points that can be identified by the firm impact the customer experience on a conscious or unconscious, rational or emotional level. Therefore, touch points correspond to the decisive moments when customers verify the extent to which the experience satisfied their expectations.

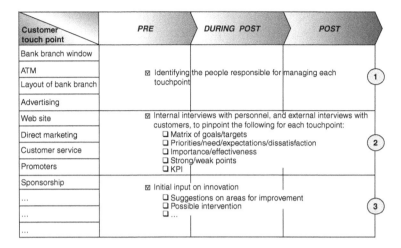

Figure 3.21 The contact point grid

By intersecting the touch points with the three phases of the experiential path, we can build a touch point grid or contact point grid (see Figure 3.21 above).

All the touch points that fall within the pre-purchase phase, from the firm's perspective, must arouse interest, create awareness, differentiate between the benefits offered, create favorable associations, and facilitate ratings and comparisons to ensure the brand is considered within the set of brands to be evaluated. For customers, instead, these touch points are useful for acquiring awareness of their own needs and solutions, generating familiarity and knowledge, narrowing down choices to a certain number of brands to simplify the evaluation processes.

Touch points activated by the firm that fall into the purchase phase signal the best offers available and how they differs from the competition's, so as to encourage confidence, create value, facilitate access to the product and service, and generate a sell out. Likewise, at this stage of the purchasing process touch points help customers trust the brand, select the offering that best suits their priorities, achieve value and simplify the purchase.

In the third post-purchase phase, the touch points serve other purposes. They help the firm keep its promises, they offer incremental value, and they delight customers to create loyalty in terms of cross-selling and up-selling. Customers, in turn, use the post-purchase touch points to confirm the choices they've made, the forms of service, assistance and support they expect, and to verify satisfaction with the continuous use of the service, consolidating loyalty to the brand.

Improving the customer's experiential path starts with a detailed inventory of touch points. This is done by determining what functions of the firm are responsible for which touch points, identifying the customer experience, and pinpointing the actions the firm can take to differentiate this experience and make it irresistible. From a careful evaluation of our customers' experiential path, we can get a more systemic view of the effectiveness of the value proposition offered to the market.

3.17   "Customer-centered reengineering"

As we saw in the previous section, managing the customer experience means rethinking all the processes that can generate value for the customer, bringing them in line with the objective of maximizing satisfaction.

A process is a set of concatenated activities aimed at producing a given result. Some processes are developed and deployed within the same function of a firm; other more strategic processes are characterized by their inter-functionality. Developing a product, reengineering an order, managing the supply chain, handling logistics, and distributing goods/providing services – all these things are done through both functional and inter-functional processes. We can categorize them as customer processes that produce an output that is furnished to an external, intermediate, or end customer, or administrative/managerial processes that relate to routines and to serving customers within the organization. A process therefore defines a value chain because each structured phase adds value to the next. We can affirm that a firm's competitiveness depends to a large extent on how effectively and efficiently it structures and manages its processes. Processes are the living, breathing part of the organization, and the most effective place for innovative planning. Naturally the most critical processes are geared to generating and transferring value to customers.

This shows that great care must be taken in managing processes, breaking them down into constituent phases, pinpointing logical and temporal links, tracking related costs, identifying the necessary skills for process implementation and improvement by setting goals and assigning responsibilities, and defining criteria for measuring the results achieved. All this, which must revolve around the focal point of customer

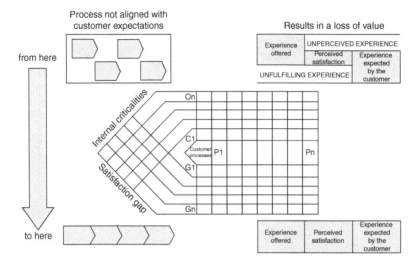

Figure 3.22 Customer-centered re-engineering: aligning customer processes

satisfaction, is a prerequisite to intervening proactively in managing the processes in an organization. In particular, we can identify three different operations for process restructuring or customer-centered reengineering. Specifically, these are those aimed at:

1. Improving sub-processes or functional processes;
2. Enhancing employee processes;
3. Regenerating processes.

The firm can then proceed with rationalization by simplifying and continuously improving processes. A higher-impact tactic would be to plan radical reengineering and regeneration, to find creative and original solutions to satisfy customer needs, thereby generating extraordinary experiences and value with respect to the competition's offer.

3.18 Incremental development of products and markets

In Movement Games, the search for adjacent opportunities in order to overtake the competition provides a great variety of options. Firms can creatively explore myriad product and market vectors, as suggested in Figs. 3.23a and 3.23b. However, we should note that at times these

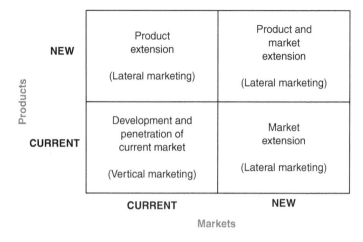

Figure 3.23A   The product/market matrix

maneuvers can become high impact, as shown in cases of a radical redefinition of the value proposition (Section 3.13) or instrumental market segmentation (Section 3.10).

The discontinuity introduced on the two dimensions of the grid, for both products and markets, discriminates between already existing and potential products – in other words, products which the company sells today (and markets being served today), as opposed to new products and markets that could be created tomorrow. The matrix cells define four different Movement Games (generally low-impact), which can be traced back to vertical and lateral marketing maneuvers.[11]

Vertical marketing implies all creative maneuvers that are designed to develop and penetrate every area of demand and offer all benefits requested by potential customers in the market defined and served by the firm. This is done by exploiting all possible modifications a firm can make to already-available products.

Movement Games through lateral marketing, instead, solicit more creative exploration, promoting the generation of adjacent options both for product and market extensions, moving away from those currently available and served.

Movement Games through vertical marketing

Movement Games through vertical marketing are based on the segmentation possibilities of the current market, and on the various competitive positioning possibilities for the firm's products and services.

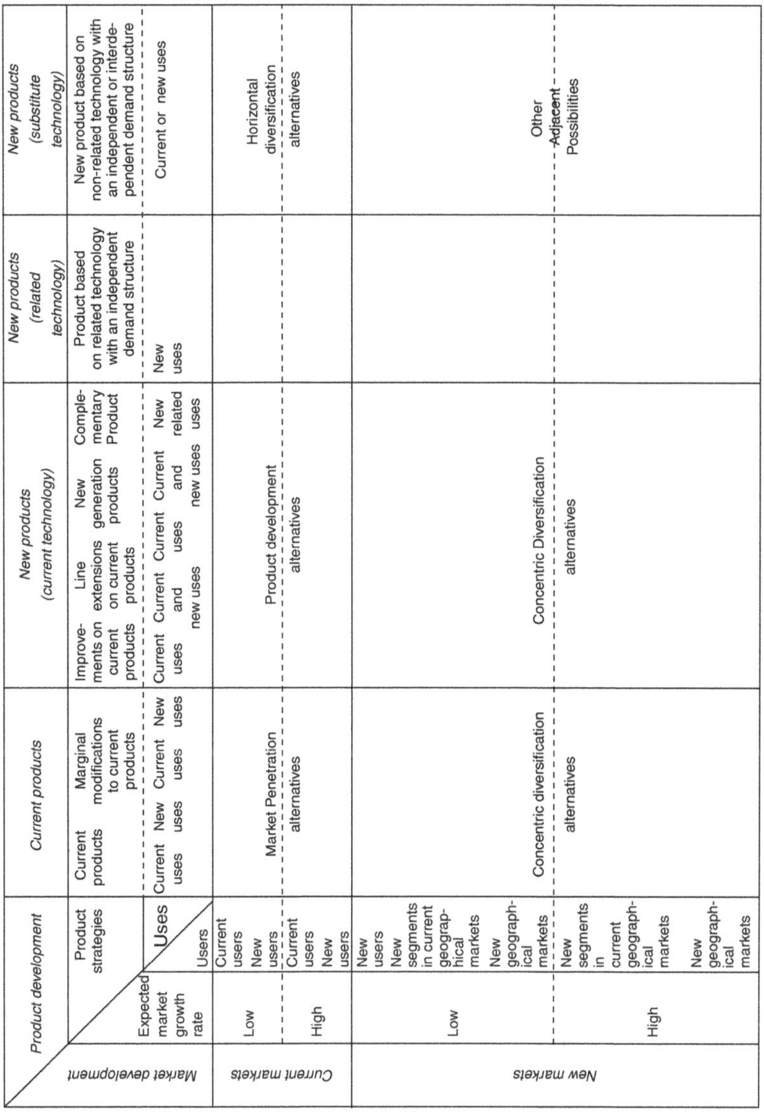

Product development → (columns)

Market development ↓		**Current products**	**New products (current technology)**	**New products (related technology)**	**New products (substitute technology)**	

Column headings (Product strategies / Uses):

- **Current products**
  - Current products — Current uses, New uses
  - Marginal modifications to current products — Current uses, New uses
- **New products (current technology)**
  - Improvements on current products — Current uses
  - Line extensions on current products — Current and new uses
  - New generation products — Current uses
  - Current products — Current and new uses
  - Complementary Product — New related uses
- **New products (related technology)**
  - Product based on related technology with an independent demand structure — New uses
- **New products (substitute technology)**
  - New product based on non-related technology with an independent or interdependent demand structure — Current or new uses

Row headings (Expected market growth rate / Users):

- **Current markets**
  - Low — Current users; New users
  - High — Current users; New users
- **New markets**
  - Low — New users; New segments in current geographical markets; New geographical markets
  - High — New segments in current geographical markets; New geographical markets

Cell contents:

	Current products	New products (current technology)	New products (related technology)	New products (substitute technology)
Current markets	Market Penetration alternatives	Product development alternatives		Horizontal diversification alternatives
New markets	Concentric diversification alternatives	Concentric Diversification alternatives		Other Adjacent Possibilities

Figure 3.23B The product/market matrix: a zoom-in

These can be marginally changed in order to create new varieties of offers. Such overtaking maneuvers set off a process of innovating the current product by extrapolating multiple versions, in order to stimulate consumption by customers who are already familiar with it, or to transform potential users into actual customers. Vertical marketing Movement Games, therefore, imply rethinking the product to make innovations based on modulation. These product modulations are all non-structural variations that may be made by upgrading/downgrading one of its features or components. To this end, firms can implement the following:

- Innovations based on formats and sizing, varying quantity without modifying other components of the product. The product or service does not change, but intensity, frequency, numbers and volumes can be modulated, multiplying occasions for use and consumption. With fast moving consumer goods (FMCGs), products are offered in a great variety of formats: 33cl, 50cl, 75cl, or 1l, 1.5l, 2l, packs of two or more cans, 35, 50, 75 grams or more, etc. Baby carrots represent a further example of this kind. As far as services go, firms can offer pre-paid cards of different value; daily, weekly, or seasonal subscriptions; internet connection at hourly rates or flat fees.
- Innovations based on packaging. How an item is packaged can impact market perception of the benefits it offers, and the enjoyment or opportunity of consumption. Here too the product stays the same; product modulation comes about by changing the packaging, amplifying the range into a greater number of consumption situations. In consumer markets, package sizes may be adapted for indoor or outdoor consumption, for personal use or gifting, for planned or impulse purchases. With regard to services, a bank can modulate a subsidiary to welcome ordinary or affluent customers in different ways; a diagnostic center can modulate the different approaches for welcoming national health or private customers. In the energy sector, gas can be distributed through a network or with large tanks to serve domestic or industrial customers, or with small cylinders for leisure or professional use.
- Innovations based on aesthetic and design components. These modulations also leave the technical or functional characteristics of the product unchanged and alter only the aesthetic aspect. This facilitates different positioning, satisfying the aesthetic, lifestyle, identity and distinctiveness needs expressed by the market. In electronic consumer goods, some brands are differentiated solely for the immense sophistication and elegance of their design. In the car market, the design of the bodywork and the interior often make the difference. In many other sectors – clothing, furniture, watches, household utensils, to name a few – the ability to reinterpret and

reconfigure product aesthetics captures the attention of customers who are sensitive to the emotionality conveyed by more sophisticated aesthetics. After years of questionable aesthetic orthodoxies in the domestic air conditioner sector, as we said before, LG led their Movement Game with success by leveraging this aspect, inventing the ArtCool line.

- Innovations based on integration. In this case, products and basic services are reinforced and amplified by adding a new "ingredient" to extend the variety offered and to revitalize customer interest. These modulations are frequent in all markets. In FMCGs, household or personal hygiene detergents are integrated with antibacterial components, conditioners, and active ingredients in the same way as food products can be combined (biscuits filled with chocolate or jam, bars of chocolate with rice or nuts, etc.). An industrial product, such as oil or gasoline can be integrated with an additive; an assistance program can be integrated with other service options.

Movement Games through lateral marketing

In the grid in Figure 3.23, three cells define the areas where a firm can search for adjacent opportunities, creatively exploring both the product and market axes, seeking: 1) new products for markets already served; 2) new markets for existing products; and 3) new markets for new products. All these operations are part of games of lateral movement. Whereas in a game of vertical movement, firms implement overtaking maneuvers that are consistent with their traditional business missions, in a lateral game, the firm proposes to develop or extend the aims of its business. In doing so, the firm explores new paths in an attempt to respond to questions such as:

- What other needs could we satisfy by changing our product or service?
- What other needs can we include in our current product?
- Can we enter new markets and win new customers by changing or modifying our product?
- If we change our product, can we use it in other situations, or in other contexts?
- What other products or services can we design and offer for the same situations and the same uses as our current product?
- What other products can we develop on the basis of the specifics of our current product?

- What new products can we develop to substitute our current products?
- What emerging markets are out there?
- What could the imaginable markets be?
- Which needs are not satisfied?

In order to generate a game of lateral movement, the firm must observe products and markets from different perspectives. While vertical overtaking maneuvers can take off from possible product modulations, lateral overtaking maneuvers are based on the adjacent possibilities of *dislocation.*

Dislocation is the process of generating a stimulus by provoking a discontinuity in conventional thought. Without going into the principles of neuroscience, we know that the brain is an extraordinarily self-organized system that constantly establishes links between thoughts, information, knowledge, emotions, and things observed or remembered. If two asymmetric, non-related ideas are presented to the mind, the self-organizational process will effect *displacements* in order to generate a logical association.

Until a few years ago, to make a call we had to use a phone connected to a cable. The provocative vision of being able to call when we're on the move, with no cables or cords, has no doubt stimulated companies to elaborate a dislocation. In fact, by modifying the original technology and service, this dislocation has facilitated the realization of an apparently impossible solution.

If "calling" represents the *focus* of our creative speculation, the "wireless" concept is the *dislocation* of a feature of the telephony system, while the *displacement* is all the changes that must be made to the system in light of the dislocation. The "mobile phone," therefore, is the *new idea* generated by logical *association*. The *stimulus*, finally, is the recognition of the gap between the idea of fixed and wireless telephony, which is the aspiration.

Innovations, therefore, are the result of abandoning logical and conventional thinking in favor of a lateral dislocation process. A creative process stimulates the combination of several ideas that have no clear relationship. In these Movement Games, to activate a process of lateral dislocation, firms have to explore several vectors: 1) the market; 2) the product; and 3) the other elements of the marketing mix. As an example we will detail the first two points; for the channel vector, refer to Section 3.16.

1. Dislocate the market

To generate a lateral dislocation on the market vector, this dislocation has to center on one or more of these aspects: (a) target, (b) needs, (c) occasions (Figure 3.24).

a) Dislocating the target means seeking new customers who were not previously considered as potential buyers of a product or users of a service. A drill designed for a professional target can be offered (as is or in a simplified version) to the DIY target. A hotel can redesign its value proposition to serve corporate customers, who have different needs than tourists.

b) Dislocating needs prompts firms to look for unsatisfied, latent, or incipient demands and modify current products or generate new ones to offer satisfactory solutions. The success of YouTube, with its slogan "Broadcast Yourself," revealed a latent (and sometimes worrying) need to be center stage, especially among young people. Some restaurants, by contrast, have dislocated their offerings in recognition of a growing need to rediscover nature while enjoying genuine food and a relaxing atmosphere, at least during the weekend. They have consequentially developed successful formulas for the conviviality and welfare of their customers, often in farmhouses on the outskirts of big cities, suitably renovated to offer massages and wellness courses, country cuisine and informal dining.

c) Consumption opportunities may trigger different lateral dislocations, especially if firms creatively explore various aspects pertaining to:

c1. Time. Dislocating time means identifying as yet unused moments for consumption. From this point of view, an interesting phenomenon emerged from RSS and Podcasting. Thanks to automatic downloads via the Internet, listeners can postpone "consumption" of a transmission until a more convenient time. Other examples are stores that open at unconventional times (think of the success of 7Eleven in the US), or banks that open on Saturdays, car dealers on Sundays,

Figure 3.24 Elements to focus on for market dislocation

laundromats that keep early hours to accommodate the early birds, hairdressers that take appointments after dinner, evening courses for executives, services offered at discounted prices in off-peak periods, product consumption that breaks with tradition (decaffeinated coffee and tea before bedtime, wine as an aperitif, etc.), instant lotteries, or sports successfully promoted out of season (skating or skiing in the summer) and so forth.

c2. Place. Dislocating the place means thinking about ways to propose products and services in a new purchase or consumption context. Distance learning; accessing a television program on a mobile phone; making purchases online; activating household appliances remotely, i.e. turning on the heating, watering the garden, taping a TV program via telephone or the internet; new packaging that encourages food consumption on the go, vending machines that facilitate purchases in the most unlikely places, and so forth.

c3. Situations. Special occasions and events are linked to special products: champagne for celebrations, eggnog at Christmas, ice cream during the summer, white wine with fish, diamonds for engagements or anniversaries. The challenge of such a dislocation is to propose occasions and events that go beyond the conventional, de-ritualizing the product in question.

2. Dislocate the product

Firms can explore the possibility of lateral dislocation of a product, whether this involves an incremental or radical move, in a market that the company is already familiar with, in the context of creating and serving a new market.

So as to avoid direct confrontation with the competition, a more radical dislocation at the product level is to develop new disrupting technologies with respect to the past, to generate true killer applications. An example in the electronics world was the transition from valves to transistors. Similar innovations translate into killer applications because they are capable of reducing the value of existing products and technologies, while offering the same functions or new ones, but with greater benefits in terms of effectiveness and efficiency.

Such product dislocation can also be associated with adjacent incremental modalities. Think of the common rail innovation, a dislocation that has significantly relaunched sales of diesel engines.

To suspend logical thought on a product and to inspire creative speculation in order to generate new associations, six different areas of investigation are useful to stimulate reflection on the adjacent possibilities: (a) replacement, (b) inversion, (c) combination, (d) exaggeration, (e) elimination, and (f) reorganization.

a) Replacement consists in eliminating or modifying one or more parts of the product by introducing components that are present in other non-related products. Examples are the replacement of watch hands and charging mechanisms with quartz technology; the replacement of glass with welded aluminum or plastic packaging for the conservation of liquids; the replacement of wood with technical materials from the aeronautical sector for skis and tennis rackets; the replacement of the cathode-ray tube in TVs with liquid crystal technology; the replacement of piano chords and hammers with electronic transistors in keyboards.

b) Inversion is the complex process of subverting the consumption or purchase of a product or service by affirming the opposite, or by adding a "not" to one or more elements. The marker that does "not" leave permanent marks, or the erasable marker for whiteboards; the glue that does "not" stick, i.e. Post-it notes; the videogame you pay for but do "not" buy, i.e. pay-to-play; digital music that you listen to on your computer but do "not" download, i.e. streaming; the home-delivered pizza that is "not" delivered, i.e. the frozen pre-wrapped pizzas you buy at the supermarket.

c) Exaggeration by contrast involves magnifying one or more elements of the product. The 4x4 that dominates the road or the minivan that carries more than four passengers; the large 50-liter water container for offices; contact lenses you change every day; Piaggio's MP3 three-wheel scooter to reduce the danger of falling over; the 100-storey building; the four-minute paella.

d) Combination instead means evaluating the possibility of adding one or more elements to the product or service to increase its potential to meet new needs and provide new solutions. Mobile phones, year after year, provide the most obvious example of this type of lateral dislocation: starting with the calculator and the alarm clock, continuing with the electronic agenda and a few videogames, moving on to internet connectivity for checking email and surfing the web, closely followed by the camera and the camcorder, adding digital music players and even surprising us with GPS.

e) Elimination is removing one or more elements of the product or service, as previously mentioned with reference to low-cost propositions. In these cases the value proposition is reconfigured with an eye to the no-frills perspective. For an extreme example, think of the "capsule hotels" in Japan. The elimination of lottery drawings has dislocated into scratch cards; electronic locks have eliminated keys. With the simplification of certain products in the electronics sector (self-installing peripherals, plug-and-play systems, simplified phone menus or "automatic" camera programs) learning, which often represents a high barrier for buying and use, has been minimized, but not always successfully.

f) Reorganization, finally, is the dislocation of products with the aim of changing the order or the sequence of one or more of the elements characterizing the value proposition. Priceline.com, for example, uses reverse pricing, where customers bid their own prices for hotel stays or air travel. Permission Marketing has reorganized the convention of advertising exposure by urging the customer to ask for ads to be delivered. This is also the case of Breezer drinks, pre-mixed with various ingredients and ready for consumption; or pre-washed and pre-cut vegetables; or, on the opposite end of the spectrum, unassembled furniture. Or soap that's already in liquid form or foam. Reorganization may relate to the promised benefits: the fun in driving a Mini Cooper becomes the primary promise, rather than a secondary benefit.

3.19　High- and low-impact: balancing risks and growth opportunities

As much as the high-impact Movement Game offers more opportunities for growth and overtaking rivals, it is also inevitably associated with greater entrepreneurial risks. To balance the trade-off between growth and risk, the company must systematically map and govern its portfolio of innovations. A simple instrument with this objective in mind is the risk matrix, as shown in Figure 3.25 (Day, 2007).

As we can see from the graph, innovations and maneuvers that distance us farthest from our current battleground (both in terms of product and market) embody the greatest risk of failure; it is equally true, however, that the only way to find the pot of gold is to venture out on new roads. The size of the circles in the example reminds us of this trade-off: the greatest opportunities are the farthest away from the origin of the graph, or rather, from what is most familiar.

To summarize, the matrix visually represents the distribution of the firm's risk according to the innovations currently in its portfolio. This serves as a reminder to management of the need to wisely balance

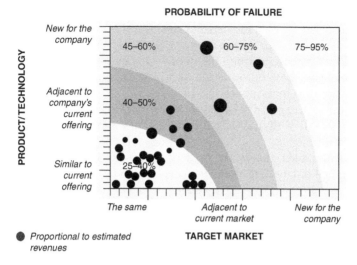

Figure 3.25 The risk matrix of a hypothetical portfolio of innovations

various exploratory paths. To place an innovation along the vertical axis, a manager could evaluate (for example on a scale of 1 to 5) the proximity of such an innovation with respect to the current:

* expertise of the firm;
* competencies in product development;
* patents;
* production systems;
* distribution systems.

In order to place the innovation along the horizontal axis, however, it is appropriate to question the following:

* similarities in purchasing behavior with respect to existing customers;
* harmony with the current positioning of the brand;
* importance and extendibility of current relations (cross selling);
* degree of knowledge of future rivals.

These preliminary intersubjective evaluations can provide valuable strategic ideas, forcing management to focus their attention on the salient points of the innovation process.

A complementary instrument to estimate *ex ante* the validity or the risk associated with a Movement Game is RWW analysis, that is, "Real, Win, Worth it", also known as the "Schrello Screen" (Day, 2007). The R is particularly useful when the unorthodox maneuver is aimed at new product launches and/or new market exploration, but it applies to any innovative business model.

The objective is to draw attention to certain key elements of the innovation, strictly verifying the existence of four essential prerequisites:

- A real market, that is, the existence of an effective need of demand, explicit or latent, not yet adequately served by other competitors.
- A real product, that is, the clarity, feasibility and usefulness of the value proposition that the firm intends to launch.
- A winning proposition, that is, the sustainability of the competitive advantage, both on the product level (the superiority of offerings) and on the business level (exclusiveness of resources).
- A worthy strategy, that is, the expected profitability of the project (estimates of the expected income flows multiplied by the expected risk rate), and consistency with the overall growth strategy of the business.

The fulfillment of these conditions, together with the determination and the commitment of the entire organization, guarantees successful market creation and market regeneration strategies in every Movement Game.

4

The Barriers to Change

4.1 Orbital inertia: the natural resistance to innovation

The high- and low-impact maneuvers of the Movement Game, as illustrated in the previous chapter, are based on the firm's ability to overcome the natural inertia that keeps us anchored to the status quo. Orbital inertia, according to physicists, is what enables a body to maintain its elliptical trajectory without any additional effort. Unfortunately, however, in the business world long-term competitive advantage actually depends on the ability to break loose from old trajectories. Referring back to our original metaphor:

- the greater the desired orbital shift (high-impact Movement Game) the greater the energy required;
- the more quickly we want to accomplish this shift (surprise effect), the greater the energy required;
- the greater our success in the current orbit, the greater the energy required to change it; and finally,
- the lesser the current financial tension, the greater the energy required to overcome orbital inertia.

All this energy will help the firm and its management to break down the many barriers to change – barriers that we will describe in the course of this chapter.

Innovation has always been critical for economic growth and social development. For this reason, and despite natural resistance, markets are characterized by constant innovative activity. The drivers of this activity are the four forces represented in Figure 4.1. Innovation is stimulated by

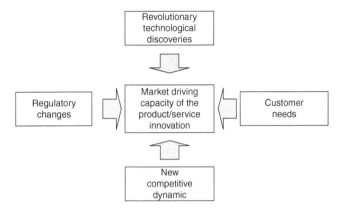

Figure 4.1   Forces that activate innovation

new scientific discoveries, by the need to overtake the competition, by the opportunity to better serve the needs expressed by customers, and, where appropriate, by favorable public policies.

These first few lines of this chapter highlight a small paradox: although innovations have always been, and will continue to be, the origin of growth and development, both the firms that launch them and the customers that benefit from them do not readily perform the necessary transactions. Innovations, in fact, require changes in the consolidated routine of firms and customers – and as these changes are emotionally costly, they generate resistance and opposition in behavior and in the adoption processes.

To be able to successfully introduce an innovation, we first have to understand the nature of the resistance to this process.[1] Some barriers are internal to the firm (Sections 4.2–4.7); others are external. The latter type include regulatory barriers (Section 4.8), barriers to market access (Section 4.9), and finally barriers erected by customers themselves (Sections 4.10–4.15).

4.2   Internal barriers to innovation

Many businesses find themselves having to face internal barriers to change that are often unexpected and sometimes insurmountable. In many cases, this paralysis can be ascribed to three barriers embedded in the DNA of many firms, which are discussed in the next sections (see also Figure 4.2).

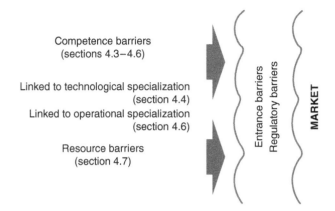

Figure 4.2 Barriers erected by the firm

4.3 Competence barriers

The greater the depth of the competencies of a firm, the lesser the probability that high-impact innovations can be introduced. When the basic technology a firm employs becomes more complex, the behavioral models and organizational routines consolidate to increase efficiency, reduce costs, and avoid errors. However, all this causes rigidity and curtails the proactivity of the firm.

Consequently, the tendency to focus on certain competencies entails two specific innovation barriers: 1) technological specialization barriers, and 2) operational specialization barriers.

4.4 Competences: technological specialization barriers

We might assume, in an era in which technological complexity is growing significantly, that technological competencies are key to a successful innovation. Often, instead, exactly the opposite is true. When firms attempt to move out of their area of specialization they are rarely successful, since the capabilities induced by specialization are not versatile enough to be transferred to similar products or markets. Pharmaceutical companies are a good example of this: the specialization acquired in a therapeutic area is often not the source of significant innovation in other areas. In the same way as IBM failed in the photocopier sector, Xerox failed in the IT sector. These firms suffered the consequences of specialization and organizational excesses, where the objective is efficiency rather than experimentation. Striving to improve production processes and enhancing the value of the offering undoubtedly encourages depth of knowledge, but sacrifices the breadth of knowledge required to introduce successful high-impact innovations. This orientation allows firms to change their established products but not to produce completely new ones. The degree of technical specialization and the effects of competence barriers are even more obvious in the service sector. For example, without acquisitions or mergers it is almost impossible for a bank to compete in the insurance industry, or in financial intermediation, or in non-bank products. Likewise, a conventional telecommunications company would find it difficult to navigate in the new multimedia world without appropriate alliances with other firms.

The difficulties that highly specialized firms face often lead them to introduce products that evolve almost naturally from their respective technological bases (low-impact Movement Game) without taking account of the dynamism of their customers' specific desires. An innovative firm must instead be flexible and courageous enough to modify its consolidated technological research and development models so that it can anticipate and satisfy changes in market demand. This behavior often presents an enormous challenge for a hyper-specialized firm. The temptation to introduce incremental innovations simply because they are compatible with the company's prevailing technology can be irresistible. Firms can overcome these competence barriers in many ways:

a) The combination of technological risks.[2] The pursuit of several technological paths may reduce the risk of competence, and in particular, specialization barriers. With such a maneuver, the firm deploys an innovative development strategy by simultaneously combining support and destruction technologies. The former, through knowledge-leveraging maneuvers, seeks to extend the life cycle of existing products and technologies. The latter, destructive (sometimes called disruptive) technologies, through processes of knowledge building, serve an asymmetrical purpose: their goal is to reduce the value of existing products, destroy existing technologies, and generate radical innovations. The combination of leveraging and building capabilities offers firms an effective way to stimulate and combine technological development and innovation. Simultaneously developing both the technological support and destruction paths creates a healthy internal competition between the two. This conflict determines the continuous improvement of existing technologies and the development of destructive technologies at the same time.

As soon as the existing technology is improved, it becomes the target of a new, destructive type of technology, which in turn triggers other innovations (see Figure 4.3 below). The stimulus provided by the new destructive technologies may therefore be useful not only to generate and introduce revolutionary products or services (high-impact maneuvers), but also to improve existing ones (low-impact maneuvers). The improvements made to existing products derive from both leveraging current knowledge and the destructive new technology putting pressure on existing technology.

b) Research alliances and collaboration. The huge investments needed to develop new technologies are often impossible for a single firm to sustain independently. Alliances and agreements are formal coalitions among firms that agree to cooperate in order to exploit specific complementarities and asymmetries in terms of capabilities. By forming strategic research alliances firms can share resources to achieve mutual benefits. Alliances enable enterprises to keep their consolidated R&D models and processes, but at the same time offer creative combinations of these models that facilitate the pursuit of the wide range of knowledge a successful innovation necessitates.

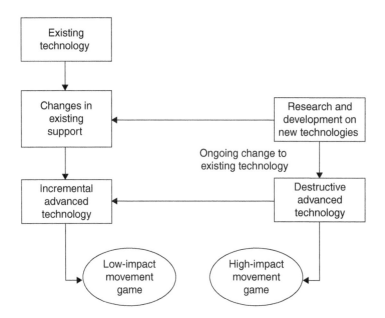

Figure 4.3 The combined dynamics of incremental and destructive technologies

c) Acquisitions. In order to overcome specialization barriers, a different solution for developing high-impact innovations involves acquiring or merging with other businesses that have the knowledge or experience that the firm is lacking. eBay, the online auction company, followed this strategy when it bought out PayPal (2002). Microsoft did the same with Skype in 2011 and, more recently, Google acquired Motorola Mobility to reinforce their position in the ICT battlefield. A word of warning: reckless acquisitions and mergers can create as many problems as they solve. Generally, this occurs when the cultural and management models of firms are unable to integrate, and conflicts or new barriers arise on the path to innovation and change. We must be equally cautious of overpriced acquisitions, as we can see in numerous cases where the synergies generated by the new acquisition were lower than estimated. (The acquisition of Skype by eBay in 2005 was probably an example of this, as was the acquisition of America On Line by Time Warner.)

4.5 Continuous and dynamic innovation of competences

The observations made above remind us that continuous innovation requires the firm to pay close attention to its internal processes. In particular, from an organizational point of view, innovative continuity is based on three stages (Figure 4.4):

- identifying specialized knowledge;
- combining specialized knowledge, and translating it into new products;
- reconfiguring specialized knowledge continuously, in order to encourage market innovations (Verona G., 1999).

In the first stage above, identifying specialized knowledge, the firm must pinpoint the competencies it deems critical for developing and launching a new product. The specialized competencies linked to technical know-how feature largely here. Research on the subject has brought to light how some of these take the form of technological expertise in R&D, engineering, and manufacturing. Others center on marketing competencies and tend to generate knowledge on controlling, diagnosing, and measuring market phenomena; formulating the new product's segmentation and positioning options; and defining its operative marketing strategy. In brief, technological and marketing competencies

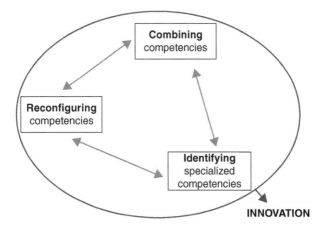

Figure 4.4 The evolutionary model of the firm's ability to innovate continuously

allow the firm to identify, develop, and formulate key knowledge linked to the innovation. At the same time, these competencies must present a technological matrix that targets an end-market and therefore includes a marketing component.

Clark and Fujimoto (1991) carried out an analytical study of material linked to different car components that underscored the key role of R&D knowledge. What also emerged was the importance of analytically understanding consumers' preferences in terms of the various components that make up a car so that the "technical" product meets their needs. Specialist marketing competencies, honed through experience and market research, complement the knowledge needed to create a perfect fit for our customers.

In addition to specialist expertise, the use of integrative competencies is essential. These allow for the unification of the technical knowledge developed and codified into specific expertise for the new product. Integrative competencies produce the organizational know-how needed to build the architecture most suited to combining and coordinating technological and market competencies in the context of the innovative project.

The wealth of empirical evidence produced in the context of the pharmaceutical sector[3] shows that the basis of a firm's greater innovative productivity can also be attributed to integrative competencies linked to the structure and processes of the organization. Here we make

particular reference to the interfunctional committees that democratic-
ally allocate resources for various scientific investments. This and other
empirical evidence linked to different sectors (including film, biotech,
medicine, consumer electronics, computers, and software) show that
specialized and integrative competencies play a key role in the innovation process in traditional environments.[4] Once the firm maps them
and uses them in a systematic way, it can plan a pipeline of products to
be progressively launched on the market.

Also emerging in the continuous innovation model is the need to
change our basic assumptions. To introduce innovations characterized by planned diversity, we should also use dynamic capabilities[5] – in
other words, meta-capabilities that enable us to change the basic logical
premises under which integrative capabilities operate.

Dynamic capabilities are the basis of a firm's creativity and are divided
into reconfiguration capabilities (linked to changes in the knowledge
architecture for the innovation) and recombination capabilities (linked
to the changes in knowledge integration methods over time).

Let's look at Figure 4.4. We can see from the arrows linking the identification, combination, and reconfiguration processes that they set a
virtuous cycle in motion that sustains competitive advantage through
continuous innovation. We can compare this to the evolutionary link
between closely interconnected processes in the business world.[6] From this
perspective, we see continuous innovation as the evolutionary cycle that
feeds a virtuous circle, thanks to the firm's ability to generate, strengthen,
and update the capabilities that fuel the innovation. The presence of
particular specialist expertise enhances the acquisition of specific integrative capabilities, which in turn, triggers the learning processes needed to
generate additional capabilities. This recurrence leads the firm to redefine
its capabilities pool on the basis of the learning activated in the course
of the innovation.[7] Therefore, we can say that the cycle is evolutionary
because it allows capabilities to evolve, and enables firms to nourish their
value-generation capabilities through innovative continuity.

It is also important to note how the cycle feeds itself: it activates a
virtuous spiral that expands over time. The model suggests that the
firm does not stop at a single innovation. Indeed, the knowledge generated by each specific innovation enables the firm to discover new forms
of specialist knowledge, and as a result new ways of combining this
additional knowledge. All this allows the firm to evolve over time,
producing innovations with continuity. This means that the firm's
competitive advantage is based on different forms of knowledge, and is
therefore easier to sustain over time.

Case 4.1 Continuously innovating and organizing competencies

Oticon, a successful Danish company in the acoustic appliances sector for decades, stands out for its ability to systematically produce a continuous stream of innovations.

Source: Verona and Ravasio (2003).

Oticon has created a context that facilitates the recombination of knowledge based on the way each individual innovative project is linked to other projects. The key to this approach is the mechanism for allocating resources among new product development projects. Any member of the company who has come up with an idea has the opportunity to present it to the Development Committee comprising the CEO, the CFO, the Director of the Research Center, and managers responsible for quality, new products, and marketing. The Development Committee decides which projects to pursue according to the priorities of the firm and the resources available. Although the criteria for project selection are substantially unstructured, the people involved in the decision-making process have solid competencies and expertise. This fact transforms a potential weakness into a strength. The Development Committee's supervision also provides help with coordinating human resources management, thanks to its global vision of current projects and the company's competencies and skills. In this way, committee members can effectively move people from one project to another, minimizing problems and sharing promoting capability. A Revision Committee, whose objective is project coordination, was recently created in order to close the gap between the Development Committee and other company functions. The new committee, besides the CEO and CFO, is made up of three people from management activities relating to sales, marketing, and IT. While the Development Committee members are all executives, the Revision Committee, which acts as the interface between top and middle management, also includes managers from the Competence Centers who contribute to aspects relating to the firm's operational management.

A study by Brown and Eisenhardt[8] relating to the IT sector highlights that firms characterized by their ability to innovate with continuity set up semi-structures in their organizations. The semi-structure concept is linked to the capacity for self-organization, supported by internal and external communication processes with no hierarchical or functional constraints. The self-learning that takes place within the semi-structured framework encourages the firm to continuously redefine its strengths.

What's more, since these structures are not rigid ones, they can easily and continually be recombined and reconfigured.

4.6   Competencies: operational specialization barriers

Other sources generating blocking mechanisms to innovation are operations. Within the framework of competence barriers, here we refer to the hyper-specialization and resistance to change that emerges further downstream in the production and assembly stages of the value chain, rather than upstream in research and development. A very specialized firm in the technological field is often just as specialized in its operations, thanks to the benefits deriving form the experience curve. Innovation, instead, often implies changes in the product portfolio. In fact, innovation triggers a process of change that spills over onto all business functions: from the supply of raw materials to the production and distribution processes. Changes that require profound innovations in the firm's operational routines may give rise to major problems. We can find confirmation of this, for example, in the obstacles that both Airbus and Boeing faced in the production and assembly stages of highly innovative products such as the A350 and the 787 Dreamliner.

Changes do not simply require improvements in production processes and management, but total redesigns. This involves transforming the organizational architecture and hierarchy which serves to coordinate various activities; the aim is to transform the firm into an agile and self-perpetuating organization. In contexts with high specialization and functional focalization, there is little chance that operations are adaptable or flexible because all routines are carried out to attain a single objective; a change to a single activity may jeopardize the unity and stability of the entire system. The desire to avoid undermining the status quo elevates competence barriers upstream in terms of research and development, and operational barriers downstream involving production and assembly. The adage, "If it isn't broken don't fix it!" explains why most recent innovations have been introduced by non-traditional firms with a more entrepreneurial spirit with respect to the established sector leaders. In addition, firms hindered by operational barriers are often tempted to commercialize "operational" innovations rather than market-centered ones. In other words, firms often launch products and services that don't call for any major retooling of the production and assembly processes involved; these innovations are easy to produce and market without due consideration to the actual needs and reactions of potential customers. By their very nature, firms that perform highly specialized operations face significant innovation barriers. Overcoming them requires maneuvers that help the firm escape from the pre-established behavior models that delay and obstruct successful innovations. This is possible by implementing the following measures:

a) Isolated activities and operational processes. This means prevailing over an operational barrier by opening a new activity that is physically separate from existing plants, and uses a different labor force and management team. The production plant where the Fiat Punto is produced, for instance, was an innovative project with sophisticated, flexible manufacturing facilities. Here the company opted to create an autonomous production unit where Fiat partners with suppliers to maximize collaboration, economy of speed, and mutual learning. This solution, which allows innovative activities to flourish without being hindered by ingrained procedures, allows already-consolidated processes to continue smoothly.

b) Modified activities and operational processes. This second expedient to overcome operational barriers, in particular in industrial areas where investments in facilities and resources are significant, involves improving and even completely redesigning existing processes in order to facilitate innovation. In cases where current activities and routines are superseded or become obsolete, an overhaul of the entire organization is the most effective way to stimulate innovation. The process of integrating new operational procedures, in any case, must be executed with great attention to people, to avoid the risk that they might refuse or resist change, due to a culture that is cemented in tradition.

c) Selectively modified activities and operational processes. In order to reduce the intrinsic risk of change generated by innovations relative to improved or redesigned procedures, these maneuvers can be limited to specific parts of the organization. For example, the firm can modify certain processes for managing suppliers' activities, or customer services, depending on whether the innovation directly involves operations upstream or downstream on the value chain. By focusing innovation selectively on specific areas according to the priorities of the moment, the firm has a greater chance of successful implementation.

4.7   Resource barriers

Akin to capability issues, the lack of appropriate stocks of resources (whether human, financial, technological, or reputational) may hinder entrepreneurial initiatives. Very few firms have adequate economic resources to ensure that innovation costs are never an obstacle to the innovation process.

How high a resource barrier is depends on how adept the firm is at generating value, or resorting to financial leverage. More generally, to overcome similar barriers, the firm can consider the following options:

a) Partnerships and cooperation agreements. Conceding technological and production know-how through licensing agreements with other firms constitutes one method for disseminating an innovation when adequate financial or organizational resources are lacking. Establishing joint ventures with other businesses with complementary or even competitive activities (see Chapter 9) is another form of cooperation which serves to develop common technology, and to potentially establish it as the technical standard in the market.

b) Recourse to venture capital. Even if this option is infrequently adopted and poorly applied in some countries, an additional solution is resorting to venture capitalist contributions. However, since investors must share the investment risks, they may not be prepared to contribute more than the absolute minimum for any given initiative. A deal's financial backers could impose strict financial and administrative controls that may hinder the development of the initiative.

4.8   Regulatory barriers

The legal context may take various forms and is often sector-specific. In fact, self-regulation is common, and normally limited to the sector's associations or business leaders imposing codes of conduct and ethics. For example, in many Western countries there are self-regulated advertising codes, and official juries or review boards to ensure they are respected. Competitive regulations exist both on a national and supranational level in the case of the European Union (starting with Article 81 of the Treaty of Rome, 1957), or on a federal level in the United States (dating back to the Sherman Act of 1890). Enforcement of these rules is generally entrusted to an independent antitrust authority. In addition, specific industries may be subject to ad hoc regulations and monitoring bodies, as in the case of banks, communications, publishing, or energy. In many countries all this is supplemented by explicit regulations for consumer protection. Other legislation on the issue of innovation pertains to the protection of patents and trademarks; ironclad laws concerning environmental protection also exist.

While we recognize the need for shared rules to ensure the proper functioning of markets and the harmonious development of our society, we also note that as the number of rules increases, so does the risk of higher innovation barriers. Policy makers should always take into account the possible trade-off that impact the entire system. In other cases, fortunately, regulations are what actually foster innovation. Some relevant examples are enterprise incentives, the protection of intellectual property, and standard-setting bodies.

In other cases, as mentioned, the legislative complexity that our businesses must face tends to make the processes of creative destruction slow and inflexible. Many cell phone payment systems, for example, are constrained by rigid monetary regulations.

There are several ways for firms to bypass the restrictions to innovation unintentionally imposed by law while staying well within the law; one option is to set up a new company. In any case communication activities to sensitize institutional bodies should be undertaken, perhaps in coordination with other firms or organizations.

The legislative authority should constantly evaluate which past rules have negative effects today that outweigh the innovation benefits for which they were designed. It was with this objective in mind, for example, that the liberalization of many former state monopolies began. In other cases, it may suffice to restructure the law or its implementation to reduce barriers for firms, by simplifying and delegating some of the associated tasks to peripheral bodies, or by making greater use of new network technologies.

4.9 Market access barriers

Additional barriers to the dissemination of innovations can sometimes arise between the firm and the market. These are called market access barriers since they hinder the firm from reaching potential customers. Such barriers can be caused by a number of factors, such as:

- the absence of a distribution network, or the resistance of retailers to give new products shelf space;

- standards that are already consolidated on the market, which makes it difficult to transition to innovative – but incompatible – solutions;
- customs barriers in some countries;
- market power exercised by certain incumbents over the entire value system (suppliers and distributors).

These barriers that elevate the cost of market access, may be reduced through:

a) Agreements and alliances. Here we refer to licensing, joint ventures, or marketing and distribution agreements. Fiat, in the postwar period, was among the first to use strategic bridges of this kind to access the former Soviet Union's markets (its main partner was Lada). Even today, Fiat has agreements and alliances to access China, India, Egypt, South Africa, Turkey, and Vietnam. Another example is Mediolanum Bank, an Italian bank with no physical branches: they made an agreement with Italian postal offices to access the market through the latter without needing their own branch network.

b) Innovative distribution formulas. Dell, even before the rise of the internet, developed a formula for direct sales to customers mainly via telephone orders and home assistance. Another example is an underwear company that sells its wares via vending machines located in hospitals. Netflix successfully attacked Blockbuster by introducing DVD rentals by mail and, more recently, film distribution by direct streaming via the internet.

c) *Pull* marketing maneuvers. Through aggressive mass communication campaigns, a firm can excite the interest of customers, who then request the product in question in stores. Retailers, in turn, solicit wholesalers to distribute such product, and so it goes until the access barrier is overcome. This was the strategy successfully adopted by Bticino when it launched its innovative Living light switches, breaking with orthodoxies on the design front for the first time.

4.10   Innovation barriers erected by customers

We have repeatedly stressed that innovation, which lays the groundwork for the Movement Game, does not necessarily involve a product. When it does, however, there may be resistance to change from the very people for whom we designed the new product or service: the customer.[9] This resistance may even delay the success of our maneuver.

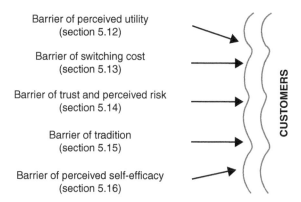

Figure 4.5 Customer barriers

The initial opposition customers may have is entirely physiological and generally justified by the fact that any change generates structural discontinuity that upsets the familiar, consolidated model of behavior. Even before this initial opposition, an awareness barrier exists – namely, an awareness of the very existence of the new product and its relative advantages.

Resistance by customers may be associated with two types of barriers: functional and psychological. As described in the following section, the first consists of barriers linked to the perceived value and to the operating costs of change (switching costs). In the second, instead, we have barriers arising from the perceived risk, trust, tradition, and perceived self-efficacy (Figure 4.5).

4.11 Functional barriers: perceived value

The perceived value barrier arises when customers do not have any specific incentive to change their purchase and consumption habits. This value is perceived instead in the best alternatives among those with which the customer is already familiar. Although this value may derive from functional benefits, it is not limited to them. There may also be symbolic benefits (think of the fashion factor that contributed to the success of Nespresso machines) or even experiential benefits linked to the intrinsic pleasure of using the new product or service. Both these go beyond functional motivations (the dissemination of chat services, for example).

New product or service launches may fail because of marginal (or perceived) improvements when compared to existing alternatives, considering the measure of value mentioned above. Among these values, the weight of the functional dimension will be greater as the level of rationality grows in the customer purchasing process, as in B2B contexts. In the case of functional and tangible benefits, the advantage of the innovation is more easily communicated, thereby lowering the barriers to perceived value.

Firms that do not entirely understand the logic behind customer behavior are likely to introduce innovations that no doubt provide advantages for buyers, but which do such a firm can erode the net perceived value barrier if it can demonstrate the value of its innovations, and make customers appreciate this value. The following maneuvers can make this happen:

a) Superior benefits. The firm can leverage significant benefits that justify and gratify value to customers with respect to the existing alternatives in terms of reliability, compliance with specifications, durability, technical/functional characteristics, performance, support services, etc. Further levers center on the symbolic and experiential value of the new product.

b) Differentiated benefits (new positioning). With this option, the innovative firm must analyze the map of already existing replacement goods and identify unserved market areas in terms of the benefits offered by current competitors. These areas, of course, must be significant in terms of the profitability and defensibility of the competitive position. Cameras built into mobile phones don't give better performance than digital cameras, but they offer different benefits instead.

c) Lower economic sacrifice. In this case, an innovation is offered at a more competitive price than current products, so as to ensure significant savings. This compensates for the initially lower performance or other adoption barriers, which are dealt with further on. An example here once again is internet telephony, with its lower quality and reliability than existing alternatives, but offered at a much lower price.

d) Effective communication. The only advantages of an innovation that really make a difference are the ones approved by customers. In this sense the firm's communication activity is fundamental, be it centered on persuasion and aimed at generating awareness and stimulating interest, or focused on information, through brochures, specialized magazines, and the internet. Here the innovation test may be key, which we will come back to later on. In the initial stages, the firms should pay special attention to opinion leaders, and adroitly manage word-of-mouth and positive feedback, online and off.

e) Legal obligation. The perceived value barrier can be annulled by making an innovation obligatory by law, where its value is clear and socially relevant to the policy maker, independently of the average individual's judgment. This is the case of digital television for example: many governments have recently forced the switch-off of analog transmissions.

4.12   Functional barriers: the switching cost

The most common justification customers give in rejecting an innovation is its incompatibility with their current processes, purchasing patterns and, more generally, with their habits. Any additional benefit, therefore, even if correctly perceived, would not be sufficient to compensate for the costs inherent to change. As a result, innovations that require a substantial adjustment in established routines have adoption cycles that extend over time and require major investments to educate the market and develop market knowledge. The reduction of functional barriers calls for various maneuvers:

a) The systemic approach. Since each new product or service interacts with other products already in use and familiar to the customer, the firm should consider beforehand whether the innovation is suitable to the existing system of products and services. Some new smartphones, for example, can be easily connected to a home printer, a TV, a car stereo, or, of course, to a computer. In other words, firms should aim for maximum compatibility (technical and cultural) with the system of products that consumers already use. From this point of view, customer involvement in the design phase of the innovation could be critical.

b) Integration with other products or services. An analogous solution is to integrate the innovation into an existing activity or product. Rather than selling the innovation directly to end users (for example, a car satellite navigator or "run-flat" tire systems), it may be more effective to sell it to other producers, such as suppliers of the original equipment (the car manufacturer in our example).

c) Reimbursement for switching costs. On the basis of good customer Lifetime Value (LTV) estimates, the innovative firm may evaluate the possibility of reimbursement for tangible costs resulting from transitioning to the new supplier. Some innovative operators, for example, offer to cover the costs to ending the customer's current contract with a competitor.

4.13   Psychological barriers: perceived risk and trust

Every innovation, regardless of the extent of change it requires with respect to consolidated routines and know-how, elevates the customers' perception of risk. When this perception grows, customers react by post-poning the adoption of the innovation until the causes that generate uncertainty are significantly reduced.

A major risk is economic. This arises every time the customer presumes that financial investment in the new product could be lost. The higher the purchase cost, the greater the perceived economic risk. The second risk is physical, and centers on the perception of foreseeable damage to persons or property related to the innovation. The third risk lies in uncertainty regarding the performance of the product or service. In other words, customers might think that the technology has not yet been properly tested. This means that the product can't initially ensure high reliability, and that the invention it's based on will be improved in the future.

There may also be a social risk associated with products with a high personal involvement. This translates into customers' fear that the innovation might not win approval in the social system to which they belong. For example, social research shows that one reason Italian consumers were slow to accept cars with automatic transmissions was their fear that others would think they weren't any good at driving a manual transmission.

There are also trust barriers inherent to the issue of risk linked to the image and reputational resources of the innovative firm. The lower the trust, the greater the perceived risk. Therefore, the barriers an innovation faces are also contingent on the image of its country of origin, its industry, and of course, the firm that proposes it. The image of the innovation, therefore, needs to be developed over time and effectively reinforced.

Low trust and, more generally, the perceptions of the risk involved in adopting the innovation may be mitigated by using the following:

a) Free testing – offering the new product or service for experimenta-tion with complete guarantees.
b) Testimonials – presenting results of clinical tests and user reviews.
c) Integrating the product into an already existing system – presenting the innovation as a component of a system so that customers do not

directly decide for themselves to adopt it. Tires using the innovative run-flat system were adopted for the first time by many consumers because they were standard features in their new cars, such as the latest Chevrolet Corvettes, or some Mercedes, and BMW models.

4.14   Psychological barriers: the power of tradition

As in the case of operational and tangible changes (Section 4.11), an innovation generates resistance when it requires changes in the tradition and values of the firm. Any cultural discontinuity, in fact, is problematic in the purchase and adoption processes of both complex and basic institutions such as families or individuals. As a country's economic development progresses, the number of customers trying to defend themselves against change can also grow; this throws up cultural barriers to the progressive variety of innovative products or services possible. Moreover, such an attitude may be amplified by more conservative personality traits, as in the case of the "laggards" indicated by Rogers (Section 4.16). Innovative firms may try to modify these psychological blocks through:

a) Understanding: Respect and the understanding of cultural traditions is the most effective way to reduce a priori resistance or rejection of an innovation. The most effective strategies to spread a new technology must be developed consistently with the specific contexts in which they are proposed.
b) Social pressures: Recourse to forces that can promote change may be effective in lowering barriers. Children, for example, may spur on their parents' adoption of new technologies. Similarly, more innovative persons may spur on their closer friends. The firm can develop specific promotional measures and incentives to activate these forces.

4.15   Psychological barriers: perceived self-efficacy

Among the most critical factors for the adoption of a new product or service are the obstacles linked to customers' self-assessments of their ability to use the innovation without difficulty ("self-efficacy" or "personal control beliefs"). In other words, customers judge whether or not they can actually enjoy the potential benefits promised by the innovation. Naturally, this judgment will depend on both how easy the innovation is to use, objectively speaking, and on how skilled and experienced customers are. In both cases, the foundation of these barriers is the fact that customers anticipate negative emotions such as anxiety or frustration associated with adopting and using the product. The maneuvers a firm can implement to alleviate these feelings are the following:

a) Trivialization, simplifying the operational and functional complexity of the new product to reduce customer resistance in terms of use. Relevant examples are Microsoft programs that have simplified access and use for all consumers, even those who are not particularly tech-savvy.
b) Training and educating the market on the use or consumption of the innovation.
c) Excellent support services, communicated prior to purchase as a "safety net" the customer can always rely on, providing reassurance even in the product evaluation stage.

4.16   Crossing the chasm

Many of the customer competence barriers previously mentioned can be summed up with the expression "technology readiness".[10] The technology readiness index, in fact, is meant to measure the natural propensity of an individual to adopt innovative technologies. It is an umbrella concept for variables such as the propensity to innovate, optimism, the discomfort caused by technology, and the insecurity that it may instill in an individual (Figure 4.6).

Rogers' model (and subsequent variations) is the best-known attempt to classify potential customers by virtue of their propensity to innovate.[11] The model represents the adoption process by identifying the categories of new customers and their relative numbers following the launch of an innovation (Figure 4.7):

1. Innovators: enthusiasts and explorers of any new technology. This category groups together all those people who are favorably inclined to every new technology a priori because they believe that any innovation will bring about an improvement in their lives. Innovators tend to enthusiastically accept and adopt each new innovation.
2. Early adopters: visionaries who develop the technology. The early adopters are all those people who see innovation as an effective way to introduce discontinuity with the past and move forward into the future. Their motivation is guided by the belief that innovation

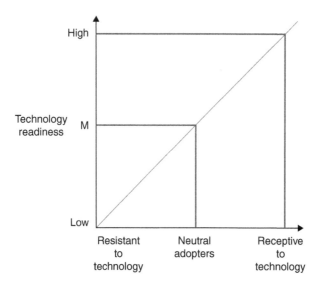

Figure 4.6   Customer types

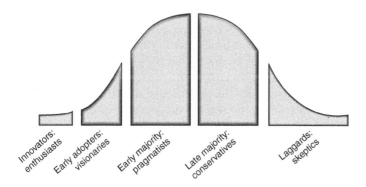

Figure 4.7   The adoption curve of an innovation

may offer the chance to achieve a significant competitive advantage over the old order. These visionaries represent a strategic segment of potential adopters because they are most willing to invest time and resources to buy the innovation and to test it.

3. Early majority: the pragmatists. This customer segment is neither infatuated with new technologies, nor easily influenced by them. These people believe that innovation provides solid, effective

solutions. Therefore, their approach to innovation is more evolutionary, rather than revolutionary, compared to innovators and early adopters. Pragmatists have an incremental attitude toward technology: they tend to adopt new technology only when testimonials on its effectiveness and efficiency are substantiated and they trust their sources.

4. Late majority: the conservatives. This customer category shows great caution in adopting innovations and resists changing their behavior in any way. They accordingly express great skepticism in evaluating the capabilities and benefits of an innovation; they become adopters only when they fear that the rest of the world is doing so and they risk being left behind. Compared to the other categories they are very sensitive to the cost sacrifice they must bear and are extremely demanding in evaluating offerings.

5. Laggards: the skeptics. This segment is the most problematic type of adopter. They are critical of all change, and very unwilling to adopt new products or services, which they buy only when they consider them essential to their survival.

This model, in its most common interpretation, tends to reinforce the idea that the process of adopting an innovation can be charted on a continuum, and is caused by reciprocal contamination of various potential customer segments. In this perspective, technology enthusiasts have the task of stimulating and educating the visionaries who, in turn, serve as points of reference for the pragmatists, whose behavior then encourages the conservatives and skeptics to set aside their distrust and embrace the change brought about by the innovation.

In real life, however, consumers do not follow this desired progression in innovation adoption. In a Movement Game based on product innovation, in fact, the firm risks plunging into the market chasm (Moore 1991, 2002). Figure 4.8 usefully illustrates the meaning of this evocative term. As we can see, the diffusion of the innovation from the early adopters segment (the visionaries) to the early majority (the pragmatists) does not progress along a self-supporting continuum. On the contrary, a chasm or behavioral abyss gapes between them.

Despite the fact that we can position these two groups of consumers in an adjacent temporal sequence in the adoption process, in actual fact, they are divided. As Table. 4.1 shows, there are deep differences in their values and how they interpret and assess a new product or service.

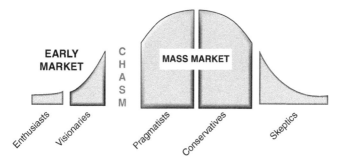

Figure 4.8 The chasm: discontinuation of the adoption process

Table 4.1 Cognitive and evaluation differentials of an innovation

Early adopters and visionaries	Early majority and pragmatists
Intuitive	Analytical
Sustaining the revolution	Sustaining the evolution
Against innovation	Conformists to innovation
Guided by instinct	Prefer the sociability of the pack
Predisposed to risk	Share their choices with others
Design the future	Manage the present
Seek out the possible	Pursue what is likely

The success of an innovation comes about when it is adopted by the early majority and laggards, in other words, by the market at large. This means that if the new product or service does not appear convincing and reassuring to these groups, it risks failing, or falling into the abyss. The innovation will earn the enthusiasm of innovators and early adopters, but it won't win over the pragmatists and conservatives. If after initial success a firm that's launched an innovation fails to establish itself on the market, this failure is due to the firm's inability to portray its product as irresistible in the eyes of the early majority and laggards.

To cross the chasm, therefore, firms must draw in pragmatic customers. To do so, the most effective form of attack is often a gradual, selective penetration maneuver, which in the next sections we generally refer to as selection and protection strategies. First of all, firms must identify the customer niches or segments (within the early majority) that seem more inclined to adopt the innovation first.

The main purpose of this behavior is to build references in markets in order to penetrate beachheads that act as bridges to win over the

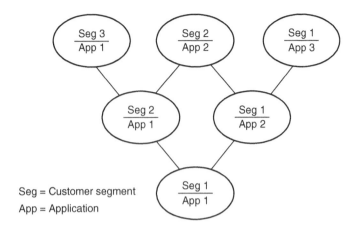

Figure 4.9   The conquest of adjacent segments in the pragmatist group

remaining groups. It is vitally important to consolidate these niches as this helps to reduce doubts and perceived risks in adjacent segments, reaffirming at the same time the firm's leadership image.

In order to conquer the "beachheads" the firm must be ready to adapt its innovation, to the point of developing ad hoc personalization for each niche where possible. In Figure 4.9, for example, to serve segment 1, the firm initially develops application 1. Although this tactic is an expensive one, it can be the most effective way to gain the confidence and the cooperation of pragmatic customers. The reason for this, as we've mentioned before, is that market development would come about through the gradual conquest of adjacent niches of customers who are favorably influenced by testimonials and word of mouth of the early adopters within the group of pragmatists, like in a bowling pins analogy (Figure 4.9).

4.17   Some tools for evaluating an innovation

To systematically and structurally evaluate how truly irresistible the innovative proposition is, we propose two simple instruments.[12]

With the first, we can use the two axes of the grid shown in Figure 4.10, relative to the B2B context but easily adaptable to the B2C context. On the vertical axis, on a scale of 1 to 4, the management has to assess the total costs for customers, including the cost of integrating the new product or service into their systems. The horizontal

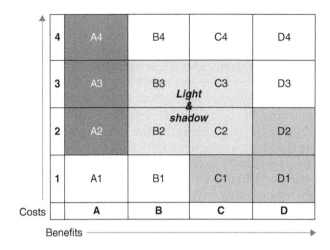

Figure 4.10   The innovation costs/benefits matrix (B2B case)

axis charts the overall benefits that may be achieved from the customers' perspective.

By examining the 16 cells of the grid, we can identify the ones that may arouse greater apprehension toward innovation. The cells resulting from the intersection of column A with numbers 2 to 4 indicate a negative area, since the products or services here are evaluated not only as costly but also as unable to provide a benefit that would justify adopting them. The four central cells show lights and shadows. The value proposition offered to potential customers by the innovation has an uncertain future, as the benefits are more or less offset by the relative adoption costs. In this area, the value proposition is not only unattractive but is also equivocal in the customer's eyes. In the other cells, the innovation indicates the various tradeoffs perceived by customers. Products in a developmental phase are located in cell 4D, where customers acknowledge that significant benefits can be had from the innovation, although at some cost. The perception of value of products located in cells D3 and D2 remains high while costs are regarded as contained. Finally, in cell D1 we find innovations that have all the prerequisites of success. In fact, these innovations can facilitate the attainment of a significant competitive advantage, without elevated adoption or integration costs.

The most critical problem the firm faces in analyzing the positioning of the innovation in the matrix is deciding how to most effectively migrate from the more unfavorable to the more promising cells.

The first area of intervention calls attention to all those innovations that should fall into the four central cells. In this case, the firm must move to improve the trade-off by lowering perceived costs and raising perceived benefits. Innovations located in cell D4 are attractive to customers with a greater inclination to experimentation, and less appealing for those who more pragmatically want to avoid integration and adoption costs. In order to facilitate the migration of these products into the lower cells of the column, the firm must redesign the innovation, improving the technology and production processes where needed so as to make the new product more attractive with respect to the cost dimension. The products located in cells D2 and D3 require a careful strategy of demand segmentation in order to guarantee those customers willing to pay the medium-high cost of integration the benefits attainable from the technology. In order to encourage the development and diffusion of the innovation in the early majority population, the firm must identify every opportunity to reduce any costs that still may represent a barrier to adoption and use. Cells C1 and D1 contain all those innovations that the market considers competitive and attractive. As we can readily imagine, these products do not require migration to other cells of the matrix, but rather, a maneuver by the firm to protect these innovations from imitation and attack from direct or potential rivals.

A further tool we can use to assess the potential for developing an innovation is presented in Figure 4.11. This matrix is constructed on

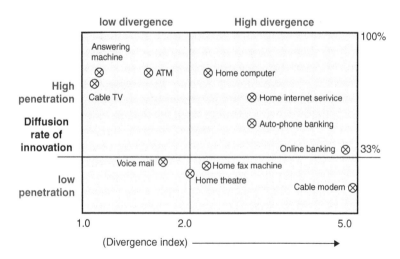

Figure 4.11 The adoption potential grid

two dimensions: the diffusion rate of the innovation among customers expressed as the percentage of adoption, and the divergence index.

This second index derives from the relationship between the percentage of use of an innovation among customers, comparing those who express a high propensity to adopt this innovation and those with a low propensity to do so. (For example, if the percentage of use of the innovation among high techno-ready customers is 26%, while among low techno-ready customers this figure is 13%, then the divergence index would equal: $26/13 = 2$.) As we can see, the matrix can suggest valuable information to the firm on the potential for developing an innovation, and on the best strategy for disseminating its adoption. In the example shown in the figure, the answering machine appears to have achieved high diffusion in all customer segments, demonstrating that its potential for development in the USA is exhausted. By contrast, online banking services have interesting potential since they have been adopted by around 35% of potential customers only, but they have a high divergence index (the numbers are for illustrative purposes only). Up to now, only customers who are more inclined to embrace technology use these services, while the greater portion of the market still waits to be conquered, with the related risks and opportunities linked to crossing the chasm.

4.18 Strategic maneuvers to overcome the barriers

In the previous section, we reaffirmed that innovations bring about discontinuity and require changes in behavior, both in the firm that introduces a new technology and the target customer. The greater the discontinuity generated for the firm, the higher the barriers it must face to develop the innovation. Similarly, the greater the discontinuity for the customer, the greater the innovation barriers created by the market and the more slowly the new technology will propagate.

If a firm wants to successfully innovate, therefore, it has to learn how to deal with both internal and external innovation barriers, beyond the specific actions already illustrated case by case. For this purpose, by intersecting the firm's internal barriers with those generated by customers, we can identify four strategic maneuvers to overcome the obstacles to change (Figure 4.12).

1. Caution and constancy (Section 4.19);
2. Selection and protection (Section 4.20);
3. Rapid development (Section 4.21);
4. Incrementalism and migration (Section 4.22).

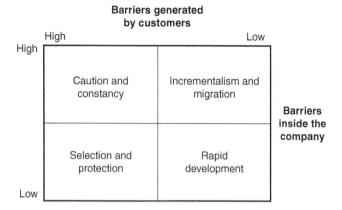

Figure 4.12   Strategies for removing innovation barriers

4.19   Caution and constancy maneuver

When an innovation has to overcome high barriers generated both by the firm and potential customers, "caution and constancy" may be the most effective maneuver.

In a context where the company is not ready to offer the product or the innovative service and the customer is not ready to adopt it, the most appropriate strategy is a limited launch. Market development is incremental, initially targeting customers who would get the most out of the product or service. The objective is to give priority to the more receptive customer segments, and subsequently to extend the offering to the rest of the market.

As illustrated in Figure 4.13, the pricing policy will also reflect this choice. The firm first proposes a higher "skimming" price to the customer who initially recognizes greater value in the innovation and adapts it over time, recognizing the lower level of interest expressed by other customer segments.

To succeed, the firm pursuing this development strategy must be protected by high entrance barriers. In fact, if other rivals are able to enter the market, caution and constancy would become a risky move. In fact, for this strategy to succeed, the firm must do business in a market without threats from rivals until it has recovered the investment in research and development and production facilities. In addition, before pursuing this tactic, the firm must be certain of the following:

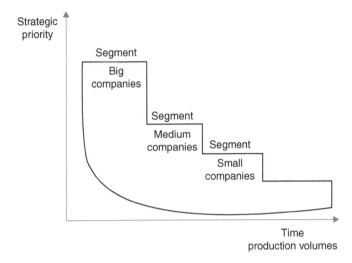

Figure 4.13 The planned sequence for the diffusion of an innovation: an example

- There are enough customers with a high propensity for using the new product or service.
- These customers are willing to pay more for the new technology than they do for the existing technology.

4.20 Selection and protection maneuver

The "selection and protection" maneuver is advisable when the firm is ready to market the innovation while customers show some discontinuity in use. In the preceding pages, this maneuver was introduced in the discussion on crossing the chasm.

The purpose of this approach is to strategically segment potential customers with respect to a particularly popular benefit. The success of the selection and protection strategy depends on the firm's ability to first understand the needs of the market, and to then personalize the innovation until it's a perfect fit with those needs.

Low entrance barriers should instead alert the company to the danger from potential rival imitators who may be attracted by the opportunities offered by the innovation. In such cases the firm must protect the market it is creating. After choosing a niche to target with its development efforts and then winning it over with a killer application, the company must act efficiently and decisively, incrementally improving the price/performance of the product to prevent competitors from appropriating the new market.

In the selection and protection strategy, the following principles must be respected. The first is not to attempt to elicit levels of demand above and beyond the production capacity of the firm. This consideration is justified by the objective of affirming the innovation as the market standard. By winning customers that the firm is not entirely able to satisfy, it risks opening the door to other potential competitors who could step in to meet the needs of the new adopters. Dominating a customer niche requires achieving over two-thirds of customer purchases of the innovation. With this level of dominance, potential competitors are contained in the more marginal and less insidious positions. We can reduce both the threat of their growth and the stature of their standard.

The second principle, which relates to the first, is not to try to penetrate too many customer niches simultaneously. Raising interest in various segments without being able to completely cover them only means, once again, creating a potential market for competitors.

The third principle is to pay particular attention to the adopted decision-making process of a potential customer in the marketing phase. Often the communication, presentation, and promotional efforts target the wrong audience, and do not take into account the various people involved in the purchasing decision: influencers, financiers, end-users, and so forth.

The fourth principle echoes what we've reiterated many times. We can more easily convince our customers to adopt an innovation if we give them an irresistible motive for doing so. To develop a selection and protection strategy, therefore, we must answer the following questions:

- Have we clearly identified the target segment? Is it accessible?
- Will conquering the identified target be useful as a promotional lever for other segments?
- Do our customers express an irresistible motive for desiring the innovation?
- Is our firm, along with our partners, able to respond appropriately to such motives?
- Are there competitors that could anticipate our firm's maneuvers or easily surpass them?

4.21   The rapid development maneuver

This strategy is diametrically opposed to constancy and caution since technological innovation must not exceed either the barriers generated by the firm or those erected by customers (see Figure 4.14 below).

The rapid development maneuver is therefore appropriate when the company is ready and able to dominate every aspect of the launch and production of the innovation, and the market is prepared to implement it.

Such a strategy involves introducing the new value proposition on a large scale in order to stimulate a rapid process of adoption and diffusion so as to immediately consolidate a dominant market position. The objective of the maneuver is to achieve the greatest market share and the highest volume in the least amount of time, and to enable the firm to exploit the benefits of the experience curve and attain a significant cost and image advantage with respect to the imitative competition.

The innovative firm introduces the product or service with a quick-penetration price policy. This means short-term losses that will be offset by long-term forecasted profits from accrued sales volume. This maneuver also impedes competitor entry and imitation by raising financial barriers that emerge from the anticipated reduction of profitability (and therefore attractiveness) of the new market.

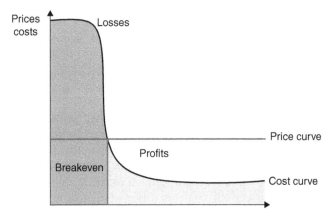

Figure 4.14   The price maneuver to accelerate diffusion of the innovation

This maneuver can be successfully adopted where the following conditions exist:

- Internal firm barriers and customer-created barriers are very contained.
- The benefits derived from the experiential effect make significant cost advantages possible by developing sales and market share.
- Access to distribution channels, to rapidly penetrate the market, is guaranteed.
- The firm, having a solid financial basis, is prepared to take higher short-term risks to achieve long-term benefits.
- The product or service must be the subject of constant improvement, so as to maintain customer loyalty and interest.

4.22   Incrementalism and migration maneuvers

When the innovation does not raise customer resistance but the firm suffers from internal barriers to change, then the maneuver to consider is migration.

With this strategy, the firm seeks to induce its customers to migrate to improved and constantly updated versions of the product. The purpose of the maneuver is to develop incremental innovations that are compatible with the internal constraints to change, and to proceed with small steps, as the resource and competence barriers allow. With sequential technological leaps leveraging on loyalty, customers can migrate up to a new generation of the product. The assumption, of course, is that constant innovation meets the needs expressed by its target and that the maneuver translates into greater value for the firm.

4.23   Barriers and opportunities in the convergence era: coevolution and metamarkets

Since the 1990s, high-impact Movement Games based on new products have often been the result of a factor generically known as convergence.[13] This is an evolutionary process of competitive dynamics that sees once-separate areas become part of a large single meta-market where the strategic boundaries are much more blurred. Although the enabling factor can be the fact that different technological trajectories come together, the key is the ability to continue to meet the needs of the separate competitive arena. If we illustrate this situation on a graph, the relevant demand curves are now interdependent and the needs satisfied by each firm become articulated clusters of needs. This means, for example, that the functional foods offered by some food companies compete with pharmaceutical products in fighting cholesterol, or mobile phone producers turn into rivals of camera manufacturers. According to the *Wall Street Journal*, "Smart phones are getting so smart that they're now outwitting other consumer-electronic devices," including GPS devices, digital music players, and digital cameras.[14]

The concept of coevolution[15] is introduced to lower internal resource barriers in an era that is seeing increasing technological convergence. Coevolution, in the natural sciences, is the process by which inter-dependent species tend to evolve reciprocally in an endless cycle. The most widespread metaphor to explain the theory of coevolution refers to what frequently occurs in the food chain. To survive, the lion hunts gazelles and the weakest animals are the first to fall prey. The survivors, the fastest and most robust, strengthen the herd and give birth to a new, more evolved species. The weakest lions of the pride, unable to catch the new breed of gazelles, in turn die out, while the rest, if they wish to survive, must produce faster lions that are able to catch their prey. In this way, the behavior and changes that occur in species A activate a process of natural selection and evolution in species B and vice versa.

Rather than evolving in the Movement Game, firms tend to coevolve, just like the organisms in an ecosystem. Organizations, in fact, interact with one another, and give chase to each other in a complex dance of coevolution. This dance produces results in nature that are only appar-ently random. Nature has created flowers that evolve thanks to the contribution of their pollinators, which in turn, thrive off their nectar. In the economic world, the dance of coevolution has also produced networks of mutual dependency between allies and rivals, customers and suppliers. Coevolution, in the Movement Game, refers to changes brought about by the interaction of two species whose evolutionary trajectories tend to cross paths. This interdependence may occur symbi-otically (each species helps the other) but could also be opportunistic (one species uses others to its own ends).

Coevolution is a typical process among species living in complex adaptive systems. In these contexts, their interdependence produces non-linear effects that result in an intensification of their respective capabilities, which may even reach exponential levels. This is demon-strated in how the agility and creativity of the system increase as the incremental connections intensify. These concepts can easily be trans-ferred to firms. In highly complex markets, in fact, firms are spurred to explore possibilities of opening new Movement Games in coevolution with competitors, whether in their own ecosystems or in new ones. In order to survive, firms must share their experiences and their capabilities, often oriented to the past, with companies in unrelated sectors, in order to coevolve and shape the future. Using a graphic representation can be useful to distinguish the significance of the sector, markets and metamarkets, and to introduce contexts in which the new Movement Games come about through convergence and coevolution processes.

As illustrated in Figure 4.15, the traditional boundaries of the sector include all firms that satisfy certain benefits for specific customers by means of a particular technology. The delineation of the market, meanwhile, transversally identifies all customers with a specific need, regardless of the technology used to satisfy it. Therefore this definition includes a set of complementary products with similar functions and benefits for customers.

Finally, firms positioned in asymmetric sectors and markets converge and coevolve in metamarkets. This coevolution process generates an aggregate without clearly defined boundaries that is undergoing a dynamic process of constant reconfiguration. In other words, sector boundaries tend to blur because they are constantly moving toward the creation of new metamarkets.

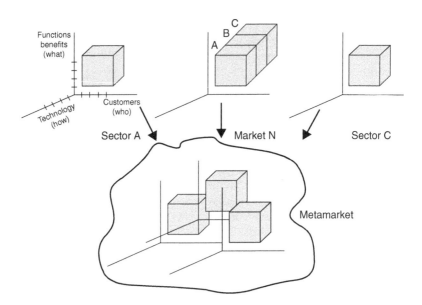

Figure 4.15 The metamarket

Through coevolutionary processes, new Movement Games begin that not only activate the transformation of individual sectors but also generate intersectoral convergence that gives rise to metamarkets. The progressive increase of knowledge that comes from coevolution accelerates the convergence process and erases the distinctions between the boundaries of traditional sectors. This is particularly relevant in sectors with higher levels of knowledge and information. The boundaries between computers, consumer electronics, telecommunications, and contents, for example, are increasingly transitory in the ICT (Information, Communication & Technology) metamarket. Other metamarkets include nutriceuticals (nutritional products and pharmaceuticals), cosmeceuticals (cosmetics and medicines) edutainment (education and entertainment), genetic diagnostic technologies (biogenetics and pharmacology), and so forth. Examples of unpronounceable neologisms are becoming increasingly numerous.

By soliciting new Movement Games, convergence and coevolution increase market hypercompetition and turbulence as it becomes more difficult to determine the boundaries of specialization on which to build defensible and durable advantages. At the same time, the boundaries of the firm's internal resources expand (Section 4.7) as the knowledge it needs is much more extensive. This leads us to the next section.

4.24   The coevolution chain

The coevolution chain, shown in Figure 4.16, squarely intersects with the traditional value system, offering useful ideas for our discussion.

In the Movement Game, in fact, the coevolution chain may be where a firm can look for the capabilities and resources it needs to generate innovations and to find less conventional answers to market needs.[16] This can be done through alliances and collaboration with competitors and partners.

In keeping with what we discussed in Section 4.7, the firm surpasses its resource barriers by planning a network of interconnections with its coevolution chain. This network may take different forms in terms of equity and non-equity, and alliances and partnerships between businesses: acquisitions, licensing, co-marketing, outsourcing, joint developments, contractual joint ventures, risk-sharing ventures, corporate venture capital, or any other relations between constellations and interconnected networks of firms.

In the coevolution chain the firm can therefore operate through simple bilateral cooperative relations or through multiple interconnected

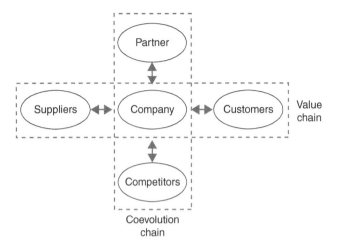

Figure 4.16   The coevolution chain

relations. Figure 4.17 illustrates the complexity of the multipolar interconnections that can be created between the firm and its potential
partners. The firm tends to build a complex network of interconnections when it is difficult to find a single partner that can provide all
the asymmetric competencies necessary to develop an innovation. The
network of firms generated in this way represents a network of opportunities. As we can see from the figure, each firm is interconnected
with other firms and has access to all the potential knowledge and
capabilities of the network to which its partner is in turn integrated and
interconnected.

When a firm decides to exploit the coevolution chain to create a
network of opportunities for its Movement Game, it must meticulously
analyze the interconnecting relations to assess not only the generative potential of capabilities and resources but also the causes of latent
conflict. The option of teaming up with a partner in the coevolution
chain requires the firm to carefully explore the value and conflict
that could arise from participating in the opportunity network. To
more fully appreciate the significance of these considerations, we
can recall the dynamics created in AOL's opportunity network when
it was bought out by Time Warner. The collaboration between these
two companies sparked a conflict with AT&T, which offered telecommunications services to Time Warner. AT&T, in fact, owned a share
in Excite Home, an internet service company and AOL had been its

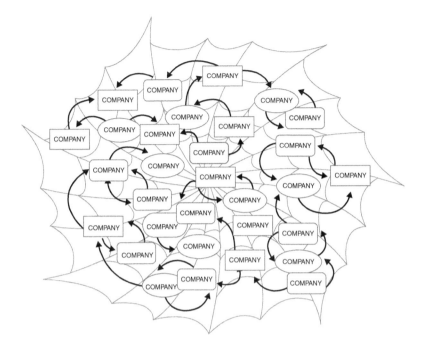

Figure 4.17 The opportunity network

competitor. A similar problem occurred in Europe, where AOL had agreements with Bertelsmann, the German publishing group who in turn competed with Time Warner, both in magazine publishing and the music industry with the WMG label. This brief example clearly shows that a coevolutionary relationship can also activate a chain of potential conflicts due to pre-existing interconnections in the opportunity network.

In order to instigate a Movement Game founded on the interconnections between coevolutionary businesses, we have to reflect on the following questions:

1. Do our partner firms, integrated into the opportunities network, compete in central or peripheral areas?
2. How can we leverage the firm capability of the network?
3. Which protective barriers to knowledge must be high among firms in the network that are in competition to avoid misappropriations and conflict?

4. Does our firm's participation in the network generate as much value for us as it does for the network?
5. Will coevolutionary participation in the network increase our firm's competitiveness?
6. Have the network partners, in turn, created interconnections with other firms that may be useful to our company?
7. Will our coevolutionary collaboration with a business partner prevent our firm from participating in other networks with greater potential?

The balance between collaboration and competition between partners in the evolutionary chain depends on the relations that each company in turn has with third parties. The collaborative relation between two firms, from this point of view, is clearly less complex than what we might find in a network with several partners.[17] In general, it is useful to distinguish between two types of relations: balanced and unbalanced. In the first case, relations between the parties that make up the opportunity network tend to synergistically reinforce each other. In the case of unbalanced relations, at some point in the network, structural tension arises that can result in conflict and annul all benefits of collaboration between parties.

In the first example on the left above, all collaborations in place are balanced, in the sense that each party works efficiently with the others. This is represented with the "plus" sign in the figure. In the scenario represented in the center, Firm A collaborates only with B, while C is in conflict with both A and B. The collaboration (between A and B) is also balanced, since the conflict with C does not undermine the relationship between the two companies. The tension that both have with C may even reinforce mutual understanding. The third example on the right has an unbalanced network. The collaboration of A with both B

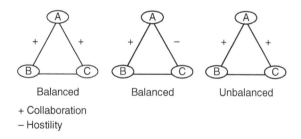

Figure 4.18 Multiple balanced and unbalanced collaborative relations

and C risks being subjected to considerable tension due to the conflict between B and C.

We've summarized the great opportunities offered by the coevolution chain in dealing with internal barriers to change above. Our final considerations focus instead on the risks that can arise among the network partners when indirect conflicts emerge due to the interconnections that each partner has with other firms.

4.25 Overcoming barriers in the Movement Game started by a new entrant

Some scholars have observed five stages that are surprisingly recurrent in the revolutionary path that leads to the usurping of a market leader and the crowning of a new entrant innovator.[18] The path tracks the evolutionary phases of the Movement Game initiated by the insurgent, and is illustrated in Figure 4.19.

At the outset of the new game, the innovator sometimes attempts to enter into a "foothold market." For example, the market for very small electric vehicles (50cc, or 0.05L) could become a foothold market for entry of these new producers into the future car market.

This stage, although often unnecessary, is in some cases the start of the Movement Game. At this point in time, the innovative firm with mature knowledge can complete its experimentation and acquire the minimum critical mass of sales to support the successive phases of development of the new initiative. By strengthening resources and expertise, the company creates the conditions to overcome their own barriers, up to the point of daring to take the next step.

The second stage coincides with the attack on the main market that the innovation addresses. A critical success factor in this stage, in addition to appropriate financial resources, is the overcoming of the barriers to market access presented in Section 4.9.

In the third stage, following entry, the value proposition of the innovator is still unattractive to most of the market. Therefore, the company at this stage serves unsophisticated customers who have not yet been served by other competitors, while continuing its technical, financial, and market expansion.

This takes us to the fourth stage, when the expansion of the innovator becomes detrimental to the previous incumbent through a growing migration of the customer base. Getting to this stage means successfully overcoming customer barriers, that is the distrust and switching costs associated with abandoning old suppliers.

In the fifth stage, direct opposition to the insurgent inevitably begins. The incumbent firms, now aware of the threat, launch full-force, defensive retaliation strategies.

When an innovator manages to endure even through this stage, then it has successfully accomplished the Movement Game. In this case, two scenarios are preferable for the ex-incumbent: (1) the old and new value propositions coexist because they target groups of customers with different requirements; or (2) the ex-incumbent, over time, manages to overcome the innovation barriers in order to imitate the insurgent and adapt to the new rules. In the worst-case scenario, the incumbent will be marginalized from the Movement Game until it leaves the market definitively.

Figure 4.19 clearly illustrates that the Movement Game can fail at any stage, but if that were to happen the threat would be thwarted before

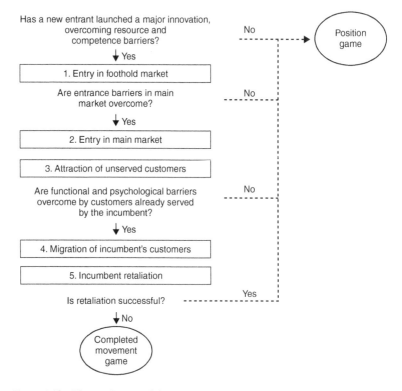

Figure 4.19 The evolution of the Movement Game started by a new entrant

generating significant damage to the current businesses. The task of the incumbent facing the threat is to evaluate *ex ante* the nature of the innovation and the probability that it can surpass all the stages described above and come out unscathed. In this case, the firm must immediately remold its coevolutionary network and develop the skills that the new game requires. In summer 2007, for example, Deutsche Telekom, via the T-online Venture Fund, became part of Jajah, a company founded in 2005 specializing in VoIP technology whose main investor, since spring 2007, had been Intel Capital.

The following chapter details the defensive maneuvers that can be deployed by the incumbent in order to mitigate the threat posed by the innovative competitor.

5
Defense Strategies in the Movement Game

5.1 Responses to change

An analysis of great historical events reveals that revolutions were often unable to achieve the changes they aimed to bring about. However, when a revolution does succeed, it is due to the inability of governments and the elite to shape history as they see fit instead of being shaped by it. The same often applies to markets. The success achieved by an insurgent can generally be attributed to the incumbent's ineffectiveness rather than to the innovator's superiority.

In current markets, dominating incumbent firms often are unprepared, and even intimidated by new emerging technologies, or by the ability of a potential rival to creatively regenerate their business models. When these incumbents succumb to widespread change, their lack of proactivity alone is to blame.

Leader firms who ignore change are destined to failure. Rather than deal with change, they underestimate the emerging threat and fail in turn to regenerate their stocks of capabilities and resources. They await devastating events without reacting, paralyzed by their procrastination. The following signals or events often precede the radical transformation of a sector (Sheth and Sisodia, 2002):

- a growth rate of new entrants consistently above the growth rate of the market as a whole;
- a prolonged period of under-utilization of capabilities;
- the rise of new technological trajectories that call into play just as many new skills;
- the expiration of key patents;

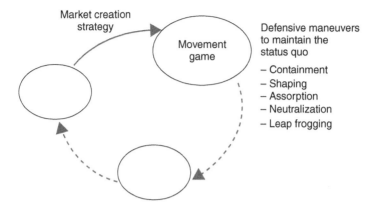

Figure 5.1   The incumbent's defense maneuvers in the Movement Game

- sudden changes in the distribution system that erode certain entrance barriers, as in the case of e-banking;
- a "shock" upstream, downstream, or in a related market, such as the 2008 oil shock that precipitated the downslide of American car manufacturers.

Between the two dangerous extremes of ignoring the change on one end and blindly embracing it on the other, the research[1] on sector change shows that business leaders tackle such challenges using a wide variety of intermediate behaviors. This conduct can be summarized as follows (see Figure 5.1 above):

a) containment (Section 5.2);
b) shaping (Section 5.3);
c) absorption (Section 5.4);
d) neutralization (Section 5.5);
e) leap frogging (Section5.6).

5.2   Defensive containment strategies

This maneuver is based on the adage that it is better to act sooner than later. The containment strategy is the first maneuver that a firm should use when a rival's innovation is being initially developed and signs of threat are still very weak. Two objectives are possible. The first is to relegate innovation to a market niche. The second, more drastic aim, is to block the evolutionary path of the new technology.

Containment is a valid option as it enables a firm to buy time to evaluate the nature and scope of the threat and to assess effective defensive maneuvers. The firm can deploy this strategy in six different ways:

1. Retaining customers. Enhancing customer satisfaction – and thus customer loyalty – is based on the principle that a satisfied customer is the best defense against the competition. More satisfied customers are less likely to want to try out competing alternatives.
2. Increasing the costs of migration (switching cost). To reduce a customer's interest in an innovation, an effective tactic is to objectively demonstrate that the costs she would incur by making the change would far outweigh the benefits she could achieve. We can also minimize the impact of a rival's offering by improving product benefits of our own, technology permitting.
3. Exploiting distribution channels. We can exploit our distribution potential to stifle an innovation via contractual pressure on our current channels. In the FMCG (fast moving consumer goods) market, firms can contain the opponent's Movement Games with aggressive strategies offering discounts, promotions, and incentives.
4. Surrounding the innovator with containment brands. If the leader firm can encircle the innovation with a multitude of new products, this is often an effective way to strengthen brand loyalty.
5. Disorientate customers. By announcing the launch of major innovations in response to an opponent's Movement Game, the leader firm can induce procrastination in customers, dampening their willingness to change in the short term.
6. Undermine the innovation. The leader firm can run an aggressive or subtle communication campaign in order to undermine the attacker. The Internet is the perfect arena for this type of maneuver.

The purpose of the containment strategy, therefore, is to shift the customers' attention away from the innovation with a set of maneuvers that synergistically dissuades them from purchasing this new product. The containment maneuver is effective if it significantly lessens the chances of the innovation's success, thereby demoralizing the innovative firm, forcing it to commit additional financial and commercial resources to support its Movement Game.

5.3 Defensive shaping strategies

When a revolutionary change cannot be contained, another option is to try to shape it. The shaping strategy involves establishing a competitive order oriented to coexistence rather than the elimination of one of the contenders. Three different maneuvers are possible to facilitate coexistence:

1. Cooperating with the innovator. Shaping an innovation means recognizing the possibilities of exploiting its revolutionary content in order to complement the firm's business model, rather than to chance being replaced by the innovation. An incumbent firm, in other words, accepts the idea that the innovation is a useful complement to the status quo. This maneuver works when competing firms cooperate with other innovators to jointly develop new value propositions. This scenario tends to create hybrid products that are an effective compromise between premature technology and mature technology in need of revitalization.
2. Guaranteeing financial support. Rather than enduring the anxiety of technological change, a firm may try to appropriate it by using its own financial resources to support venture capital strategies. By creating an incubator for development and experimentation, the firm can have hands-on contact with the innovation and directly monitor it, assessing its competitive potential and development opportunities.
3. Integrating the value system. A firm can shape an innovation by serving as a strategic supplier to the innovative firm. The incumbent firm can thus turn a potential threat into an opportunity by participating directly in the development of the innovation, and in doing so get the chance to access knowledge. Conversely, the firm may also convert a rival innovator into a strategic supplier.

5.4 Defensive absorption strategies

When the threat of an innovation can't be eliminated through shaping, the absorption strategy is another option to consider. In this case, the firm can pursue two distinct maneuvers:

1. Acquire new skills. The firm promotes the acquisition of new skills and new technologies in order to improve the competitive content of the current value proposition or business model. In absorbing the

new technology, the firm exploits the potential innovation without destroying its original stock of resources and capabilities. The aim of this maneuver is to quickly integrate tradition with innovation, reducing both the competitive threat of the revolution and customer diffidence.

2. Create blocks to facilitate the acquisition of revolutionary firms. A fast and efficient way to remove the threat of an innovative firm is to acquire it. To do so, the incumbent needs to reduce the innovator's maneuvering room so as to force it to accept an alliance or to pave the way for a buyout. The incumbent can effectively restrict the innovator's freedom of movement by creating a network that integrates suppliers, distributors, and strategic partners, impeding access to customers, raw materials, and other collaborations.

5.5   Defensive neutralization strategies

If containment, shaping, or absorption maneuvers prove inadequate or ineffective, the firm can turn to more radical options. The neutralization strategy can be employed when the innovation is in a rapid development phase and the firm decides that it does not have the time to deploy an effective alternative strategy. This strategy is pursued in following ways:

1. Using legal initiatives. The serious threat induced in the record industry by digital music exchange programs is being addressed through extensive legal actions aimed at stopping their spread.

2. Offering the same benefits promised by the innovation free of charge. To cancel out the perception of the value of an innovation, the incumbent firm can offer the same benefits in its value proposition, thereby removing any competitive advantage achievable from the rival's Movement Game. This strategy is often adopted by Microsoft, which has increasingly integrated applications into its Windows operating system: Media Player, Instant Messenger, Movie Maker, Malware removal and so on.

5.6   Defensive leapfrogging strategies

This option becomes necessary when neutralization maneuvers prove ineffective or unworkable. The objective of leapfrogging is to render the innovation irrelevant, thanks to the incumbent's more advanced technological development, which now supersedes the insurgent's innovation. Due to the sizable commitment of resources and higher levels of risk it entails, leapfrogging should be deployed only when there are no other alternatives and the firm's very survival is at stake.

Leapfrogging is a metaphorical term representing how the incumbent reacts to the innovation – either by increasingly improving the innovator's technology (incremental leapfrogging), or by proposing a radically new and superior innovation (radical leapfrogging). The former is generally the right course of action when the incremental cost of imitation is much lower than that of a radical innovation, and the benefits achieved are sufficient to neutralize the competitive threat. Otherwise, resources should be channeled into the latter option, the development of more efficient and effective cutting-edge technology. An example of leapfrogging is Microsoft's Office Excel spreadsheet, which supplanted the original Lotus 1-2-3.

In conclusion, an incumbent's defensive strategy, when threatened by an innovator's Movement Game, requires a careful selection of the different maneuvers suggested in the previous pages. Clearly, such maneuvers should be used in combination to exploit synergistic effects and to increase competitive and interfirm pressure on the innovator. Finally, remember that it is possible to win a battle against an innovator, but the war against change is in vain. Here, as always, the only weapon guaranteeing victory is proactive innovation.

6
The Imitation Game

6.1 Pursuit strategies: players and types

The success achieved by a firm that starts a Movement Game, be it low- or high-impact, spurs the competition to pursue the innovator, thus activating the second game: imitation.

Imitators, in general, can be:

a) Newcomers: These firms, previously extraneous to the competitive confrontation, like the innovator, sense the significance of the revolution. They enter the new competitive arena, launching their pursuit maneuver or flanking attack on the first mover's as yet-unprotected market. In Italy, for example, Lino's Coffee was a newcomer in the breakfast market, in an Imitation Game modeled after the American company Starbucks, which does not currently operate in the Italian market. Newcomer imitators can most often be found in the wake of a diversified Movement Game. Think, for example, of Samsung entering the new digital cameras' market: the Korean company, following a diversification strategy, was a newcomer for that market. b) Incumbents: Feeling threatened by innovations in their market, incumbents may either imitate immediately, or do so after first (unsuccessfully) attempting to thwart imitators by strenuously defending their original technology (confrontational phase). Nikon, for example, was an incumbent that belatedly imitated the Movement Game set off by newcomer Sony with digital photography. (The Sony Mavica was launched in 1981, while Nikon's Coolpix debuted in 1997, almost a year after Canon's PowerShot.) c) Retailers: Often big organized distribution (BOD), these organizations increasingly use their own tangible and intangible resources to imitate the best-selling branded products. Among the numerous examples are Costco's or Carrefour's ready-made starter meals, following Findus' Movement Game that we referred have to previously.

By analyzing the phenomenon in more detail, we can make a further distinction among imitators, particularly with reference to new product launches. The generic "imitator" label applies to three different types of firm:[1]

1. The pioneering imitator (or early-entrant imitator), who by exploiting its own skills imitates an innovator who is still testing the technology or the market. This imitator may even succeed in pre-empting the commercial launch of the product in question, and by so doing, emerge as the actual pioneer.
2. The follower imitator (or later-entrant imitator), who enters the market after the innovator and employs a maneuver that is more or less imitative, as described in the cases below (pure or marginal imitation).
3. The innovative imitator (also called follower innovator), who takes a competitive innovation as the benchmark and tries to overtake it by introducing innovative improvements. (See also the incremental and creative imitation cases described in the next section.)

	Innovator	Imitator
Pioneer	The firm that innovates in a technological field and first commercializes the resulting products and services	The firm that commercially pre-empts the innovator by imitating products or services that are still being tested in terms of technology or market
Follower	The challenger firm (early or later entrant) that attempts to overtake the innovator by incrementally improving the innovator's products or services	The firm (later entrant) that enters the market only after the innovator, with an explicit imitation maneuver

Figure 6.1   Innovators, imitators, pioneers, and followers

The strategic motivations behind an imitation maneuver are what determine the timing of an imitator's market entrance and the role it plays.

As we shall see, in some cases the imitator awaits an environment conducive to the acceptance and growth in demand of the innovation, recognizing that waiting doesn't mean losing out on opportunities in the short term, and may even reduce entry costs. In other situations, the delay is motivated by the dynamism and instability of the technological evolution of the innovation, which may not necessarily open a window of opportunity in the new strategic market. The imitator may also decide to delay entry until the opportunity arises to achieve significant sales volumes. This may come about with a price penetration maneuver in order to stimulate the adoption of the new product in unserved segments, which would in turn spur development of primary demand. To summarize, imitators often seek a more strategically favorable scenario in which they can drive the growth of the whole market. The objective is win/win for all firms. This is what happened, for example, in the mobile phone market in the second half of the 1990s.

At this point, we should introduce further classifications regarding the innovative standard chosen by the imitator. There are three ways to pursue an innovator (see Figure 6.2 below):

- Unsolicited imitation of the dominant standard;
- Incompatible imitation;
- Solicited imitation.

The Imitation Game of the dominant standard takes place when imitators pursue the innovator by adopting a very similar standard, the so-called "dominant design." Think of the successful concept of the SUV (Sport Utility Vehicle), and the numerous imitators who have gradually followed suit in producing similar models. Car manufacturers who failed (or were late) in doing so, such as Saab, lost out on valuable market opportunities.

Non-solicited imitation occurs when the pertinent legal or knowledge-based innovation barriers are low and indefensible; this facilitates quick replication. However, even though imitators copy the innovator's maneuvers, these firms can provide a value proposition that customers may appreciate more for its incremental improvements in how the offering is bundled, or for its relative price advantages.

We have a game of incompatible imitation (sometimes called tautological imitation) when the imitator responds with an innovation that

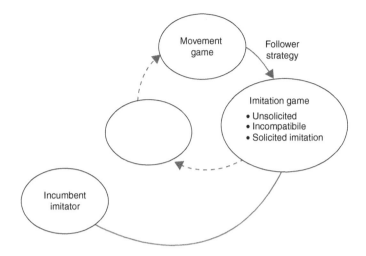

Figure 6.2 The Imitation Game: pursuit strategies

is technologically incompatible with the innovator's original product. This imitation-offering satisfies the same functions and provides similar benefits. When there are network economies (network externalities) or more generally, significant positive feedback (see below), the innovator's technology faces off against the imitator's to see which will become the market standard. In this case, what is known as a standards war[2] is waged. For example, Microsoft's answer to the success of Sony's PlayStation was the XBox console, but each has its own mutually incompatible standard. In fact, at launch, the Play Station 3 and the XBox360 were not even compatible in terms of the high-definition video players they used: the first used Blu-Ray, the second HD-DVD (optional). The game of incompatible imitation may end with a truce, with a duopoly, or often with the defeat of one of the contenders. In the high definition video market, for example, in February 2008 Toshiba withdrew its HD-DVD standard, conceding victory to Sony's Blu-Ray technology.

The game of solicited imitation correlates to some extent with the standards war. This is evident in contexts where the innovative firm facilitates and accelerates the transition from the Movement Game to the Imitation Game, by recognizing that this is the most effective, and perhaps least costly pathway to setting the standard or quickly developing the mass market. In this respect, see also the concept of positive feedback in Section 6.7.

Market histories abound with standards wars. A classic case is the reproduction of video images in the 1980s that kindled the confrontation between the VHS standard offered by Philips and Matshushita and Sony's Betamax. On par is the audio reproduction battle between Sony and Philips' CD technology and vinyl record and magnetic tape technologies. In both cases, the winning firms adopted a strategy that fostered an Imitation Game by guaranteeing user licenses and technological assistance to any interested rival.

Equally important is the support of content providers such as record companies, and film or software houses. In all these cases, the winning firms were not fighting against another technology. Instead they were interested in cornering market demand, convincing potential purchasers and users that it was more convenient to abandon the old and adopt the new technology, because it offered a better value proposition.

In conclusion, we should clarify a further, radical distinction in Imitation Games. The imitation that we have discussed up to now develops within the legal boundaries of fair competition. However, as we all know there is imitation with illegal intent, or counterfeiting. As stipulated in many legal systems, such imitation is considered an unfair threat when it is *likely to cause confusion* in a consumer of average attentiveness.

Counterfeiting in the broadest sense involves different players and typologies; in particular:

- Dishonest competitors, sometimes with the complicity of dishonest employees, counterfeit an exact copy of a product in order to appropriate a third party's brand. This also applies in cases of copycat imitation, which is clearly intended to create confusion for potential customers but without appropriating the brand.
- Dishonest suppliers. Here we refer to overrun, in other words, when contractors manufacture in excess of the product ordered by the brand owner. The surplus products are then channeled onto the black market. Similarly, some ex-suppliers may continue to produce and sell products even after their license has been withdrawn.
- Dishonest customers. This involves domestic piracy of copyright products or under-licensing of software products.
- Dishonest distributors. An example is when expiry dates are replaced on perishable products (tampering, i.e. counterfeiting packaging), when products are reintroduced on the market after being withdrawn or, when second rate products are sold as top quality.

As regards Imitation Games, there is a gray area between fair and unfair competition: the so-called asymmetrical competition, that originates from firms located in developing market contexts such as those of the Pacific Rim, is a case in point. These governments are often accused of fostering social dumping (i.e. unacceptable working conditions), environmental dumping (inadequate rules to protect the environment), and in some cases currency dumping (unrealistic official exchange rates). For follower competitors from these regions, naturally, such factors guarantee a position of artificial advantage and as such are arguably unfair.

6.2 The object and scale of imitation

Imitation can be extended beyond products and services to the innovator's procedures, processes, organizational models, and market strategies. Beyond the imitation of a quantum leap (high-impact games), this chapter refers to imitative strategies in general, including smaller, low-impact maneuvers.

The lawful imitation of products and services can be more or less original, as we can see from the examples below:

- Clones: These are legal copies of the original product, but marketed with the imitator's trademark or with no trademark. Examples are windshield wipers for the Volkswagen Golf, HP printer cartridges, and so forth. In some cases, the clone may have qualitative characteristics that are different from the original.
- Marginal imitations: An innovation can be imitated by modifying the peripheral factors, developing an aesthetically different design, reconfiguring the product, using alternative materials, or perhaps activating different production processes. Samsung's Galaxy Tab has been seen as a marginal imitation of the Apple's iPad.
- Incremental imitations (also known as innovative imitations, technological leaps or leapfrogging, as mentioned in the previous chapter): In this case the imitator enters a market in the development stage but makes a significant technological contribution, innovating and overtaking the pioneering innovator's products. As already mentioned, Microsoft Excel made a technological leap over the pioneering spreadsheet Lotus 1-2-3.
- Creative imitations: These represent the most innovative copies of a pioneering product. In this case, the imitator makes modifications to the original concept, but the aim is to create new applications of

the pioneering product to serve new customer segments, to enter new markets or new sectors. An example of this type is the Tuk-tuk (or 'auto-rickshaw'), a licensed imitation of the Piaggio *Ape*, a three-wheeled work vehicle. The Tuk-tuk is sold in many Eastern markets, successfully reconfigured as a taxi for local residents and tourists.

Illegal copies or counterfeits are proliferating at an alarming rate in more sectors than ever before, and with higher quality.[3] Up to the 1980s, the phenomenon essentially impacted on luxury items, but since the 1990s it has encompassed mass markets and industrial goods as well. More recently this phenomenon has extended to the web, and to services and distribution. There is even a copy of Disneyland in China and fake Cartier stores have sprouted up in Mexico.

Going back to lawful imitation, we mentioned how it can involve not only products but also the strategies, organizational models, and processes that distinguish the market success of the innovator. For example, competitive intelligence and benchmarking actions purport to learn the market-driving capabilities of rivals or other excellent firms in different industrial sectors with a view to replicating them. Asian companies are often accused of systematically pursuing the Imitation Game. However, we must admit that their international market success has stimulated many European and American enterprises to follow their lead. Western firms are striving to broaden their stock of skills and capabilities that produce these exceptional results, with the aim of reengineering their most critical procedures and processes. There is no doubt that it's easier to imitate a product than a process or procedure. The latter are in fact defined by intangible resources that are the fruit of constant investment in the firm's distinctive culture, climate, and organizational mechanisms. All this makes replication difficult. As some scholars observe, the complexity and causal ambiguity of a successful strategy – "What lies behind it?" – serve to protect against imitation.[4]

6.3   When to imitate and why: behavioral drivers

Firms play the Imitation Game for different reasons. First we need to draw a distinction between incumbents and other organizations, such as newcomers and large retailers.

Newcomers may recognize new diversification opportunities in the first mover's innovation. The innovation offers the opportunity to surpass the sector's old entrance barriers, often placing these companies in an advantageous position over incumbents. Think, for example, of the skiing or tennis racket sectors in the past, when great wood-working skills were required to produce these items. The innovation in materials introduced by the first mover naturally threw the door open to newcomers with skills and resources from the world of plastics. Similarly, digital photography has paved the way for imitators from the electronics industry, such as Panasonic and Samsung.

Even big distribution increasingly exploits opportunities for upstream integration through strategies of parasitical imitation of best-selling products and brands. This is the so-called private-label phenomenon which, according to AC Nielsen data, in North America in 2010 attained nearly a fifth of the market share of all consumer packaged goods with an average annual growth of 7%. The share attained in the frozen food sector, for example, is now 30%, while for cosmetics it is only 2% but with a growth rate of over 20%. This trend accelerated with the economic downturn: according to a 2011 Nielsen global survey, while more than half of consumers surveyed online said they purchased more private label brands during the downturn, almost 90% said they would continue to do so when the economy improves.

The motivations of large retailers are clear: to capitalize on resources such as contact with end-customers and their trust in the distributor's trademark. These retailers exploit integration opportunities with particularly low risks. In fact, production investments are flexible; and retailers only imitate goods, brands, or formulas that have already proven their profit potential.

Behavioral motivations may differ with reference to the imitative strategies adopted by incumbents. We can classify these strategies as follows:

a) Reacting only when success is evident, after initial paralysis. Many firms are taken by surprise with the introduction of an innovative product or service by small enterprising innovators. This happens when the market potential of the new product is understated or not recognized at all. Reaction is delayed until sales and demand explode. Sometimes in these cases the firm does not react because it considers the success of the new product to be simply a passing fashion, or it fears compromising and cannibalizing sales of its current products. In such cases, an incumbent imitator reacts only when the change taking place in the market clearly exposes the risk of a significantss of market share and market domination.

b) Choosing to wait until success is evident. In this case, the firm decides to wait on the market development of the innovation.

This move is typical of a firm that has significant stocks of resources and capabilities but decides that it is more appropriate to leave the market development costs to the innovative firm. The idea is to enter the market when the innovator makes its first error, or when sales of the new product start to take off. At this point the incumbent exploits its speed of reaction and imitation capability. Vodafone, for example, did this for the third generation mobile telephony (UMTS) market, where the firm deliberately left the burden and the risk of opening the market to newcomer Hutchison 3G ("3").

A critical factor in this maneuver, obviously, is timing. Although avoiding the risks of failure characteristic of the first mover, the imitator firm in this case exposes itself to a different risk, namely, that of waiting too long. The incumbent's imitation, in fact, could come too late, when the margins, the experience economies, or the number of early imitators have eroded the best opportunities opened by the innovator. (Refer to the first mover advantages outlined in the chapter on the Movement Game.) Ideally, the underlying logic should be to weigh the probability of success of an innovation at a certain point in time and the potential profits obtainable from an innovative strategy in this scenario at that time.[5] Such an imitation may then become a systematic choice. However, this choice must be accompanied by refining the firm's capability of exploiting economies of speed with regard to the imitation. This refers to technical and production development, to flexibility of processes and, more generally, to time-to-market. An excellent example here is Zara, the clothing company. A systematic imitation, by contrast, is not likely to be very effective with innovations that involve greater set-up problems, considerable capital requirements, or products that cannot be easily or quickly copied.

c) Choosing to imitate even when success is still uncertain. The reasons for this interesting and very common strategy are varied:

c1) Imitation based on implicit information. In contexts of high uncertainty, a follower may observe the actions of first movers and decide to imitate them, irrespective of the exclusive information they possess. (This is especially common if first movers are authoritative players.) The follower's assumption is, of course, that the first movers have better information at that moment in time. For this reason, once imitative firms have reached critical mass, what some economists call "information cascades"[6] may occur. A clear example is the hasty and blind entry into e-business by many firms, until the dot-com bubble burst in early 2000. Information cascades are imitative processes based mainly on the assumption that first movers are working in the right direction. In similar scenarios, sectors are exposed to high overall risks; if the trail blazed by first movers proves to be the wrong one, the overall industry may incur substantial costs.

A similar phenomenon in contexts of environmental uncertainty is mimetic isomorphism, studied by some organizational sociologists.[7] In this case, the object of imitation is the organizational model. This strategy again allows cost savings for finding the best solution in response to the existing uncertainty. Often, however, the process becomes more ritualisitc than rational. Here also, in fact, the structure being imitated may not prove optimal, although verifying this is much more difficult and time-consuming than in the case of product imitation, for example.

c2) Legitimacy or status. As in the previous case, some companies (or some managers) follow the behavior of others to legitimize their institutions and their public in order to anchor their status to other well-established players (institutional theory). This is a phenomenon akin to emulation and aspiration in social consumption mechanisms. Many Internet websites in the 1990s were developed following this logic. Here, the imitation assumes a signaling function with the intention of avoiding a negative market reputation (economic theory of herd behavior). In contexts that remain uncertain, some studies have revealed that first imitators are driven by more rational reasons, as in the previous case, while latecomer imitators are motivated by more symbolic reasons, as described above.[8]

c3) Preventive defense of the status quo and downplaying rivalry. An incumbent may follow an imitator's every move even before knowing what the outcome may be. To use a sporting metaphor, this means to run a tight defense. If an innovator decides, for example, to explore a new market segment or geographical area, the imitator may immediately decide to do the same, so that regardless of the success of the operation, their relative positions remain unchanged. The idea is to maintain a level playing field, naturally with the aim of containing the firm's risk levels. This could be the case of current imitations of hybrid cars, where Toyota/Lexus was the first mover.

In concentrated markets reciprocal imitation may become a form of tacit collusion: "Divergent strategies reduce the ability of the oligopolists to coordinate their actions tacitly (...) reducing average industry profitability."[9] This has given rise to the more recent idea of "mutual forbearance."[10] Simply put, firms imitate their mutual presence in different markets in order to have more contact points that facilitate collusion, since this increases the likelihood of retaliation.[11]

In the cases we have discussed so far, the imitators take advantage of the innovative firm's early efforts, in terms of financial factors and market dominion. Figure 6.3 intersects innovators and imitators with the results of the competitive confrontation, providing some well-known examples of successful and failed imitation wars. (See also Table 6.5 in Section 6.7 showing how the follower can win even in the presence of positive feedback.)

As a case in point, many innovations in domestic electronics (CDs, the VCR, etc.) have been developed in Philips' laboratories. However, in actual fact it was their rival firms, solicited imitators, who later exploited the new technologies more fully.

The reasons, illustrated in the figure below, provide the main motivations for the Imitation Game which complement the specific considerations outlined in the first part of the section.

First of all, firms who play the Imitation Game justify their behavior by citing the metaphor of an explorer who, like the pioneering firm, must bear the higher risks and uncertainty resulting from the journey into unknown, often hostile, territories. The explorer enjoys public recognition for the resulting discoveries, but this search could also benefit those who follow and exploit them more fully.

	INNOVATOR	IMITATOR
WIN	Du Pont (teflon)	IBM (personal computer)
LOSE	Xerox (office computer)	Kodak (instant photos)

Figure 6.3   Winners and losers in the war of imitation

The imitator can in fact:

- Learn from the innovator's mistakes, and avoid expending resources on developing products without market potential; the imitator prepares better products and services that give greater satisfaction and more benefits to the customer;
- Avoid or reduce the financial burden that must be borne by the first mover in the early stages of research and development, and plant engineering;
- Focus attention and resources on developing technological processes rather than product or service technology, improving both production quality and efficiency;
- Avoid the inertia trap; this is where the innovator may end up if it neglects making improvements to the innovation;
- Avoid the innovator's cost of educating and familiarizing customers with new products;
- Exploit experience consolidated in other markets. The more experience and knowledge an imitator has gained from producing and selling similar products, the easier it will be for this firm to break into a new market, responding with greater skill and speed to the first mover's initiative. This experience may center on technology, marketing, or reputation.
- Achieve greater maneuvering room and change the rules of the competitive game set by the innovator. The pioneer, due to its size and available resources, is often forced to initially take refuge in a market segment. The subsequent development of demand can create new entry opportunities for later entrant imitators. These firms may occupy more desirable and attractive positions, investing in all other unserved market segments that guarantee large sales volumes.

The logic behind the Imitation Game is also related to the very idea that innovation is comparable to a process of incremental improvements rather than radical technological discontinuity. Although radical discontinuity does sometimes occur, it is quite a rare event. In fact, products do not normally come to market as the result of a radical technological breakthrough. Instead, they are often the outcome of a long, incremental process of continuous technological and manufacturing improvements following the pioneer's product launch. The reason for this is that initially groundbreaking products are technically imperfect and still primitive in terms of features and design; they offer benefits that are not entirely satisfactory with respect to the expectations of target customers. These defects allow the later entrant imitator to develop products and services that may better meet the needs of the market.

Lastly, motivations for unlawful imitations are rooted in the contrast between the enormous illegal profits that these provide and the relatively low risks run by counterfeiters: "Counterfeiting is better than selling drugs because the penalties are not as stiff and the money is just as good."[12] Extra profit is, of course, also guaranteed by cost savings in terms of marketing, research and development, post-sale services, and taxes. We must also note that more and more often these profits are used to finance other criminal activities.

6.4   The enabling factors: what favors innovation

How quickly newcomers or incumbents can appropriate the first mover's innovation depends on several factors:

- Lack of legal protection for manufacturing secrets or innovation patents;
- Suppliers that provide and disseminate raw material and critical technologies for the production of new products or services;
- Production processes that are easy to replicate;
- Dissemination and ownership of the innovation's know-how;
- Lack of ability (or of desire, in the case of solicited imitation) of the first mover to create entrance barriers.

Moreover, as mentioned above, environmental uncertainty is also a factor that can promote imitation, as is demonstrated by the phenomena of mimetic isomorphism and information cascades. A final condition that may encourage particular imitative strategies is a concentrated and static competitive environment. As we have seen, the reason for this lies in the preventive defense of the status quo guaranteed by systematic and reciprocal imitation.

What all this means is that advantages for the innovator are not significant unless they can be transformed into solid barriers to block rival imitations. In fact, the greatest concern for an innovative firm is how effectively it can protect the advantages it gains from exploiting an innovation. Table 6.1 lists various protection mechanisms and their relative effectiveness.

Empirical studies reveal the limited effectiveness of the legal protection guaranteed by patents or licenses. According to firms in twelve

Table 6.1 Efficacy of the protection mechanisms

	Effectiveness of:	
Appropriation method	Processes	Products
Patents to prevent duplication	3.52	4.33
Patents to guarantee royalties	3.31	3.75
Secrecy	4.31	3.57
Lead time	5.11	5.41
Rapid descent on the experience curve	5.02	5.09
Marketing investments	4.55	5.59

1= ineffective 7= very effective.

Table 6.2 The time required to replicate an innovation

	Less than 6 months	6–12 months	1–3 years	3–5 years	More than 5 years
New products protected by patents	2	6	64	40	8
New non-patented products	3	22	89	12	1
New patented processes	0	4	72	37	9
New non-patented processes	2	20	84	17	2

different sectors, these protections were a valid defense against imitation to the following degrees: [13]

- 65% in the pharmaceutical sector;
- 30% in the chemical sector;
- 100% in the oil and steel industries;
- less than 10% in industrial machinery, textiles, automobiles, tires, office supplies, etc.

Other research shows that 60% of innovations and patents are imitated within four years, and that the imitator's development costs are less than 35% of the innovator's.[14]

These studies also demonstrate that in the case of innovations that are not legally protected, the imitation period is less than a year.[15] The table below clearly illustrates the range of effectiveness of different innovation protection barriers and the average time it takes to circumvent them (Table 6.2).

To conclude this section, let's look at the factors that encourage unlawful imitation, a phenomenon of alarming proportions. The OECD, in fact, estimates that the counterfeit market is worth 450 billion dollars, and has grown by more than 1500% over the last 10 years. Some counterfeiting drivers are linked to demand: (1) the trend toward consumer opportunism, and in some cases the growing disaffection with respect to the original brand, which translates into a strong willingness to purchase counterfeit products; (2) the tendency of society at large to downplay the fact that purchasing a counterfeit product constitutes criminal behavior; (3) the globalization of consumption and brand, which in turn globalizes counterfeiting markets.

Other trends that favor the spread of the phenomenon are linked to supply: (1) new organizational models, in particular the delocalization of production and licensing systems, which reduces direct firm control; (2) the intensification of marketing activities to enhance the intrinsic value of the brand, which paradoxically fuels interest in illegal appropriation.

Finally, there are exogenous factors that encourage counterfeiting – for example: (1) technological developments that reduce costs and increase quality; (2) limited enforcement of anti-counterfeiting laws in many countries, or the lack of coordination among the different institutional bodies responsible for enforcement; (3) the growing availability of illegal workforces; (4) the interest of organized crime and terrorist groups in counterfeiting activities.

6.5   Competitive imitation maneuvers

In implementing an imitation maneuver, the follower can pursue diverse marketing strategies that must convince customers to take the risk of abandoning the innovator's products or services. Possible paths are numerous. Some successful ones are listed in Table 6.3, and generally involve:[16]

1. Exercising market power, which enables the follower to compete head-on with a similar product and similar position to the innovator's.
2. Repositioning the innovator's product. The product remains essentially the same, but the follower repositions it by offering a lower price and/or quality, or higher quality, or new ways to use the product.
3. Lateral entry, either competing on the same needs satisfied by the innovator but with different technologies and products, or moving into untapped markets.

Table 6.3 Maneuvers for overtaking the innovator

Product	Lower Prices	Imitate and improve	Market Power
1. 35 mm cameras	x	x	
2. Automated teller machnes (ATMs)			x
3. Ballpoint pens	x	x	
4. Caffeine-free soft drinks			x
5. CAT scanner (computed axial tomography)		x	x
6. Commercial jet aircraft		x	
7. Computerized ticketing services		x	
8. Credit/charge cards			x
9. Diet soft drinks			x
10. Dry beer			x
11. Food processors	x		
12. Light beer			x
13. Mainframe computers			
14. Microwave ovens	x		
15. Money-market mutual funds			x
16. MRI (magnetic resonance imaging)	x		x
17. Nonalcholic beer			x
18. Operating systems for personal computers		x	x
19. Paperback books			x
20. Personal computers	x		x
21. Pocket calculators	x		
22. Projection television	x	x	x
23. Spreadsheets		x	
24. Telephone answering machines	x		x
25. VCRs	x	x	
26. Videogames		x	
27. Warehouse clubs			x
28. Word processing software	??	x	??

Source: Schnaars S.P. (1994).

Now we'll illustrate these options.

1. The imitator's first mode of behavior, using market power, means entering the market created by the innovator, demolishing the protection barriers and leveraging the entire critical mass of resources and market-driving capabilities. We'll discuss this move at length in the sections dedicated to the Position Game and market sharing strategies.

2.1 Repositioning may take place, firstly, with a lower price and/or quality strategy, involving three distinct tactics:

- Same quality, lower price: The imitator offers a product that is very similar to the innovator's but at a more competitive price. This was the strategy originally adopted by Lexus, Toyota's luxury brand, offering customers quality products with characteristics very similar to the Mercedes and BMW, but with more aggressive prices. Now they aim at a higher quality for the same price.
- Impoverishment: The imitator, rather than imitating the innovator, downgrades product features to offer a version of the innovator's product at a more accessible price for sizeable market segments. An example was Amazon's Kindle Fire tablet launched in 2012 at $199.
- Compatible products: This relates to the behaviors mentioned above. In order to reduce the customer perception of incurring high costs to substitute the innovator's products, the imitator launches "compatible" products or clones (e.g. IBM compatible) that are perfectly substitutable or compatible with technological systems already adopted by the user.

2.2. In the higher quality repositioning maneuver, the objective of the imitator is to be recognized as second best, or "second, but better". To do so, the imitator neither clones the innovator's products nor instigates a price confrontation, but instead elicits customer interest by making incremental improvements to the pioneer's offering. (See the concept of incremental imitation introduced above.) In these cases, we often refer to "second-generation" products. The imitator focuses on areas where it can strengthen product/service features or performance, launching a second generation of products recognized for their significant improvements when compared to their predecessors.

2.3. Another way for followers to reposition the imitation is to reconceptualize the product. The imitator exploits the product innovation but changes its intended use and application. This is done by redefining the structural characteristics or performance of the product in question, and leads directly to the concept of creative imitation described above (and also exemplified by the Tuk-tuk taxi).

3. Last, lateral entry is the strategy pursued by the imitator who enters a geographic market that is not protected by the innovator. This is

the case with Lino's Coffee in the Italian market, left undefended by Starbucks.

As we have seen, there are a wide variety of maneuvering options for imitators. These options require market-driving capabilities and very different resources that help the follower demolish the competitive advantages acquired by the innovator. Thanks to its relatively consolidated position, the first mover can defend its market dominance by raising barriers to block competitive challengers and imitators. This firm can also develop preventive defensive and lateral maneuvers to forestall potential attacks.

Finally, counterfeiters can also make a variety of moves. These warrant explanation because they each have a different impact on costs and risks to the imitated firm and to the consumer.[17] As Figure 6.4 shows, we should underscore the following:

- The level of customer awareness that the product in question is counterfeit. While in consumer products the purchaser is normally aware of buying a fake, in industrial goods the buyer is often an unwitting victim, although reduced prices should raise a red flag.
- The quality of the product. The counterfeiter's "strategy" may be more or less oriented to quality, safety, or functionality of the copy. This is conditioned by how easy (and expensive) it is, in technical terms, to copy the original item.

Level of customer awareness that the product is counterfeit	Low	• VERY HIGH potential damage for **consumers** • VERY HIGH potential damage for the **brand** (loss of sales and greater loss of image)	• LIMITED potential damage for **consumers** • HIGH potential damage for the **brand** (loss of sales and greater loss of image)
	High	• HIGH potential damage for **consumers** • LIMITED potential damage for the **brand** (partial loss of sales and no loss of image)	• LIMITED potential damage for **consumers** • VERY HIGH potential damage for the **brand** (greater loss of sales)
		Low	High

Figure 6.4   The potential damage of counterfeiting

Naturally, the greater social costs involve low consumer awareness and the low quality of the copy sold. For the imitated firm this means a loss of revenue because the buyer would have purchased the original product. Also the firm's image is seriously damaged: customers who unknowingly use a counterfeit product have a bad experience, which they then associate with the copied firm's brand. The least worrying scenario for the brand is when the buyer's awareness is high in the face of a low quality offer. In this case, it is likely that the counterfeiter's public target is different from the firm's and the loss of turnover is therefore negligible. What is more, the brand image, as an object of desire and aspiration, may even benefit in these cases.

6.6 When to imitate, and when to attack laterally and enter a niche market

In defining its market entry strategy, a firm can decide to launch an imitation to pursue the Position Game, or to open new fronts by entering a niche market with lateral attacks to generate new opportunities (see Figure 6.5 below).

The two alternatives present the firm with market and technological risks, and consequently different economic and financial returns. As we can see from Table 6.4, the Imitation Game and the successive Position Game offer a much larger market size than does a Movement Game.

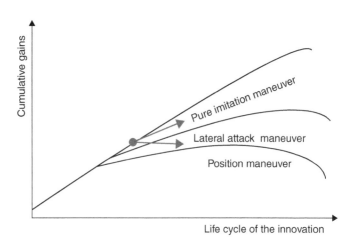

Figure 6.5 Confrontational maneuvers

Table 6.4 Innovator and imitator opportunities and risks

	Game of imitation and position Imitator	Game of movement Innovator
Market size	Large	Small
Market uncertainty	Medium-high	Medium-high
Competitors present	Many	Few
Cost structure	Higher than the dominant firm's	More contained
Price structure	Lower than the dominant firm's	Higher
First mover advantages	Reduced	Possible

Clearly the intensity of competition will also be higher than in the case of a Movement Game.

Technological risks and cost structures differ in the two areas of Table 6.4 below. In the Imitation Game, as we've already noted, the technological risk for the imitator is often contained. When firms pursue incremental technological strategies, on the other hand, they have to contend with greater uncertainty when entering a niche market with a lateral maneuver, or by developing new versions of a product.

The imitator's cost structure may therefore be higher than that of the dominant innovative firm. The latter can also take advantage of the legal protection of its inventions and a more favorable position on the cost curve.

A firm maneuvering in niches can generally set sales prices higher than an imitator firm; with this price lever the firm can rapidly fortify its market position.

To evaluate the financial returns that these two strategies afford, it can be useful to apply the formula for return on invested assets.

The formula, as we know, is as follows:

$$ROA = \text{Net Profit/Assets} = (\text{Net Profit/Sales}) \times (\text{Sales/Assets})$$

To compare the expected return generated by the imitation strategy with that achievable via lateral maneuvers, we need to rewrite the two formulae denoting the imitator with "i" and the nicher with "n".

$$ROA_n = (\text{Net profit/Assets})_n$$

$$ROA_i = (\text{Net profit/Assets})_i$$

Hypothesizing that the expected returns of "n" are higher than those of "i," we come up with the following ratio:

$$ROA_n/ROA_i > 1$$

which we can rewrite as:

$$(m/a) \times (Sales)_n/(Sales)_i > 1$$

where "m" summarizes the relation between the margins achievable by the two maneuvers and "a" the relation between the assets invested in the strategy.

Further, for $n > 0$ and for $a > 0$, we can once again rewrite the ratio above as follows:

$$(Sales)_n > (a/m) \times (Sales)_i$$

Based on all this, we can assert that lateral niche attack maneuvers allow firms to achieve higher margins than imitation maneuvers when sales expectations are greater than the a/m ratio multiplied by the imitator's expected sales.

6.7   Positive feedback in the Imitation Game

In the Imitation Game, challengers and innovators fight to take advantage of the positive feedback effects arising from the innovation, and strive to develop the kind of demand that favors their technology and offerings. Positive feedback (as in the case of network externalities) is based on the principle that success breeds success. This means that strong firms get stronger and the weak get weaker.[18]

Positive feedback translates into fast growth for businesses, and allows their technology to set the standard because success feeds on success and initiates a virtuous cycle. In the Imitation Game, the amplified effect of positive feedback for the firm can translate into market dominion, and for the technological innovation this can mean setting the bar. When a number of firms or technologies compete in a market characterized by strong positive feedback, it is very unlikely that they will all survive, because only one or a few can be winners. In extreme forms, positive feedback can lead to a winner-take-all market. Figure 6.6 illustrates a market scenario impacted by positive feedback that leads to the marginalization of a contender.

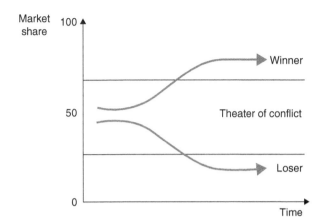

Figure 6.6 The positive feedback effects

The firm or technology that consolidates an advantage at the outset of the competitive game may win a dominant position by capturing, for example, 60% of the market due to the positive feedback effect. By contrast, the firm that is unable to take advantage of the same effect may regress to a marginal market share.

Positive feedback is self-sustaining thanks to two types of economies of scale, on the supply side and on the demand side. Supply side economies of scale result from the firm's attaining an optimum size in terms of production capability. This makes it possible to control costs better than competitors, and then use the margin differential to leverage prices and make commercial or innovation investments. Demand side economies instead influence potential customers to buy and use a product or service. A product or service that exceeds the point of inflection of the curve in Figure 6.7 and enters the virtuous stage of development, appears in the eyes of a potential customer to be a very successful product that has passed muster as far as market credibility is concerned. This product acquires even more value as it is disseminated. Positive feedback can therefore also be expressed through economies of scale on the demand side. If an asset is placed in the middle of the curve and customer perceptions favor its adoption, then it will generate a propulsive effect due to the process of reciprocal influence that activates the virtuous development cycle.

By contrast, if consumers foresee failure for the product, it will enter inexorably into a phase of vicious regression. Economies of scale on

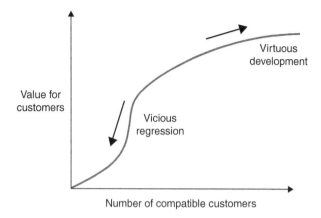

Figure 6.7　Virtuous development and vicious regression

Table 6.5　Leaders, followers, and winning firms in Imitation Games

Product	Innovator	Imitator	Winner
Jet airliner	De Haviland (Comet)	Boeing 707	Follower
Float glass	Pilkington	Corning	Leader
X-ray scanner	EMI	General Electric	Follower
Office PC	Xerox	IBM	Follower
VCRs	Ampex/Sony	Matsushita	Follower
Diet cola	R.C. Cola	Coca-Cola	Follower
Instant camera	Polaroid	Kodak	Leader
Pocket calculator	Bowmar	Texas Instruments	Follower
Microwave oven	Raytheon	Samsung	Follower
Plain-paper copier	Xerox	Canon	Not clear
Fiber-optic cable	Corning	Many companies	Leader
Video games player	Atari	Nintendo/Sega	Followers
Disposable diaper	Procter and Gamble	Kimberley-Clark	Leader
Web browser	Netscape	Microsoft	Follower
MP3 music player	Diamond multimedia	Sony (&others)	Followers
Operating system for hand-held digital devices	Palm and symbian	Microsoft (CE/ pocket PC)	Leaders

Source: Schnaars S.P. (2002).

the demand side show that the success or failure of a product is due primarily to the expectations of potential customers. In the end, they are the ones who define the actual value of the product with their buying behavior.

For this reason, a firm's ability to reduce customer barriers and define a successful marketing strategy is fundamental. A slight shift in the direction of virtuous development can activate and amplify the effects of positive feedback. With electronic products and in the new digital economy markets, demand side economies of scale are far more critical than those in more traditional markets. Potential high-tech consumers are very suspicious of products or technologies that are still in their infancy.

However, economies of scale on the demand side may not be potent enough to discourage an imitator. Positive feedback is neither fast nor predictable, meaning that it does not allow winning firms to instantly position themselves as such; nor does it convince rival firms to give up without a fight. There are many examples we can cite where two or more technologies battled head-to-head for market control for years, with neither one taking a clear lead. Being the first on the market is certainly an advantage, but being the first mover is not a sure-fire way to avoid an Imitation Game or to keep the leadership position. An illustration of this is found in Table 6.5, which very clearly shows how often followers emerge as winners at the end of an Imitation Game.

7
Creating Barriers to Imitation

7.1 The principles of defensive strategies

Competitive confrontations in dynamic markets consist of a succession of innovation and imitation maneuvers. Knowledge of the logic behind such maneuvers is useful for both the innovator and the imitator. While the imitator seeks out the weak points of the first mover's strategy in order to identify strategic windows that allow successful entry into the market, the pioneer must develop defensive and preventive maneuvers to reduce such threats.

Defensive strategies in the Imitation Game are based on a thorough understanding of how a rival could undermine a firm's positions, and how productive various available options may be. An effective defense strategy must always contain an offensive component. A company that continuously invests in gaining and maintaining its advantage is already in the best position to effectively defend itself. Unfortunately, established firms have a tendency to respond passively, thus allowing challengers to assert themselves with little difficulty. Therefore, we need to keep certain imperatives in mind in order to prepare to best defend our position:

1. Courage to attack ourselves. The best defensive strategy is to constantly question and attack our own position, even destructively, pre-empting the obsolescence of existing products by introducing new ones and redefining the rules of the competitive game. Such behavior may also involve a profit sacrifice in the short term, but it can be useful for defending positions in the long term, rendering imitation or pursuit more difficult for rivals. This is called the

moving target strategy, which runs counter to the soccer maxim, "Don't mess with a winning team."
2. Principle of force. A defensive strategy necessitates a significant initial investment. In fact, victory favors the contender that is able to qualitatively and quantitatively deploy the greatest possible resources and capabilities.
3. Concentration. This consists in amassing the greatest strengths and superior skills with respect to a specific point, typically the attacker's strength or weakness.
4. Speed of execution. A firm can often manage to foil an offensive action because of the difficulty an aggressor has in launching a surprise attack. The element of surprise, closely related to the speed of execution, wears off quickly if the tactic is not followed up with further timely action. Those defending themselves through competitive intelligence try to penetrate the secrecy of their rival's intentions, so they can determine the direction and the actual danger posed by the threat. In other words, the two factors that may hinder effective defense are:
   a) a delay in understanding the magnitude of the threat;
   b) a delay in executing a response.
5. Degree of determination. This refers to how committed the defending firm is to a given reaction. Commitment is a form of explicit communication that unequivocally makes the firm's resources and intentions known. This enables the firm to base its own defense strategy on rational, credible foundations. *Si vis pacem, para bellum:* if you wish for peace, prepare for war. The deterrent effect of the degree of determination therefore depends on:
   a) The irreversibility of the commitment. This effect grows with the increasing certainty of the behavior that ensues from the commitment. Think of sunk investments, that is non-recoverable outlay in large production infrastructures.
   b) The credibility of the threat of retaliation. An example is that of an army burning its bridges after crossing them. This forces the enemy to realize that the army it's facing does not have any means to retreat (from a particular market, in our case), making the threat of a fierce battle before any kind of surrender highly likely.
6. Customer value generation. A defensive maneuver can only be effective if it creates perceived value for the buyers, strengthening their confidence and loyalty.

7. Creation of cost asymmetries. A defensive strategy must be able to put challengers in a position of relatively greater cost. The efficacy of this defense can be measured in terms of the difference between the costs to the firm and the operational costs that the challenger must bear.

8. Sustainability. The competitive advantage resulting from defensive maneuvering must be as enduring as possible, without requiring continuous expenditures to defend it. (This is different from the opportunity to invest in the search for new market opportunities, mentioned above.)

7.2   Strategic behaviors in the Imitation Game

In the Imitation Game, the innovator firm is subject to attacks from rivals that are spurred on by the success of and enthusiastic market response to the innovation. (Other motivations are described in Section 7.3.) These imitators start to pursue the innovator.

In this game, to maintain market leadership, the innovative firm must dominate the arena with a controlling share of 70–80%. In a growing market, this share can only be defended with appropriate commercial and production resources. When the market share falls to around 30–40%, it means that the Imitation Game has evolved to the point of destabilizing the market and the innovator's leadership position. Figure 7.1 serves to illustrate the transition from the Movement Game to the Imitation Game. With progressive competitive crowding of the market, there are two types of follower firms in the new game: the more aggressive and threatening ones that take on the role of challengers, and other less hostile enterprises that take up marginalized positions. As we saw in the previous chapter, imitator challengers may pursue two different strategies: 1) to consolidate the innovative standard

Figure 7.1   Market dominance in Movement Games and Imitation Games

introduced by the innovator, possibly making incremental improvements, or 2) to establish a new standard.

Marginal follower firms leverage the heterogeneity of the needs expressed by demand. They look for market niches consistent with their size and resources where they can entrench and defend their competitive advantages.

We can come up with some innovator rules of conduct from analyzing the competitive maneuvers in the Imitation Game:

1. Attack the imitator with great commitment.
2. Rapidly penetrate and extend existing distribution channels.
3. Paradoxically, ignore the customer.

The logic behind the first principle is intuitive. If the innovative firm wants to avoid the destabilization of the Imitation Game, it must develop effective countermeasures to minimize the aggression and efficacy of the rival's imitation strategies. Every customer the innovator loses in this game is likely to be lost forever.

The second rule is consistent with the first. The Imitation Game is triggered when a large portion of the preliminary market demonstrates that it clearly accepts the innovation, which is then adopted and disseminated at a higher rate. In this competitive context, with demand and potential competition rapidly rising, a small number of distribution channels with uneven geographical coverage may compromise the firm's development and defense strategy. Customers have limited access to a firm's products if it lacks access to key distribution channels, or if it's distribution policy doesn't guarantee satisfactory service levels. More importantly, inadequate distribution leaves an area of the firm's competitive arena unprotected, exposing a weakness to rivals.

The third principle, ignoring customers, may appear to be a paradox, but at this stage, it may be a logical response. When an innovation is successful and enters into the take-off phase, the real problem is not to create demand but to meet it. Customers, in this phase of the innovation's lifecycle, do not desire differentiated products, nor do they express needs that require a sophisticated segmentation of demand (think of the original success of the T Ford): they just want access to those products or services.

7.3   The potential for a sustainable advantage

In order to manage the Imitation Game, the innovator must run an in-depth analysis of the sustainability potential of the competitive advantage it has achieved after activating the Movement Game.

Figure 7.2   Sustainability potential

The sustainability potential, as suggested in Figure 7.2, must be measured on the extension of three vectors: the heights of preventive barriers, the heights of asymmetric competitive barriers, and the strength of the link with current customers.

The first vector refers to the time needed for potential competitors to replicate and imitate the firm's strategic initiative. The imitation time horizon corresponds to the ease with which a rival, collaborating with partners and suppliers, can develop or acquire the market, driving technological and business capabilities necessary to replicate the innovative firm's Movement Game.

The second vector refers to any structural imbalances enjoyed by the innovator with respect to rivals, such as exclusive or privileged access to certain resources (also in terms of cost). These are the mobility barriers that defend the firm from potential competitors. Measuring this vector requires in-depth competitive intelligence activities that analyze the rival's capability and resource stocks in order to estimate beforehand its potential to damage or destroy the defender's competitive advantage.

The third sustainability vector is linked to the preventive barriers and first mover advantages that the firm can claim with respect to its customers and imitator competitors. These advantages, as we see in the Movement Game, raise customers' psychological and economic costs

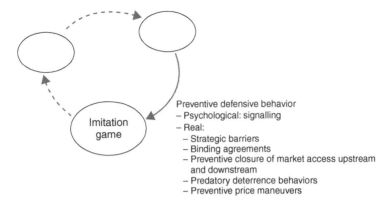

Figure 7.3 Defensive maneuvers in the Imitation Game

of buying from a competitor (switching costs). These barriers, however, may not be sufficient in cases where the value proposition offered by the firm proves significantly lower than that of the imitator. They may also be inadequate in cases of high customer dissatisfaction caused by the product itself or due to a perceived opportunistic attitude of the firm.

7.4 Preventive behavior

Through behaviors based on prevention mechanisms, the defender tries to create conditions in order to arrive at an all-out confrontation with challengers, reducing their incentive to attack. This objective can be achieved with two types of operations: (a) "psychological," described in Section 7.5; and (b) "real," discussed in Section 7.6. With the former, the firm tries to prevent the conflict by sending discernable "signals," by its actual behavior and through communication with its environment, to underscore its commitment to defend itself. With "real" maneuvers, the firm tends to reduce the competition's willingness to launch the attack, lessening *ex ante* the benefits the attacker may obtain.

7.5 Psychological preventive maneuvers: "signaling"

The leader firm often puts targeted communication mechanisms into action in order to signal to potential rivals its commitment and determination to strongly resist any possible attack. These signals directly or indirectly express the leader's intentions, objectives, and the nature of its future strategic behaviors.[1]

Beyond the context of this chapter, signals are also used to create a state of tacit collusion. This occurs, for example, when a firm announces its intention to concede certain markets to a competitor rather than putting up a fight, or when a price increase is proposed in order to reveal the competition's willingness to "toe the line."

The signals may be a precise indication of the firm's intentions, but they may also be a bluff. Being aware of this, attackers must carefully evaluate the credibility of the firm, while taking into account the possibility of a disinformation strategy. Some time ago, for example, Vodafone's Director of Corporate Strategy released the following statement: "VoIP is not a service. It's a technology which provides only one thing – cheaper calls – and we can provide cheaper calls very easily by cutting prices" (Bobby Rao, 24 November 2006). For these signals to be effective, the challenger must be able to detect a decisive and immediate retaliation capability in case of attack. Probably, in the case of Vodafone, the credibility of that signal (i.e. their willingness to start a price war) was not so high, due to the disadvantageous differences in the companies' cost structures.

The leader firm must carefully manage the image that it projects to competitors. In order to do so, it must use all the available communication channels to achieve the greatest defensive impact possible: public statements, specialist press, distributors, and customers. The more official the announcement, the greater its power to dissuade rivals from attacking. Some of the psychological deterrents available to the defender are public statements and announcements underscoring the following:[2]

1. The firm's commitment, as affirmed by company executives, to defend its market position.
2. The achievement of production capacities able to absorb future growth in demand.
3. The strategic importance of a given business unit.
4. The erection of protective barriers, such as the launch of new products or investments in new technologies. This behavior, however, in addition to having deterrent effects on rivals' perceptions, creates expectations in consumers, who in the meantime are inclined not to buy the competing products in expectation of those announced by the leader firm.
5. Price reductions or information on own cost structure. The market leader, leveraging economies of scale and experience, and by taking advantage of information asymmetries, can communicate to rivals

that should they decide to launch an attack, they run the risk of appreciable cost disadvantages or even losses.
6. The state of the sector. This involves evaluating the market's economic situation, which the firm expresses publicly in order to disseminate transparency between competitors, thus encouraging greater discipline in maintaining the status quo. The signaling strategy in terms of preventive maneuvers aims to create uncertainty in behaviors and to raise the threat of reprisal for breaking the rules of the game. At the same time, the firm retains maximum maneuvering room for future initiatives.

7.6   Real preventive maneuvers

A challenger may know how to launch an attack, but until this firm can muster the necessary resources, the leader remains safe – even more so when it controls the resources in question. To defend its positions the leader must therefore try to appropriate valuable resources before competitors understand their value.

A preventive maneuver is defined as real when it anticipates competitors' moves in order to defend the firm's dominant position that has been secured by first-mover status. This gives the leader firm a dual advantage:

1. The other competitors must compete for less effective positions with decreasing marginal returns.
2. The firm that first wins the best market position extends its revenue base to cover fixed costs, and then creates sizeable barriers.

This maneuver consists in launching an offensive against a competitor firm before it has the opportunity to begin an attack.

Since the benefits of such a move are not permanent, it is important to carefully assess response time, that is the time it takes competitors to react.

In the consumer goods market, the advantages of taking up the first position arise from three orders of variables:[3]

• The first of these results from greater freedom in the use of the marketing mix. The pioneer may exploit the experience effect and provide a better quality product at the same cost; or this firm can saturate the market space by occupying the more profitable positions. For certain products it can be advantageous to secure key distributors; at the same time, high investments in advertising may raise entry barriers.

- The second order of variables is linked to the opportunity for exploiting absolute cost advantages and economies of scale. The pioneer can thus increase market share through a low price policy (predatory pricing).
- The third source of advantage comes from demand. Uncertainty of the quality of the new product confers lasting benefits to brands first consolidated on the market.[4]

This behavior is based on the assumption that "the best way to defend is to attack" and that prevention is the most effective way to discourage hostilities. This conduct works against rivals who threaten to achieve a level of market share that constitutes a genuine danger to the firm. In other situations, such behavior is activated by the leader firm to dissuade competitors beforehand from pursuing an attack strategy on its positions. An ideal pre-emptive strategy must be characterized by the following:[5]

1. It must facilitate rapid acquisition of the desired positions.
2. It must prove difficult for most competitors to penetrate the positions occupied by the firm.
3. Conditions must exist that delay the response of rivals who are in a position to implement a similar strategy.
4. It must be relatively easy for the firm that activated the strategy to return to its original positions, if necessary.

Real preventive behaviors are manifested in five different ways and illustrated in the following sections: 1) creating strategic barriers, 2) binding agreements, 3) market closure, 4) predatory behavior, and 5) preventive price maneuvers.

7.7   Real maneuvers: creating strategic barriers

The competition's willingness to attack is based on the benefits they assume they can achieve. If these benefits are minimal, then the defending firm's position is safe. Strategic barriers therefore represent defenses erected with the intent of restricting the entry of new competitors or discouraging the attacks of rivals already present in the sector.

We can classify the main types of preventive investments designed to create defensive barriers by distinguishing between those leveraging cost and those leveraging demand.

(a)   The effect of preventive investments on the imitator's costs

If the firm expects very fast growth in demand, a useful tactic may be to invest in large-scale plants and equipment in order to create excess capacity before the competition is able to respond. The aim here is to increase the level of production output without causing a rapid increase in costs, and to reduce the market space for potential competitors. Equally, investments in the learning process aim to acquire pertinent advantages of experience. This move may discourage a rival's overly aggressive behavior, because the defender firm is in a position to charge lower prices. Another way to build strategic barriers is to invest in research and development. "Pre-emptive patenting" is an example. The firm tries to maintain its monopolistic advantage by patenting new products or new technologies before potential competitors do so. Such conduct allows holding a portfolio of "sleeping patents," that is innovations kept in the drawer, left unexploited either by the firm or by its competitors. A similar strategy was adopted by Rank Xerox, which obtained a patent for all the alternative technologies in the early stages of development of the photocopier sector. At other times the firm can invest to protect its exclusive know-how by restricting access to plants and vertically integrating components in order to avoid leaking knowledge to suppliers.

The localization of plants is another source of preventive barriers. Markets tend to take on a local dimension when substantial transport costs have a significant impact on total production costs. In this situation, potential competitors can enter in some local markets that are not adequately served by the leader firm, reaping the benefits of being close to their customers. The leading firm can therefore draw up deterrence strategies in order to occupy the most strategic geographical niches first.

(b)   The effect of preventive investments on demand

Investments of this type must include policies to extend the leader firm's product line. Often firms that want to enter a new market look for unoccupied niches in terms of product features and benefits. If consumers have to use products that differ greatly from their ideal product profile, they experience a *product usefulness gap*. To prevent the potential competitor from filling the offering vacuum, a consolidated firm can occupy the product benefit space by increasing the variety of its offering. This strategy is also known as product or brand proliferation. In this way it is no longer profitable to serve residual demand because it doesn't adequately remunerate the costs of a product launch. In the market development stages, the barriers erected with this move can be extremely effective. So much so, for example, that in 1972 the Federal Trade Commission expressly reprimanded the four major American breakfast cereal producers because of the systematic use they made of product proliferation.[6] A similar strategy, although reactive and not preventive, is what we can call *self-harming*. In this case, as soon as the newcomer decides to launch a new product targeting an unoccupied market space, the leader immediately counterattacks by introducing a better product and positions it against the attacker. In this case also, the niche residual demand would no longer be sufficient to reward both players, thus placing the new entrant in serious jeopardy.[7]

As a consequence, preventive investments (in marketing, communication, promotion, and trade marketing) enable the firm to strongly differentiate its products in the minds of consumers in order to protect its market power.

A defensive strategy centering on these barriers must take into consideration two things: the unpredictability and the inevitability of the competition's entry in the market. The rapid course of technological change makes it hard to predict where the next competitor will come from; competition can come from the most unexpected directions. This in turn makes it very difficult to know how long existing barriers will be effective.

7.8   Real maneuvers: binding agreements

Contractual agreements, stipulated with specific binding clauses, are another type of real preventive defense. To this end, long-term supply contracts for example may include what is referred to as the "meeting competition clause."[8] This states that if the buyer demonstrates that a supplier's competitor has offered an equivalent product or service (in terms of quality and quantity), but at the same or at a lower price, then the seller undertakes to accept the new price or to allow the buyer to obtain his supplies elsewhere. A greater deterrent may be achieved by reinforcing the contract with a "non-release meeting competition clause" that obliges the seller to accept the new price. This is a strongly binding commitment: in case of a price attack by a rival, the company is obliged to sell at any price, even at a loss. The potential challenger, knowing that the clause can be exercised, may be dissuaded from attacking.

7.9   Real maneuvers: preventive closure of market access

Preventive closure of market access constitutes trade practices that block entry to competitors with the aim of producing asymmetries in costs and reducing expected profitability in case of attack. These limitations, generally defined "vertical restraints," may be created by limiting: (a) supplier access to a purchaser (downstream closure), or (b) purchaser access to a supplier (upstream closure).[9]

a) *Downstream closure.* With this maneuver, the producer's aim is to make it more difficult for the challenger to access distribution channels. In this case, the defensive strategy must be directed not only to the firm's own channels, but also must block access to lateral entry in key channels. The producer imposes an exclusive right on the retailer that prevents the latter from selling substitute products and brands that are in direct competition with the producer's. Examples include the "slotting fee" contracts proposed by Coca-Cola in the United States; Coke offers financial rewards to its big organized distribution to prevent other cola branded products from accessing store shelves. The stipulation of long-term lease contracts or provisions for high penalties for breach of contract can be regarded as obstacles to access new suppliers in the downstream market. Instead, when a manufacturer's customer uses several production factors of the end product, a different type of competitive restriction may apply: associated sales (tie-in sales). In this case, the supplier of a strategic component with such a contract obliges the downstream firm to buy the other components as well. This technique is also called bundling rebates (discount packages), referring to discounts that are contingent on the purchase of a package of products. Market share discounts (volume discounts) provide a sliding discount linked to volume and customer market share. Exclusivity incentives are another form of market closure because they translate into a form of payment (advertising or promotional contributions for example) connected with the promise not to handle competitor products. Other forms of downstream market closure include:
   - granting aggressive volume discounts, or discounts based on the total purchases made by the channels so as to discourage sampling other suppliers;

- supplying firms selling private brands in order to prevent access to a challenger.

b) *Upstream closure*. In order to defend its monopolistic power, a firm can develop binding agreements with input suppliers, excluding competitors by implementing an upstream closure of market access. The purpose of such agreements is to produce cost asymmetries in supply in order to decrease forecast returns for potential competitors. Among the various forms of contractual upstream closure, we note the following:

- acquiring strategic terrain to circumvent competitors;
- stipulating long-term supply contracts to saturate the supplier's production capacity;
- encouraging suppliers to modify their value chains in order to bind the supplier to fulfilling their own needs and to hinder the transition to other customers;
- underwriting exclusivity contracts with top suppliers.

In the last case, contracts make provisions for the exclusive right to the supplier's input (exclusionary right contracts). Besides the physical supply, the firm acquires the right to exclude some rivals from access to the supplier's input or to restrict the supply of specific strategically important production components.

Finally, vertical integration is a form of upstream market closure of a non-contractual nature. The hypothesis is that vertical integration increases entrance barriers and limits growth opportunities for competitors who do not control all the stages of the value chain.

In conclusion, it is worth noting that, when implementing preventive strategies like downstream or upstream closure of market access, companies must be careful to avoid infringing competition law. The example of Intel can serve as a very useful warning in this sense. In 2009, the world's largest chip-maker was fined a record anti-trust penalty by the European Commission for abusing its dominant market position. Intel's *closing strategies* against its competitor, AMD, involved a two-pronged defense:

- On one hand Intel offered conditional rebates to *computer makers* with no models (or very few models) embedded with AMD chips.
- On the other hand, Intel offered direct payments to *computer retailers* such as MediaMarket on the condition that they exclusively sold Intel-based personal computers.

These strategies were very effective, but they cost Intel a € 1.06 billion fine!

7.10   Real maneuvers: predatory deterrence behaviors

With predatory behavior, the firm signals its intention to defend itself by using the price variable as a deterrence weapon. The defender, by reducing prices to below the cost level of its rivals (predatory pricing), forces other firms to take refuge in marginalized positions or, more dramatically, to abandon the market altogether. The firm is prepared to withstand interim losses, provided that this will protect it from future attacks. The strength here lies in the defender's greater financial resources, which allow it to sustain losses even for prolonged periods. Predatory behavior is used to deter potential rivals from pursuing attack strategies for fear of suffering the consequences. Also in this case, the mechanism that determines the dissuasive effect lies in the credibility of the firm's willingness to defend itself. The theoretical justification of the maneuver is based on the assumption of an asymmetrical distribution of information held by rivals. In the presence of incomplete information, fixing a low price becomes a credible signal that can prevent entry or attack by firms not fully informed as to the demand curve or the firm's cost structure. An aggressive price policy reinforces a reputation for toughness: potential attackers, on the basis of the leader's past behavior, foresee all-out responses to any threats. This reduces their willingness to commit to an attack.

7.11   Real maneuvers: preventive price strategies

To discourage a rival's entrance and exploit the benefits of the experience effect, the innovator may pre-empt a sales price reduction

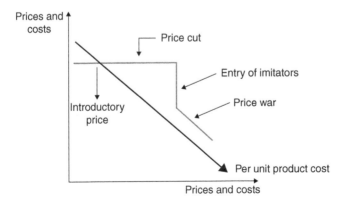

Figure 7.4   Preventive price maneuvers

policy (Figure 7.4). This maneuver corresponds to the rapid development maneuver introduced in Section 5.21.

As we can see, the entry price set by the innovator's product is lower than the product's production cost structure. This is a deterrent to rivals because the imitators' entry at a lower price is problematic and will likely incur losses. In the next phase of the sales strategy for the new product, the innovator plans to set an "umbrella price" to recover investments in research and development and recoup the losses accumulated in the introduction phase. By leveraging the monopoly it has created, the innovator can maintain the price at a level significantly above costs until imitators enter the market. Benefiting from the accumulated experience effect, the innovator can in turn pre-empt a new price reduction maneuver that can deflect the threat of competitor attacks. Also in this case, when the first mover wins a reputation as a determined defender of its hard-won positions, imitators realize that serious consequences may result from any offensive maneuvers.

8
The Position Game

8.1 Competing within the dominant frame of reference: the Position Game

In the first chapter we discussed the battle of the video game consoles between Sony and Microsoft in the early 2000s. This case exemplified the most common and dangerous approach to the Position Game: incessantly improving performance while relentlessly lowering price to win market share. This rationale prompted Sony to react to Microsoft's imitation of the original PlayStation by developing the PS2 and PS3 versions; Microsoft in turn followed the same line of reasoning with its Xbox and Xbox360. The two contenders consequently became entrapped in the Position Game, with margins and maneuvering room constantly contracting (Section 1.3).

This example underscores that in the Position Game, the key word in the definition of strategic orientation is *more: more* performance, *more* functionality, *more* affordability, *more* communication, *more* distribution coverage. Or *more* collusion, in the case of a non-belligerent game of position (or *limited conflict*). In any case, the Euclidian axes of the competitive space are given, embedded in the history of the sector; they are not a matter of debate. Sooner or later, as the rivalry intensifies, maintaining control over this space equates to continually offering more for less.

Sooner or later, the *more* of the Position Game actually turns into *less*, meaning lower margins, fewer profits, and a weaker defense against the ever-present threat of *non-orthodox* attacks on the status quo by insiders and outsiders alike. In the long run, even monopolies are destined to disappear, whether they be institutional (such as British Telecom in phone services, until the 1990s) or natural (like the "Baby Bells" in the

US local telecommunications market). Like the Roman Empire, the final destiny of the Position Game lies in ruins; unlike diamonds, the status quo and our competitive barriers are never forever.

The contrast between the Position Game and the Movement Game lies in the key word: *more* in the former vs *different* in the latter. In the Position Game, in fact, movement is bounded by the conventional coordinates of competition; in the Movement Game, on the other hand, the entire frame of reference shifts. The aim becomes, alternately or conjointly, to realize the following: a *different* value proposition, not a *more* powerful one (see the Wii console); a *different* pricing strategy, not a *more* aggressive one (books sold in installments); a *different* communication policy, not a *more* intense one (think Zara, with zero investments in traditional advertising); a *different* distribution system, not a *more* penetrating one (e.g. Ing Direct, which uses the Internet); and so on. To sum up, firms seek out a *different* market space (*market creation* or *regeneration*), not a greater share of the old market (*market sharing*).

This is the state of play in the Movement Game until competitor initiatives inexorably erode the barriers erected by the innovator. Imitators will eventually succeed in accumulating and replicating the same *market driving* capabilities of the *first mover*, through learning and by unwaveringly pursuing their strategic intent. This marks the onset of a more direct and dramatic confrontation. In fact, when the defensive barriers protecting the innovative space finally fall, and new market orthodoxies win consensus, a new Position Game inevitably results.

Despite its name, it is clear from our description that the Position Game is not necessarily a static state. On the contrary, this contest is often a hypercompetitive one, spiraling toward the final frontier of value, as described in the following chapters. It is also a dynamic game, but the rules only allow players to move along conventional axes of competition in their relative sectors – axes that are well-known; coordinates that are consolidated, canonical success factors. Every move a firm makes in this space, that is every *move* along the established axes (e.g. Sony offering a better price or a bigger hard drive) can be seen as a *Movement Game in Position;* in other words, a low-impact Movement Game within the existing frame of reference. It follows that Microsoft's reaction to Sony's lower prices and larger hard drives represents an *Imitation Game in Position.* So, we can see that our Position Game is anything but static. In fact, here too we find a succession of *competitive micro-cycles* that accelerate as the levels of rivalry and dynamism of the environment at large intensify.

We can intuit, then, that the incremental movements within the context of the Position Game fall into the following categories:

- Price cuts (primary preoccupation for firms striving for cost leadership);
- Conventional increments of the value proposition (the primary preoccupation of firms striving for product leadership);
- Combined actions on price and value (for firms that have the strength, ability, or imperative to govern both dimensions, as we will see shortly).

Market sharing strategies translate into a sequence of offensive and defensive maneuvers that can exacerbate the level of competition to an extreme, when worst case scenarios arise in which profits are nil. In these circumstances, the leader would find it extremely difficult to resume normal market behavior with respect to challengers. The reason is that each rival, regardless of its current position, may have different *aspirations* (expansion, consolidation, or retreat), as well as multiple strategic objectives. This forces firms to play on offence and defense at the same time.

Here's an example. In the early 2000s, the multinational Unilever sold off several brands to focus on its more profitable products. At the same time, Nestlé opted to hold on to its vast portfolio, while simultaneously implementing four maneuvers: (1) retreating from less lucrative markets; (2) consolidating profitable positions by aggressively recovering cost efficiency; (3) reinforcing certain key markets; (4) expanding new emerging lines with high profit potential. With regard to the first, Nestlé spun off its pasta and canned tomato business. To implement the second, the company introduced centralized procurement, a new IT system and specific incentives for management. Nestlé made the third move through major acquisitions in the ice cream and pet food sectors. Finally, for the fourth maneuver in the Movement Game, Nestlé attacked segments that placed high value on health and wellness, with products such as Nesvital for diabetics, or via the Inneov joint venture to develop "beauty supplements" with L'Oreal (nutricosmetics).

Often, in any case, the leader prefers to play defense and preserve the status quo, while the challengers are usually the ones who take the initiative. After securing a stronghold in the arena in question, these challengers can go on to win domination and assume the leadership position.

8.2   The survival zone of the firm: the price, quality, functionality triad

As briefly mentioned above, to play offence and defense in the Position Game, firms have to leverage price, value, or both – moving along the established axes of the sector.

As a simplified representation of this highlights (see Figure 8.1 below), success in this game depends on the firm's ability to maneuver in three dimensions:[1]

1) the cost structure;
2) product quality;
3) product functionalities, with respect to those already available in the market.

Clearly the first aspect impacts a firm's freedom of movement on pricing, while the second and third affect value. As Figure 8.1 shows, these three elements taken together delineate a three-dimensional space that is useful in representing the perspectives of both the firm and its customers.

The expectations that the firm and its customers come to hold regarding the extension of the three dimensions give us the *zone of*

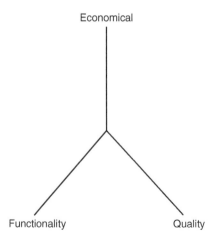

Figure 8.1   Competitive dimensions of the triad

competitive survival. We can map out this zone, represented by the shaded area in Figure 8.2 below, by identifying the following:

• The profile of expected demand. This profile reflects the minimum offering required to earn customer satisfaction, that is to meet the target's expectations in terms of quality, functionality, and price. Expected demand, illustrated in Figure 8.2, is represented by the inner border of the survival zone, staking out the minimum level of quality and functionality customers will accept, and the maximum price they are willing to pay for it.

• The profile of the potential offering. This profile corresponds to how far the firm can extend its offering, depending on its stock of capabilities and resources. The potential offering, then, represents the maximum value that the firm can offer its customers in terms of quality, functionality, and price.

The space that separates the potential offering profile from the expected demand profile for each dimension is the *competitive survival zone*. Any products or services that are not positioned inside this zone would not be attractive in the eyes of the consumer, even if there were no competitor offerings. By the same token, the distance between the

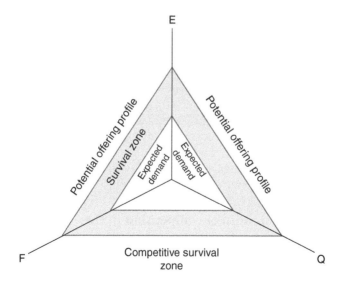

Figure 8.2 Survival zone

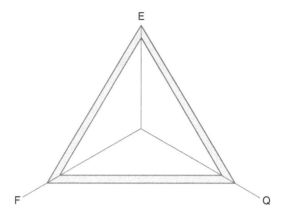

Figure 8.3   The shrinking survival zone: effects of the Position Game

two profiles determines the firms' *freedom of movement* in satisfying customers, differentiating offerings, and reinventing competitive strategies. The wider the spread in question (on at least two of the three dimensions of the survival zone), the more freedom firms enjoy to pursue cost leadership or differentiation strategies alternately – in the latter case leveraging the quality and functionalities of their offerings.

Unless firms adopt collusive behavior (either tacitly or explicitly), this space is liable to shrink due to the effect of competition, which deteriorates, as it intensifies, into a brutal Position Game (Figure 8.3).

Wide profile spreads, instead, provide ample freedom of movement. This leeway allows firms to creatively harmonize their market behavior with their stock of resources, and obviously with competitors' potential offerings. In light of these factors, a firm might decide to focus on one or more dimensions, opting for differentiation through superior product design that betters competitors in terms of quality and functionalities, or price and quality, or price and functionalities, and so forth. As we can see (Figure 8.4), the possible combinations and variations are endless, depending on the choice of positioning on the three axes.

8.3   Direct and indirect competition in the Position Game

As we'll see in the next section, as far as market behavior is concerned, it is not necessary or even advisable to invest the same resources in all components of the triad. One of them in some cases takes precedence

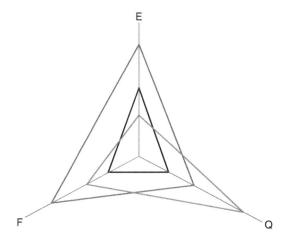

Figure 8.4 Countless positioning possibilities in the Position Game

over the other two. During times of economic crisis, for example, a cost-cutting orientation might prove more astute than a focus on functionality. In other circumstances, instead, to achieve a competitive advantage the firm may need to develop products with an eye to functionality or quality.

The choice of positioning relative to the three dimensions is contingent on the firm's strategic intent, and also on whether the competition it faces is *direct* or *indirect*. To define these concepts, two firms are in *indirect* competition when they pursue different strategies, albeit in the same market. For example, a company that adopts a generic cost leadership strategy, aiming for a low-price supplier positioning, would only indirectly compete with a firm that accents functionality and quality differentiation in its offering. A price competitor and a differentiator are therefore in indirect competition. But if one or the other makes a move to improve performance on one of the previously underdeveloped dimensions, the competitive survival zones of the two firms are liable to implode, with the situation degenerating into one of *direct* competitive confrontation.

Let's take the current Position Game underway in the car industry as an example. Despite the excess production capacity accumulated in recent years, we can easily discern different strategic clusters with varying levels of rivalry. For instance, Mercedes, Audi, BMW, and Lexus are in direct competition with one another, but only in very indirect competition with the price-oriented Kia, Tata, Hyundai, and the Dacia cluster.

Drawing general conclusions from these observations (and representing them on the vertical axis of price, i.e., the inverse of affordability in the previous figures), we can establish three rules to determine whether the competitive confrontation is direct or indirect:

1) If there is no overlap in the survival zones of two products, they are not in competition because they satisfy the needs of different customer segments (Figure 8.5).
2) If strategic survival zones overlap on only one dimension, the products do not compete directly as long as they remain *unmistakably distinctive* on the other two dimensions (Figure 8.6).
3) If there is an overlap in the survival zones on two dimensions, the products in question can coexist only if the differentiated dimension is functionality (simplified vs complex, for example; see Figure 8.7). In the other two cases, we would have an identical product with a higher price or lower quality, and the weaker competitor would be driven out of the market.

Ultimately, the more similar the moves along the three axes, the more direct the confrontation. In terms of similarity, all the firms that

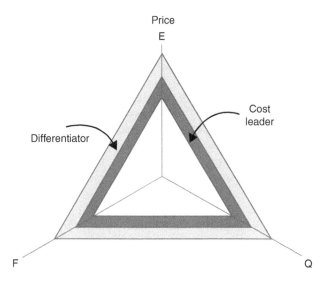

Figure 8.5 Positioning of a cost leader and a differentiator

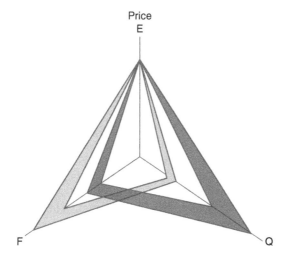

Figure 8.6   Overlap on one dimension

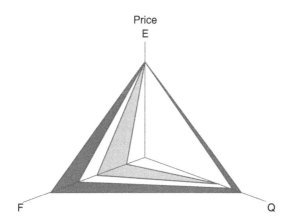

Figure 8.7   Overlap on two dimensions

offer comparable prices, quality, and functionalities make up a strategic cluster – that is, a group of companies that choose the same positioning and, inevitably, the same target.

When firms engage in direct competition and invest resources in order to progress along *all three dimensions* of the triad *at the same time*, the conflict spirals downward toward the final stages of the Position Game. Consequently, before instigating a direct confrontation, a firm should selectively invest in the dimensions that are vital to attaining a differential competitive advantage and to satisfying its customer base.

8.4 Basic strategies in the Position Game

In the first section, we reiterated how players in the Position Game can set in motion a sequence of *competitive micro-cycles* reminiscent of the high-impact Movement and Imitation Games of the *Competition Based View*. Naturally, in the Position Game we see lower impact maneuvers as well, which typically respect the status quo. Within this context, we also discussed how these maneuvers can engage other competitors more or less directly. *Initially*, in fact, firms that play the Position Game seek out differentiated market spaces, to avoid the pitfalls of battling rivals head on. The traditional strategic options, according to this rationale, are the following (Porter, 1985; Grant, 1994; Treacy and Wiersema, 1995):

- *Price Leadership.* Erecting barriers by means of:
  - excellence in operations;
  - exploiting economies of experience, scale, and/or scope;
  - reducing margins (in distribution as well) to leverage volumes.
- *Value Leadership.* Erecting barriers by means of:
  - differentiation in terms of conventional product features (incremental improvements in quality and/or functionality);
  - customer Responsive Management;
  - placing the accent on customers, their every need, their experience; focusing on service and personalization; striving to "delight" them in the different phases of their relationship with the firm.

Figure 8.8 represents this stage of the Position Game. On a hypothetical value map (see Chapter 10), we can identify three strategic clusters in the figure. The first, in the lower left corner (B) might represent the competitive space of Kia, Hyundai, Dacia, and Tata; in the center (A) we have Fiat, Renault, Toyota, and Volkswagen; in the upper right (C), Mercedes, Audi, BMW, and Lexus.

In these market spaces, firms attempt to avoid direct conflict with their rivals, even while competing in the same market. This is why strategic clusters emerge, serving distinct customer segments by implementing appropriate positioning strategies. Competition within each cluster can vary in intensity, depending on the structural conditions and customer characteristics of the segment in question. Gradually, however, offensive maneuvers within the same cluster escalate, setting

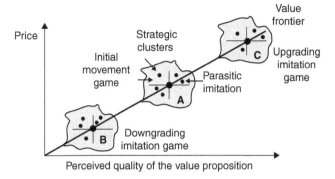

Figure 8.8 Value map

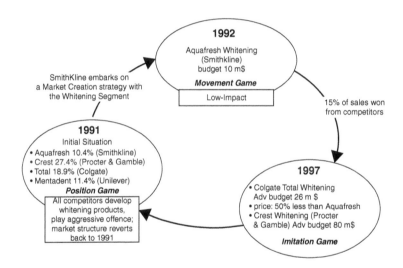

Figure 8.9 Competitive micro-cycle within the Position Game

off the micro-moves and micro-imitations mentioned above. Another example will help clarify this concept.

Consider the case of SmithKline (today GlaxoSmithKline) illustrated in Figure 8.9. In the mature market of toothpaste, this company began playing a low-impact Movement Game by launching a line of tooth whiteners. As this new product line began eroding the competitors' market share, the major rivals within the strategic cluster recognized the impending threat and initiated an Imitation Game. In no time at all, the confrontation reverted back to the *status quo ante*. This is a typical example of competitive micro-cycles in the Position Game.

As the rivalry within the strategic group progressively intensifies, the conflict relentlessly degenerates into *direct* competition. In this phase, firms become entirely engrossed in exploring *every possible increment* of quality/functionality *or* price cutting applicable to their offering, depending on the initial tactical orientation (i.e. *value leadership* or *price leadership*, respectively).

During the more frenzied phases of this escalation, when it seems there are no more improvements left to be made, a third strategy often emerges in the Position Game, aimed at breaking free of the *trade-off* between value leadership and price leadership:

Combined Price/Value Strategy. In this case, the firm acts in a very real sense like a *Value Net Integrator*. The challenge here is to simultaneously combine the different sources of competitive advantage (innovation, cost, customer satisfaction) in order to strike out on a bolder evolutionary path (Valdani, 2000; see Figure 8.10 below). In the compact car segment, for example, the Toyota Yaris won customer satisfaction thanks to product and process innovations that led to superior performance and a lower average price tag than competitors. Likewise, Samsung took the same path in mobile telephony. In 2010, for example, the company began offering touchscreen mobile phones with performance and functionality on par with the top smartphones, but priced for the lower end of the market.

1) In the first scenario, the idea is to defuse the situation by taking a collaborative approach, be it tacit or explicit. In these circumstances, firms recognize that ramping up the competitive confrontation is useless when:
- The cost of winning over market share destroys value for the firm and for the market.
- The newly-won share is difficult to defend, even when backed by sizeable investments.
- The market is in a recession.
- Every action made by a rival triggers an immediate reaction by other competitors to preserve the original status quo.

An example of the first and second points is the price war over online music. In May 2005, Yahoo launched its new low-cost, unlimited access music service. For Yahoo's competitors, this move triggered losses across

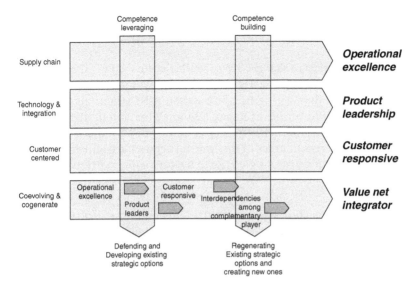

Figure 8.10 Basic strategies in the Position Game

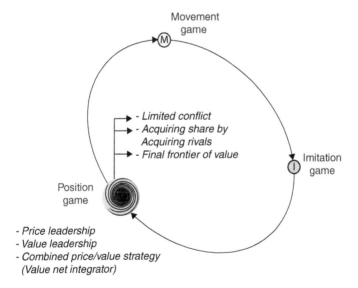

Figure 8.11 Basic strategies and evolutionary scenarios in the Position Game

the board, in some cases dramatic ones: Apple (–2.2%), Warner Music (–3.5%), Napster (–27%), and Real Networks (–21%). Yet Yahoo made no market gains.

Instead, *limited* or *non-belligerent conflict* occurs when all competitors recognize, tacitly or explicitly, that acting individually would not afford better results than acting in collaboration with others; all the players realize that the game has become a lose/lose situation. In this case, obviously, no one has sufficiently deep resources or asymmetrically differential advantages in order to instigate an aggressive competitive game.

Two different situations give rise to *limited conflict*, with the following results:

- a *truce*, when contenders recognize – in good time – the need to cap the level of competitive confrontation to avoid disastrous losses for everyone;
- a *stalemate*, when battle-fatigued competitors realize – too late – that they've completely depleted their resources.

2) The Position Game can also evolve into a second possible scenario: *acquisition of adversaries*. In mature markets, the need to grow inevitably impels the stronger and more aggressive players to expand by incorporating or merging with direct competitors. As a result the configuration of the sector becomes increasingly concentrated, as far as antitrust rules will allow. In more developed economies, we can find examples of actual "acquisition campaigns" and the consequent financial competition that leads to market growth for more promising firms. In similar circumstances, realizing added value from such acquisitions is clearly an extremely arduous undertaking, due to the major pre-venture outlay required. More and more often, for example, we see prices up to ten times the cash flow of the acquired firm or twenty times its net profits.[2]

Taking into consideration these numbers, most likely the only added value of the deal is the influx of new vitality that initially reverberates throughout the management structure, and the organizational cross-fertilization that may follow. (Although just as often cultural differences are what cause these ventures to fail.) In other words, the firm has to see the acquisition as an opportunity to rethink its destiny, to reorganize, to merge different perspectives and know-how – essentially to create the proper *cultural humus* for a Movement Game. If instead the firm simply uses the acquisition to consolidate the Position

Game, it is only postponing the inevitable downslide toward the *final frontier of value* (D'Aveni, 1994).

Given all this, clearly to maximize the potential for revitalization in an acquisition, while steering clear of the risk of failure, firms have to strike a fine balance between homogeneity and heterogeneity with the target firm. For example, some research suggests a *partial* convergence on the following aspects, avoiding both total overlap *and* total divergence:[3]

- customer base;
- geographical presence;
- product portfolio;
- distribution channels;
- work systems and processes;
- organizational culture.

Taking these considerations even further, we can say that the bigger the target firm, the more the homogeneity that there should be with respect to the acquirer (due to a higher risk of cultural incompatibility). The smaller the target, the greater the possible heterogeneity (thanks to more opportunities for cross fertilization).

3) Direct confrontation in the Position Game can lead to a third scenario: the perilous path toward the *final frontier of value*. In the last chapter of this book we give a detailed description of this state of affairs, which arises when the battle for market share becomes a lose/lose situation, and firms are unwilling or unable to keep a limited conflict regime intact.

As the market evolves toward the final frontier, there is an escalation of maneuvers which are non-defendable. As such, they are immediately replicated as rivals launch counterattacks, propelling the sector toward implosion.

8.5   Causes of the Position Game

Customer expectations evolve with the passing of time and the ongoing competitive confrontation. As this evolution takes place, the expected demand profile and the firm's potential profile move closer together, contracting the competitive survival zone. As this space shrinks, so too does the firm's freedom of movement, making it more and more difficult to pursue generic cost leadership strategies or to attempt functional/qualitative differentiation. Direct, head-to-head confrontation becomes inevitable.

The evolution of the competitive confrontation is also shaped by the speed of market change, and the determination of the firm to gain an advantage over its rivals. When customers demand products that require investments in quality, functionality, or price, the firm must drive and satisfy this demand with competency, sensitivity, and speed. By the same token, to achieve a competitive advantage, the firm must pre-empt demand, moving along the competitive dimensions of the triad. However, this option triggers an imitation process that can quickly degenerate into a Position Game of the most brutal sort. Consequently, the survival zone is shaped by both competitive pressure and market demand.

The most dangerous stage of the Position Game, therefore, is when contenders *have to abandon basic price/value strategies*, when they realize that if they want to survive, they have to tackle all three components of the competitive triad. The evolution of competition toward this final stage is best explained by two phenomena: 1) the success of the hypercompetitive firm; 2) the rapid convergence of *know-how* (in particular technological) within the sector. Both factors have *permanently* limited defensive options as far as sources of competitive advantage, as detailed below.

The rise of the *hypercompetitive firm* is the fruit of the strategic intent and creative commitment that has inspired myriad organizations to reengineer processes of research and development, production, and commercialization. All this has materialized in the form of programs such as *Total Quality Management* (TQM), *Zero Defects* (ZD), *Just In Time* (JIT), *Personnel Empowerment* (PEP), and so on. These efforts to renew organizational, productive, and commercial models reflect the desire to do more, do it better, and do it with less. The hypercompetitive firm has also acquired and perfected the ability to refocus all its activities on the needs of its customers (*Loyalty Management, CRM, Customer Satisfaction Management, etc.*).

By honing these abilities, with the support of much more flexible technology, these organizations have effectively implemented cost-cutting strategies while simultaneously establishing new paradigms of quality and mass personalization, breaking the value/cost trade-off.

This radical change of behavior has impacted demand in surprising ways. Customers have shown great appreciation for the improved products and services offered by hypercompetitive firms, preferring these

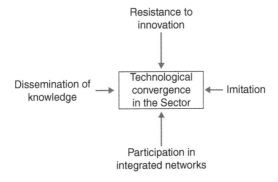

Figure 8.12 Determinants of intra-sector convergence

upgrades when making their purchases. This in turn has boosted the market share of hypercompetitive players, consequently triggering imitation processes. The reorientation of firms toward customer needs has made *demand* even more *demanding*, with preferences and expectations as regards quality, functionality, and affordability higher than ever before. With several competitors equally matched in terms of resources and capabilities on the playing field, and customers' superior bargaining power, a firm has less chance to differentiate its offering. All this has brought about a more aggressive competitive confrontation, opening up the most lethal phase of the Position Game.

The second factor that propels many markets toward a scenario of final, full-scale conflict is a phenomenon known as inter-industry *convergence*. Here, the term refers to technology and know-how in a single sector, not convergence among sectors (as discussed in Chapter 5). Below we describe the various causes underlying this process (Figure 8.12).

a) Resistance to innovation and radical change

In many companies, there is a pervasive sense of hostility and fear of *radical* innovations, those that profoundly alter the conventions that guide market behavior. This attitude raises barriers and fosters resistance to change, encouraging inertia and a partiality for *incremental* innovation alone. The reasons behind this mindset to change are primarily four:

1. Many firms keep on satisfying the same segments and the same market needs, year after year.

2. The people responsible for managing the innovation process have a similar professional background.
3. Firms use standardized methods for analyzing and generating innovation (for example, analyzing the value of competitor products, *house of quality*, etc.).
4. Firms exploit similar sources of technology.

In light of all this, we can see why firms have a propensity to develop products that converge in terms of their technological and functional content. When one firm dares to launch a revolutionary product, competitors can quickly and easily follow suit, thanks to their comparable competencies and know-how. In some cases this goes beyond imitating to anticipating, by developing products that are similar in almost every way. This leads us to the next point.

b) Dissemination of knowledge and speed of imitation

Ease of access and appropriation of scientific, technological, and commercial know-how allows every firm to quickly kit itself out with the competencies it needs to become a player in competitors' Position or Imitation Games.

How quickly imitators can appropriate a *first mover's* innovation depends on various factors (see Chapters 6 and 7), such as:

1. the lack of patents or legal protection for manufacturing secrets;
2. non-exclusive suppliers, who can sell and disseminate raw materials and critical technologies needed to manufacture the new product (see Point C below);
3. inability of the *first mover* to erect defensive barriers against potential imitators.

All this means that the advantages gained by the innovator will not be sustainable unless they are transformed into solid barriers that impede imitation.

c) Participation in an integrated network

When a firm and its rivals are all part of the same networks, the dissemination of technology and knowledge is facilitated. In these networks, in fact, suppliers, producers, transformers, and distributors all cooperate closely through integration or reciprocal dependency. Cooperative relationships are established among members that contribute to promulgate knowledge and propagate new technologies. All this expedites the transfer and appropriation of ideas, manufacturing secrets, innovations, and asymmetrical competitive advantages. Sharing information and technology in this way enables firms to quickly develop products that end up resembling one another.

To sum up, the behavior of both the firm and demand narrows the survival zone. Consequently, prices are driven down and functionality and quality ramped up, fuelling the growing expectations of the public (Figure 8.13). On one hand, the convergence of know-how makes it difficult, if not impossible, to gain and sustain a competitive advantage over time. On the other hand, the strategies and the capabilities of the hypercompetitive firm set into motion a spiral of incremental and imitative maneuvers by all the contenders in motion.

Nonetheless, we should not draw any hasty conclusions from these considerations. Functional product innovation is still a highly strategic competitive maneuver for the firm. In fact, constantly renewing and improving the innovative content of the offering is essential to survive. If the firm does not follow this path, it would find itself being relegated to the farthest fringes of the survival zone of the cost, quality, and functionality triad, with the very real risk of being forced out altogether.

To successfully compete in the Position Game, the firm must also know how to integrate and manage critical underlying processes. Since the *response time* to current market changes is a critical success factor in this game, these processes have to give the firm considerable flexibility in terms of acceleration or deceleration. In times of economic crisis and

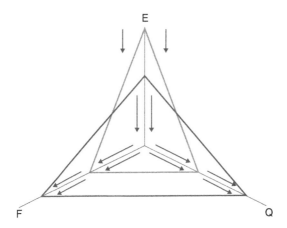

Figure 8.13 Transformation of the competitive survival zone

depressed demand, the firm also needs to be able to quickly compress its cost structure without desperately abandoning its position on the other dimensions.

In order to survive in the Position Game, the firm must also know how to deal with the *improvement coefficient* it needs to pursue in each of the critical dimensions to rapidly develop a sequence of competitive advantages, albeit only temporary ones. The *time* factor proves critical in explaining the changes in relation to the three dimensions of the survival zone.

The *economies of speed* that distinguish one firm from another measure how fast a firm can change its market positioning, and they represent a major source of competitive advantage. In this regard, note that the *time-based coefficient* (referring to how fast the firm repositions itself along one dimension of the triad) can temporarily compensate for delays on the other two. For instance, a rapid reaction in terms of functionality would buy the firm time to lower prices.

9
Offensive and Defensive Maneuvers in the Position Game

9.1 Introduction

In order to win the Position Game, a firm needs to deploy our resources and capabilities to leverage:[1]

- its knowledge of the playing field, that is the competitive arena where we do business
- the element of surprise, achieved through an unexpected attack
- a multi-pronged campaign
- fortification of ground gained
- collaboration from all personnel
- determination and high morale

Whether playing offence (vying for market share) or defense (holding position), firms have to take these points into consideration. In this chapter, first we introduce the concept of the Principle of Force and the formula for quantifying it (Sections 9.2, 9.3, and 9.4), and then we detail strategic options available to the firm in the Position Game, which can be outlined as:

- offensive moves (Sections 9.5–9.10):
  - direct attack
    - frontal attack (pure, limited, on price, or on R&D)
    - encirclement
  - indirect attack
    - flanking attack
    - guerrilla warfare
- defensive moves (Section 9.11–9.18):

- preparing for an attack (*ex-ante* defense)
  - deterrence (or pre-emptive) strategies, either psychological (in the minds of the enemy) or real (in the field) – introduced in Chapter 7.
  - static or passive defense
  - flank positioning (or lateral defense)
- responding to an attack (*ex-post* defense)
  - strategic compliance
  - Strategic withdrawal and retreat
  - counterattack
  - creative mobile defense

9.2   The principle of force

In order to determine whether a firm's competitive maneuver is offensive or defensive, we need to measure the magnitude of its marketing investments *relative* to its competitors. For example, let's say the *i*-th firm is spending €1 million on marketing, and then decides to ramp up this amount to €5 million. To assess the offensive intent of this move, let's look at how much its competitors are spending. If the investments in the *i*-th firm's sector or strategic group total €10 million, the firm's share of the total would equal 10% before the increase and 50% subsequently. With reference to a specific competitor, this relationship can also be expressed using the identity below (Cook 1983, 2006):

$$I\ mktg_i = d \cdot I\ mktg_n \tag{1}$$

Where:

I $mktg_i$ = marketing investments of the i-th firm
I $mktg_n$ = marketing investments of the n-th firm, rival of i.
d = marketing investment multiplier

The value of "d" denotes the orientation and intention – offensive or defensive – of the firm's market strategy. A value of 3, for example, means the firm in question is investing three times more than its competitors, a very aggressive strategy indeed. The level of ambition being equal, "d" varies in value depending on the degree of effectiveness and efficiency of the competitive weapons employed, and the conditions of the "battlefield". In a military theater, for example, rugged terrain would require a heavier deployment of resources. In the competitive arena, on the other hand, the value of "d" in the identity above is significantly impacted by customer preferences, specific characteristics of the

Table 9.1 The "d" coefficient and competitive ambition

Strategic Retreat	Defensive Containment	Offensive Attack	Dominate Destroy

distribution network, product or service features, the size of competitive barriers, and the defensive stance of competitors.

Table 9.1 shows the general relationship between the arithmetic value of the coefficient "d" and the competitive orientation of the firm. Values below 1 correspond to marketing investments that are lower than competitor resources, and therefore denote non-aggressive behavior or even strategic retreat, which we'll discuss further on. If a firm's strategy centers on defending or consolidating market share, the "d" would be near 1, indicating investments that are in line with competitors. Higher values signify offensive behavior. As we will see in the following sections, the more direct the attack, the higher the coefficient, which could increase to or even exceed 3. This is in keeping with the Principle of Force derived from the study of warfare.

Up to this point, we've talked about *total* marketing investments. Clearly, however, to gauge the offensive/defensive intent of a firm, we can break down the marketing budget into individual components and apply the same scale as in Table 9.1. In other words, we can compare investments with competitors per single cost item, such as communication, customer care, promotion, trade marketing, and so on. The "d" coefficient, for example, might be 3 for television advertising (attack) but only 1 for investments in the sales force (containment).

9.3 The formula for the Principle of Force

The most difficult marketing decision often lies in the answer to this seemingly simple question: "How much should we earmark for marketing, taking into consideration the offensive/defensive intent of the competitive maneuver we plan to implement?" A pragmatic tool for finding an answer is the *formula for the Principle of Force* as expressed in the identity below (Cook, 2006):

$$\text{I mktg}_i = \frac{S_i}{(100 - S_i)} \times \text{I mktg}_n \tag{2}$$

where:

  I mktg$_i$ = marketing investments of the *i*-th firm;

I mktg$_n$ = marketing investments of the n-th rival firm;
S$_i$ = i's strategic ambition in terms of market share.

We derive the formula for the Principle of Force from Identity (3) below, which we use to estimate market share relative to competitors' marketing investments:

$$S_i = \frac{I mktg_i}{I mktg_i + I mktg_n} \tag{3}$$

To see how the formula for the Principle of Force (2) works and how useful it is, we'll apply it to a real-life situation. Let's suppose, for example, that our firm has 10 salespeople to serve our customer base, while a competitor has 90. In this case, our share of sellers would be 10%, as shown below:

$$\frac{10}{10+90} = 10\%$$

Now let's say we decide to implement an offensive strategy with the aim of higher penetration and greater coverage of our client portfolio; we want to know how many sales people we would need to triple our share over our rivals. The Principle of Force, Formula (2), gives us the answer:

$$38.57 = \frac{30}{(100-30)} \times 90$$

So, according to the formula, we would need to increase our sales force from 10 to 39 (rounding up) if our intent is to boost our sales efforts up to 30% of the overall industry efforts (assuming only one competitor in the industry).

The identity S/(100 − S) gives us the multiplier "d" (which we saw in Formula (1)), referring to marketing investments needed to pursue offensive/defensive objectives.

Obviously, the deterministic result of the formula for the Principle of Force must be interpreted in light of reason, experience, specific characteristics of the market context, and the effectiveness of the strategy in question. This said, the formula provides the firm with useful information that serves as a frame of reference for further reflection and future decisions. Referring to the example above, for instance, we learn that to boost commercial pressure with respect to our rivals from 10% to 30%, we need to train and deploy 29 new salespeople.

We can use the formula for the Principle of Force to calibrate the resources we need to allocate for a specific competitive tool, to "raise the stakes" with respect to competitor investments. Similarly, we can apply the formula to all marketing investments. In this case, we may want to know how much more we need to spend overall on marketing to grow our market share by a given percentage. Let's assume for example our ambition is to win a 40% market share and our rival's current marketing investments are €10 million. According to the formula for the Principle of Force, it would take €6.66 million to achieve our aim:

$$6.66 = \frac{40}{(100 - 40)} \times €10\text{m}$$

9.4 Efficiency in marketing investments

As we've seen above, the formula for the Principle of Force gives us a *deterministic* notion of the magnitude of marketing resources we need to invest, depending on the share we want to attain or defend. However, this result is a numerical simplification that obviously does not factor in the reactions of rivals or the quality of resources in terms of efficiency or effectiveness. For instance, if we apply the Principle of Force to communication investments, the formula would suggest a certain quantity of financial resources, but naturally the effectiveness of the campaign slogans or the media we use could potentially magnify (or quite the contrary, nullify) this investment.

The same holds true for the efficiency of the investment, which can be measured with the Marketing Efficiency Ratio (MER). This indicator reflects how competently a firm actually employs its marketing resources as compared to a theoretical cost or a rival's investments (Cook, 2006).

The MER is calculated as follows:

$$MER = \frac{I\ mktg_i}{I\ mktg_t} \qquad (4)$$

where:

$I\ mktg_i$ = firm i's actual marketing investment (cost of sales personnel, advertising or promotional campaigns, total cost of marketing resources);

$I\ mktg_t$ = theoretical marketing investment (theoretical cost of salespeople and promotional/advertising campaigns, total theoretical cost of marketing resources), that is the estimate of marketing investments exactly as the formula of the Principle of Force (2) suggests.

The resulting value can be more than, less than, or equal to 1. If the outcome is 1, there is no difference in efficiency between the firm's actual marketing investments and the theoretical value, that is the average efficiency of the firm's strategic group or direct competitor. If the MER is greater than 1, this means that the firm is spending more than it should; its current investment is higher than the theoretical level needed to maintain its current market share.

There are three possible reasons for a higher MER:

- The firm is paying too much for its resources. (For example, wages for sales personnel are higher than the market average.)
- The firm is paying the same as competitors for resources that are less effective. (The sales force is less productive, so the firm has to hire more salespeople than its rivals.)
- The firm is investing to win a greater market share, so it applies an investment multiplier to step up the pressure on its competitors.

An MER value lower than 1 indicates that the firm is spending less than it should relative to its current market share. Possible explanations for a lower MER:

- The firm is paying less than the market value for its resources.
- The firm's resources are more effective than those of its competitors.
- The firm is divesting or leveraging its position, and investing less than its rivals.

All this reminds us that the competitive confrontation is a game based on the players' capacity not only to invest more marketing resources, but also to achieve higher productivity from these resources, with respect to direct competitors.

Moving from theory to practice, let's apply the MER formula in a real life situation. A firm has an 8% market share; its competitors' marketing investments (its strategic group) total €8.5 million; the firm's marketing investments are €400,000. By applying the formula for the Principle of Force (2), we find the *theoretical* investment the firm needs to make to defend its 8% share.

$$\text{I mktg}_i = \frac{S_i}{(100 - S_i)} \times \text{I mktg}_n = \frac{8}{(100 - 8)} \times 8,500,00 = 739,000€$$

Now we take the firm's actual €400,000 investment in marketing resources and the estimated theoretical investment of €739,000 to come up with the *Marketing Efficiency Ratio*:

$$\text{MER} = \frac{\text{Current Investment}}{\text{Theoretical Investment}} = \frac{400}{739} = 0.541$$

The result here shows that the firm is more efficient than its rivals, who have an MER of 1.48 (8,500,000/5,750,000). The difference of €339,000 (739,000 – 400,000) reflects the economy of efficiency of the firm's *marketing model*. This is a helpful introduction to the different *market sharing* options, from a more qualitative perspective, for firms playing the Position Game.

9.5   Offensive maneuvers

As we noted in the previous chapter, offensive maneuvers in the Position Game are actions aimed at winning market share within the framework of existing orthodoxies. Movement is made along conventional axes of competition, under the assumption that current critical success factors are constant (Figure 9.1).

The equations we presented in the previous sections remind us that a firm's market share in the Position Game is solidly anchored to its percentage of total market investments in the sector, taking into account its Marketing Efficiency Ratio, that is its ability to maximize return on these investments. It follows that every added effort made

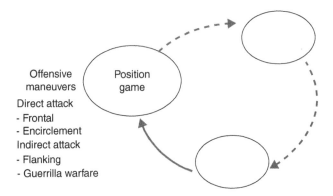

Figure 9.1   The Position Game: offensive maneuvers

by one or more competitors has negative repercussions on the firm's market share, unless it adjusts its investments accordingly.

In light of these considerations, the only real advantage of an offensive maneuver is often the element of surprise. There are two reasons why surprise has the impact it does. First, some key aspects of the attack will be intrinsically unexpected, such as:

* where the attack will take place;
* when the attack will take place;
* how big the attack will be, in terms of resources and market-driving capabilities.

Added to this would be the non-orthodox content of the maneuver (if we were playing a Movement Game), neutralizing the opposition even more completely.

The second is the psychological element of surprise, which affects the morale and the behavior of the adversary. When surprise is particularly acute, it leaves competitors feeling lost and confused, weakening their courage and determination to react.

For a competitive maneuver, the principle of surprise calls for deploying large-scale activities, fast decision making, and "forced marching" to rapidly achieve goals and facilitate the effect of surprise. If our firm already has the upper hand in intimidating the competition, we would have an easier time successfully employing the elements of surprise. We should also remember that only the players who set down the rules of the game for the others can create a surprise. Also, to establish and enforce these rules, we must act consistently and effectively. Even if our firm surprises its rival(s) by breaking the rules, surprise alone would not be enough to ensure success.

Just as no defensive maneuver involves exclusively defensive actions, the same can be said for offensive maneuvers. In fact, if an offensive move does not open up a new competitive game, it will only end up fortifying a defensive position. At the conclusion of an offensive action, in fact, the biggest threat is to the defensive position, which is at risk if the firm fails to achieve its objective, just like a counterattack on the soccer field. Direct attacks are launched against rivals' fortified positions (products, markets, competitive advantages, etc.). This in itself is an inherent drawback. When an offensive move is made against fortified positions and competitive advantages without a substantial competitive potential for attack, the result may well be catastrophic.

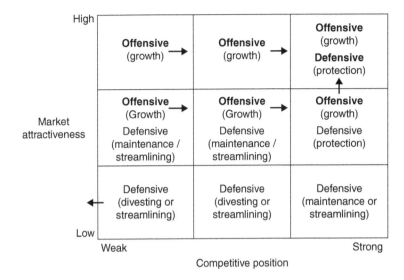

Figure 9.2 Market attractiveness and offensive and defensive strategies

Therefore launching a direct attack against an established adversary with its guard up is an extremely perilous undertaking.

Fortunately for the attacker, not all defensive positions are inaccessible or unassailable. In fact, a firm on the offensive could hit the mark without directly engaging the enemy on its fortified positions. Other offensive options are available, such as planning a flanking attack, evading rivals' competitive advantages, or training all available firepower on weak spots. Only after exhausting these possibilities should the attacker consider a head-on confrontation.

The aim of offensive maneuvers is to win new positions, penetrating and developing markets where the firm deploys its competencies and concentrates its business. We find such maneuvers particularly in markets with a medium to high attractiveness. In these arenas, in fact, both challengers and leaders pursue offensive strategies. The former may currently hold marginal positions, but intend to develop them; the latter aim to consolidate their position and dominate the market (Figure 9.2).

9.6   Direct attack

As we've noted, the kind of indirect attack a firm launches often depends on its competitive situation and available resources. If this strategy is successful, a more direct attack may follow to consolidate and extend the ground gained.

Firms that undertake a direct attack presumably have the resources and competencies needed to take down rivals' defensive barriers. There are two types of direct attack: a) frontal, and b) encirclement.

9.7   Frontal attack

While an indirect attack capitalizes on the weaknesses of potential rivals, a frontal attack *targets strengths*. For this reason, it is an extremely risky and challenging strategy that should only be implemented under certain conditions. A successful and speedy outcome depends on the following:

a) Solid superiority of resources and competencies; these provide the firepower needed to break down the resistance of rival opposition. A study of 280 military campaigns shows that in only six did a frontal attack end in a decisive victory. According to military theory, in fact, the attacking force must have three times the firepower to defeat the enemy and secure a victory. If not, the frontal attack may deteriorate into a war of attrition, which could result in dramatic losses on all sides. This 3-to-1 ratio corresponds exactly to the coefficient "d" from Formula (1) discussed above and illustrated in Table 9.1 above. This proportion is cited explicitly in the management literature (Cook, 1983) and can be interpreted as an estimator for evaluating the resources needed for a head-on confrontation.
b) Exclusive competitive advantages, that is those defendable against competitor imitation.
c) The possibility of undermining customer loyalty toward competitor brands and value propositions.

There are four different types of frontal attacks: 1) pure frontal attack, 2) limited frontal attack, 3) frontal attack on price, 4) frontal attack on R&D.

1. Pure frontal attack

Superior resources and solid competitive advantages are critical success factors here. Two different strategies can be used in launching pure frontal attacks: *acquisition* or *head-to-head confrontation*. In the first, as we have already discussed in the previous chapter, the attacker opts to follow the path of mergers and acquisitions rather than engaging its

Table 9.2 The head-to-head confrontation between Time Warner and Walt Disney

Time Warner	Walt Disney
Cartoons, movies	Cartoons, movies
Television:	Television:
– CW Television Network (50% con CBS)	– Disney Network
	– ABC
– Time Warner Cable (cable TV and bundled TV packages)	– ESPN
Publishing:	Publishing:
– Time	– Hyperion
Chains and megastores selling gadgets and apparel emblazoned with the company's characters	Chains and megastores selling gadgets and apparel emblazoned with the company's characters
Theme parks	Theme parks

adversaries in a long, arduous, offensive campaign. Albeit it is a costly strategy, with M&A the firm aims to avoid a confrontation that not only risks becoming a protracted one, but may also generate negative fallout for sector and firm profitability due to the grueling conflict that would result. In the second case, *head-to-head confrontation*, the firm implements a blow-by-blow imitation strategy, engaging its adversaries in the same markets and on the same targets. We can find strategic similarities in the historic clash between Time Warner and Walt Disney (see Table 9.2). In this case, however, it is interesting to note that Disney did not follow the lead of its competitor in acquiring an Internet Provider, thereby capitalizing on the negative experience of Warner with its buyout of AOL (America Online).

In light of these considerations, we can assume that the differential of resources and capabilities employed is sufficient to capture an adequate market share (in terms of products, investments, communication and promotion, prices, sales force and access to distribution channels, customer assistance, technical/production resources, quality of personnel, etc.).

The Principle of Force applies to the pure frontal attack, as the great military strategists knew well. Sun Tzu and Napoleon both affirmed that when one's army is inferior in numbers or skill, it is critical to avoid a direct conflict and better to elude the enemy. In a competitive confrontation, the magnitude of the superiority of forces to deploy in the battlefield is quantified by *Lanchester's Square Law*, which affirms that the *firepower of a force is equal to the square of the number of members of that unit* (Lanchester, 1956).

Let's use a numerical example to illustrate this concept. Imagine two armies on the battlefield, the first (A) with 2000 soldiers and the second (B) with 1000, both equally skilled. Since both are protected on their flanks by natural barriers, they can only engage in head-to-head combat, in close ranks. With every volley, assuming that all shots hit the mark, the B army would lose two soldiers, while the A would only lose one. The outcome is obvious. The A army would win the battle with 1000 survivors, while the B army would be wiped out completely. In a war zone this would normally never happen (unless surrendering were tantamount to certain death). In fact, when faced with a more powerful enemy, a military force would recognize its inferiority and opt for surrender or evasion. Even if the opponents do not engage in close ranks, the advantage of the bigger contender is clear.

Let's take our military scenario even further. Now we'll assume that the A army's 2000 soldiers can fire at will on the 1000 B soldiers, that each soldier is armed with a similar weapon, and that one of every five shots kills an enemy. A five-shot volley would result in the following:

- A would inflict 400 B casualties (2000 × 1/5).
- B would inflict 200 A casualties (100 × 1/5).

So, the A army would be reduced in number to 1800 [2000 − (1000 × 1/5)], while only 600 of the B army would survive [1000 − (2000 × 1/5)]. The initial 2-to-1 ratio would become 3-to-1 in favor of A (1800:600). After the next five shots, A would lose 120 men (600 × 1/5) and B 360. The forces on the battlefield would drop to 1680 for A and 240 for B, and the fire power ratio would rise 7-to-1 to A's advantage (1680:240).

The disproportionate advantage that comes with a substantial superiority of forces should serve as a warning to any firm with inferior resources or size, regardless of comparable competitive advantages. If two firms have the same capabilities and neither one can generate a sustainable competitive advantage, it is very likely that the larger firm will defeat its smaller competitor. The advantage deriving from the Principle of Force lies squarely in the greater availability of resources. This is what enables the firm to sustain the financial losses, even in the long term, that may ensue from an intensely competitive confrontation. A firm with fewer resources, on the contrary, will rarely emerge victorious over a bigger rival. Thanks to deeper financial resources and other competitive advantages, a powerful player can not only imitate the successful behavior of a small competitor, but could even opt to acquire it.

2. Limited frontal attack

In this case, the firm's offensive efforts are brought to bear on a particular customer segment, in order to win it over from a competitor and take up a position of dominance; this kind of attack may also target a specific geographic area. In Europe, for example, the attack on the automotive market, started in the 1980s by some Japanese manufacturers, was limited to the off-road segment (4x4), with successful models like the Suzuki Santana and Mitsubishi Pajero.

3. Frontal attack on price

This maneuver leverages prices, which the attacker slashes to undercut rivals. It is generally a risky move, only effective in the following situations:

- The market leader does not react likewise with an immediate price cut of its own.
- The market recognizes that the challenger's value proposition, also considering reliability and accessory services, is comparable to the leader's.
- The price differential is such that the buyer is willing to sacrifice quality, albeit not below the minimum acceptable threshold.

To avoid a swift reaction by the rival firm, during price wars contenders often use maneuvers that don't explicitly reveal their intention to launch a direct attack. For example, a firm may apply *camouflaged prices*; services such as installation, assistance, and financing are added to lower the price without actually stating this as such, thereby modifying the list price. There are myriad examples of this strategy, such as offering zero-interest financing or including new accessories as standard for the same price, with cars for instance. (In this case the camouflaged price also helps lessen the disappointment of prior buyers, who won't see a drop in the retail price.) Various kinds of supplements can also be combined with periodical publications. For the normal price of a newspaper, for example, publishers can offer incentives that actually lower the real price. This serves to capture customers who are oriented toward competitor products, or to enhance loyalty in one's own customers.

4. Frontal attack on R&D

This maneuver consists of continual, systematic incremental improvements in technology to enhance product design, performance, and functionality. The aim is to demonstrate to competitors' customers the attacker's ability to create value through continuous improvements, while underscoring its rivals' obsolescence. A well-known example is Toyota, the Japanese car manufacturer that enjoys constant growth and boasts a capacity to redesign its models faster than any of its rivals.

In all the cases described here, the frontal attack in the Position Game does not generate any radical innovation: the competitive frame of reference, the critical success factors, market structure and segments remain the same; the only possible exception being that companies change places as they vie for position in these segments.

We conclude this section with an exemplary case that sums up the importance of the Principle of Force in frontal attacks during the Position Game. We refer to the devastating consequences for Netscape when Microsoft decided to develop Explorer, in direct competition with Navigator. In fact, just a few weeks after Microsoft's announcement, Netscape stock plummeted by 50%, and in six months' time the company lost 50% of its market share as well, which exceeded 85% in the mid-'90s, and has disappeared today.

It is interesting to note Microsoft's single-minded determination in its head-on aggression, as evidenced by how the company went about securing a key customer, the accounting firm KPMG. This client, after considering the proposals of both Microsoft and Netscape, verbally agreed to commission the latter in order to create an Intranet to link its corporate offices all over the world. In order to win back this client, Microsoft applied the Principle of Force, deploying all of the weapons in its arsenal, illustrated in Figure 9.3, with easily imaginable results. The point is that in a direct attack, significantly superior resources translate into victory in almost every case for the contender with the greater firepower.

9.8 Encirclement

Encirclement is an appropriate strategy when the attacker considers a head-on offensive too risky, despite having superior resources and competencies as compared to its rivals. A valid alternative in this case is launching an attack on several different fronts (products, distribution channels, market segments, etc.), while expending minimal resources on each.

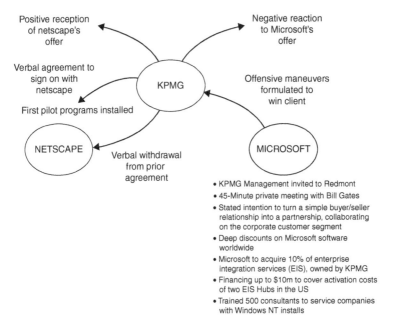

Figure 9.3   The determination of Microsoft in winning back KPMG as a key customer

The primary aim in implementing this approach is to incite competitors to react by shoring up fortifications, forcing them to squander resources. The attacker then waits until the adversary is financially vulnerable, and when the time is right, capitalizes on weakened market or product domination, bringing this maneuver to its conclusion.

Encirclement strategies focus on either a) products, or b) markets.

a) In the case of product encirclement, the idea is to undermine the rival's brand, making customers more fluid in their loyalty to it. This is done with a "pincer movement" of product proliferation, initially differentiating only a few product features, then "encircling" the adversary with a higher-quality, higher-priced offering (*upgrading* with respect to the competition). Finally "closing the circle," the attacker launches a product with higher customer satisfaction at a lower price (*downgrading*). This tactic can be supported by multi-channel distribution. In the end, rival products will be "surrounded" by differentiated offerings in terms of product design, features, or image. All this is achieved through the use of aggressive pricing, hard-selling policies, or rapid-fire technological changes, forcing the rival onto the defensive. A classic case in the literature is Komatsu, whose attack on Caterpillar can be summed up with the internal slogan *Maru-c*, which means *Encircle Caterpillar.*[2]

b) In the same way, encirclement can be based on markets (instead of products). This involves proliferating aggressive offerings in order to attack all market segments to surround and encroach on the rival at a national or international level, implementing a scorched earth policy and minimizing the maneuvering room of the firm under siege. While in the previous case, the attacker encircles rival products, here action involves target segments. Figure 9.4, which illustrates the underlying premises of this approach, shows sales volumes, costs of commercial development, contribution margins, and cash flows following a new product launch.

Figure 9.4 highlights, perhaps even optimistically, that in some cases it takes up to four years to go from product launch to positive cumulative cash flows. If the attacker is financially solid, rapid-fire product launches in different market segments could prompt rivals to attempt imitation, depleting their cash reserves as a logical consequence. This shortage of funds would limit the rivals' ability to repel or resist further aggression by the attacking firm, which in turn would achieve greater bargaining power and freedom of movement.

We should emphasize that to implement an encirclement strategy, the newcomer has to take into account certain conditions that can facilitate or compromise such an approach. First, as with any kind of direct attack, encirclement is only an option when the attacker has greater financial resources than its adversaries, and the determination to persevere over an extended period of time, if need be. But adequate financial resources are not enough. The firm must also have an exceptional capacity for research and development in order to sustain the technological innovation needed to introduce new products. Additional prerequisites include marketing competencies, access to distribution channels, and a professional sales force with consistent performance, enabling the firm to operate in dissimilar markets. To all this is added the commitment of the organization and morale of management, which must be high and remain so for what might prove to be a very long campaign.

To mitigate potential risks, the attacker often combines the strategies described above with forms of cooperation and alliances. This translates into the possibility of spending fewer resources, and more importantly ensuring the collaboration of other firms, even potential rivals,

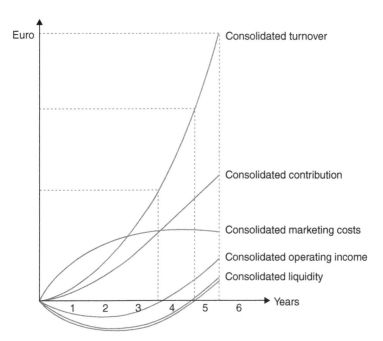

Figure 9.4   Encirclement strategy and financial results

who already do business in the market. By using this approach, a firm can support and integrate its competencies and resources (financial, technological, distributive, and marketing) with its ally's asymmetrical competencies and resources, giving rise to reciprocal advantages and benefits.

As a final consideration in this description of the different strategies for direct attacks, we must remember that taking opponents by surprise is no easy task. The inherent risk, common to every type of offensive behavior, is triggering a violent, lengthy, defensive reaction.

A direct attack calls for long preparation and deployment of organizational support that may have to be kept in place beyond the short term. Adversaries would have the time they need to set up market defenses and to block any attempted incursions, which in turn would result in higher costs for the aggressor. Once again, we have to remember that this maneuver makes sense when the attacker can invest the necessary resources over a long period of time to create and grow significant competitive advantages that are defendable against rival imitation, reaction, or counterattack.

9.9 Flanking attack

Avoid strengths and attack weaknesses: a central tenet of the military philosophy inspired by Sun Tzu to achieve a rapid and effective resolution. A market maneuver that targets a rival's weaknesses allows the attacker firm to employ fewer resources, focusing and limiting investments for acquiring and employing competitive weapons. In the competitive confrontation, like the military theater, an offensive move often aims at the rival's strengths, while logic dictates that the enemy's weaknesses should be targeted first. On one hand, the tendency to undertake a direct, head-on attack reflects a cultural value that, in the western world, is inspired by legends of knights-errant, or by sports competitions. We are prone to rush into battle, primed for rapid and decisive victory. On the other hand, this inclination is in line with the reasoning that prompts us to imitate a successful competitor, in either its ability to innovate or to operate efficiently. The underlying assumption is that we can not only do as well as our rivals as far as these success factors are concerned, but we can do even better.

Every move we make to follow a rival's business model leads us to attack its strongest points. Instead, everyone knows that a lion never chases the fastest antelope, just as an invincible army lies in wait only to attack when the enemy is at its most vulnerable state. We can discover our competitor's weaknesses by analyzing its business model and its value chain configuration (Figure 9.5).

If our intention is a flanking attack, we need to focus on how our rival manages its most critical processes, with special attention to integration. In fact, we may find weak points in coordination, in regarding functional responsibilities, or between subsidiaries and headquarters. A watchful attacker can identify these shortfalls and concentrate its competitive resources to exacerbate them.

In fragmented markets, another possible strategy for a flanking attack (at a sector level in this case) calls for launching an offensive against

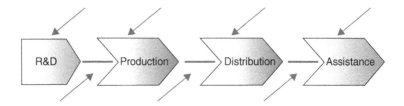

Figure 9.5 Potential weaknesses in a competitor's value chain

smaller, weaker rivals in order to win market share without triggering direct, immediate retaliation by bigger competitors.

9.10   Guerrilla warfare

Guerrilla warfare is an indirect offensive strategy that aims to change a firm's weakness (e.g. small size) into a strength. The objective is to seek out market niches that competitors do not adequately serve where a firm with limited resources can find room to grow.

In this scenario, the battlefield is divided into *bases* and *fronts*. The *bases* are the customer segments that are crucial to the future of the guerrilla firm. *Bases* are its home positions, small as they may be, to defend even at the cost of sacrificing resources, while avoiding any form of conflict. The objective for the guerrilla warrior is to scale down the field of action and gain superior strength; in other words, to become a big fish in a little pond. The *fronts*, on the other hand, are the segments and groups of customers that are attractive only for guerrilla incursions. This strategy unfolds in a series of minor but unrelenting attacks against the adversary in the target segments.

Guerrilla attacks can take the form of various micro-marketing measures such as: slashing prices unexpectedly and selectively, running aggressive promotions, headhunting, or launching a *fighting brand*. This last move consists of a line extension with autonomous brands with respect to the lead brand, designed to attack a specific competitor brand generally by leveraging price.

Military theory holds that a constant bombardment with a series of small-scale offensives can disorganize, confound, and demoralize the enemy much more than a few violent attacks. Translated into marketing terms, a guerrilla firm can successfully invade small, specific, poorly defended market segments rather than by confronting the adversary in areas where it is deeply entrenched. If a rival realizes that the cost of repelling guerrilla attacks is higher than the potential financial returns from a given niche or market share, that firm will be much less willing to defend its positions.

In international marketing too, firms adopt guerrilla tactics to convey their intention to open a front in a rival's key foreign market. This behavior is used as a retaliatory move when competition in other critical markets intensifies. We discuss this in the chapter on imitation strategies (see *mutual forbearance*). Simply put, when the conflict heightens in our key markets (i.e. our *bases*), we respond by opening bridgeheads in our competitor's strategic segments, forcing that company to back down or risk negative fallout for its *bases*, thereby putting a squeeze on cash flows. In an advertising campaign in Italy a few years ago, for example, Unilever's Algida (an ice-cream brand) positioned its Magnum Chocolate Pralines in direct competition with the famous Perugina Baci (Kisses) (with the claim, "I won't settle for just a kiss"). Perugina, owned by Nestle, quickly responded with an incursion into its rival's territory by launching "Ice Cream Kisses" (for a limited time and in a limited geographical area, but the offensive sent a clear signal nonetheless).

Beyond the cut and thrust of these tactics, they can be viewed as defensive counterattacks (see Section 9.14). Systematically engaging in guerrilla warfare is the strategic option of choice only in the following circumstances:

• Our firm is small, but instead of behaving like our successful rivals, we think and act like a guerrilla warrior.
• Our tactics will disproportionately drain our adversary's resources, should that firm decide to follow our lead.
• We can avoid battles of attrition, and keep an exit route clear if we need to abandon our newly-won positions due to intensified loss-generating competition.

An additional critical success factor is maximum flexibility and rapid reaction in utilizing capabilities and deploying resources; also key is the commitment of the company management in giving their moral support to the "soldiers" sent into a battle when the outcome is uncertain.

9.11   Defensive maneuvers in the Position Game

Marketing literature on occasion associates offensive maneuvers with the ability to acquire new customers, and defensive maneuvers with the capacity to keep them (Woodall, 2004; Rust, Zahorik and Schibrowsky, 1994). In a military context, the Prussian theorist General Clausewitz held that defensive behavior tends to be more effective than offensive conduct (*Vom Kriege*, 1832); Sun Tzu claimed that the *possibility of victory* lies in attack, but *invincibility* lies in defense. In the managerial arena, too, when opponents have the same type and depth of offensive resources, the firm that knows how best to defend its positions is likely to dominate over other competitors. In this sense, we refer to the tactical primacy of defense.[3]

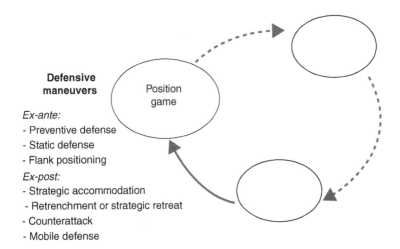

Defensive maneuvers

Ex-ante:
- Preventive defense
- Static defense
- Flank positioning

Ex-post:
- Strategic accommodation
- Retrenchment or strategic retreat
- Counterattack
- Mobile defense

Figure 9.6   The Position Game: defensive maneuvers

The art of defense is based on four principles:

- Being prepared to wait (i.e. *competitive intelligence* and peripheral vision);
- Knowing the territory (i.e. marketing research and *customer-driven insights*);
- Fortifying competitive positions (i.e. innovation, *customer satisfaction* and *loyalty management*);
- Averting offensive maneuvers by adversaries (i.e. *pre-emptive strategies, signaling* and *commitment*).

The first point takes us back to the pages of Buzzati's *The Tartar Steppe*. In competitive markets, however, time spent waiting must always be active. In fact waiting passively with no activity whatsoever would run counter to the intrinsic dynamism of the competitive game: if you wish for peace, prepare for war.[4]

In order to do so, we must first draw a distinction between two kinds of defensive maneuvers: those used to discourage an attack and those used to respond to an attack. More specifically, we can break down the first type into the following:

- **preventive maneuvers**, both psychological and real (*signaling* and *pre-emptive strategies*), which we already discussed with reference to imitation initiatives by new entries (Sections 9.4 to 9.11). Such moves are also valid options as *ex-ante* defense against competitors in the Position Game. The more explicit a firm's commitment to defending its current positions, the more effective these maneuvers will be. To offer another military example, think of an army that burns the bridges behind it to destroy any possible escape route. Voluntarily minimizing options (*locking out* the "retreat" option) conveys the utmost determination in pursuing current objectives (strategic *lock-in*). Given this commitment, any firm playing the Position Game and contemplating an attack on our firm must be extremely wary.

- **static defense** or passive defense is an inert defense, based entirely on the superiority of our value proposition. This naïve, often subconscious attitude is discussed in the next section.
- **flanking position (or lateral defense)** is a maneuver by which the firm attempts to reinforce its weakest positions in order to deflect an attack on its flanks. This tactic is detailed in Section 9.13.

In order to build our defensive architecture *ex-ante*, we need to periodically ask ourselves a number of questions, listed in the box below. To answer competently, the management must look beyond its market horizon, and be constantly attuned to what is happening on the periphery of its field of vision (Day and Schoemaker, 2006).

Questions for organizing an *ex-ante* defense

- What are the strengths and weaknesses of our firm?
- Which ones could potentially provide a foothold for a competitor to build a competitive advantage?
- If we were our rival, how would we attack our company?
- Which potential competitors could threaten our firm?
- What is the likelihood of an attack?
- What are we planning to do to prevent an attack? Which resources and competencies do we need to improve on?
- What is the potential cost of the self-competition that might result from planned maneuvers?
- What cost/loss would our firm incur if the competitor attacked our positions and achieved some level of success?
- Why would a customer abandon our firm and turn to a competitor?
- Does our firm really focus on fulfilling customer expectations?
- What do we need to do to enhance customer relations?
- What barriers can be rapidly and effectively erected to defend our firm's positions from attack by potential rivals?

9.12 Static defense and market leader inertia

Static, or passive, defense is based on the false premise that there is such a thing as "permanent barriers" that can protect a position, making it impervious to enemy attack. The analogy with military strategy brings to mind what happened during World War I, when the Germans outflanked French forces stationed along the border between the two countries and invaded Belgium without warning. The element of surprise in this offensive, which neutralized all defenses, was based on the violation of Belgian neutrality, a contingency that the French dismissed. In order to avert future invasions, having learned from the earlier error, in the 1930s the French/German border saw a huge French defensive buildup with the famous Maginot Line, which extended into Belgium. When World War II broke out, the passive defense erected to protect the border proved an utter failure. In fact, in May 1940, the Germans flanked the Line and penetrated the French back roads through mountainous and wooded regions of the Ardennes Mountains. This was the only section of the border left undefended as it was mistakenly considered too treacherous for an army to cross in order to launch an attack. In both cases, history dramatically proved that all static defensive maneuvers are useless, as they cannot effectively thwart a military invasion. A static or fortified defense is a competitive practice typical of a firm that has come to believe its offering cannot be imitated or improved.

This mindset, when it permeates the firm, leads to what we might call the *invincible product syndrome*: we are so satisfied with our results that we become complacent, convinced of our customers' undying loyalty. So, we are no longer concerned with evaluating or reacting to threats or changes in the market or in competitor behavior. On occasion, this attitude can be found among companies that do business in sectors in the maturity phase. In this context, the firm may assume that long-term demand will hold steady, continuing to generate acceptable profits. Such circumstances could lead the firm to adopt a *"defend what we have"* policy, unwisely cutting back on investments to energize its position.[5] Often it's the market leader who is the last to notice the destructive potential of a rival's innovative or imitative maneuver, as empirical research has demonstrated time and time again.

Due to the intrinsic *rigidity* of the static defense, it represents one of the riskiest defensive behaviors of all.[6] This attachment to existing products and blind faith in tactical routines fuel a form of organizational inertia that can lead to three equally dangerous situations:

1) The firm fails to perceive peripheral signs of threats, because it focuses entirely on its traditional field of vision, that is on its more direct competitors. Excessive selective attention means a compromised view of the bigger picture and the risks that may lie in wait. Consider record companies, for example, and how long it took before they finally recognized threats emerging from the "far away" world of information technologies.
2) The firm recognizes a threat, but doesn't consider it dangerous. Often times, in fact, successful companies justify their cautious "wait and see" behavior by citing past innovation failures. In the history of a company, the larger the number of failed innovations, or false alarms, the greater the risk of dangerous levels of defensive inertia. It's the dramatic, inexorable "cry wolf" effect of Aesop's fable. This is in part what happened with the innovation of Internet phone service provision. Traditional carriers sat on the sidelines, watching and waiting to assess the scope of the threat. But passive companies, paralyzed with surprise, risked being wiped out by the speed of dissemination and success of an innovation.
3) Again, the firm recognizes a threat, but it hesitates or doesn't react at all. This may happen because the firm is afraid of cannibalizing its current product line, and refuses to consider the "creative destruction" of its existing business. Think of the ignoble end of some prestigious encyclopedia publishers as a result of the Internet revolution. Similarly, in the late 1990s countless newspapers were reluctant to seize the opportunities offered by new media.

Whatever the reason, concentrating all resources to build static defensive fortifications represents a form of market myopia. In fact, environmental changes, whether endogenous or exogenous, can always alter a firm's *relative* ability to satisfy market demand. Therefore, it is utterly useless to build extensive fortifications only to discover that the battle is being fought elsewhere, on some other competitive orbit. No firm, not even the market leader, can protect its positions by adopting passive defensive behavior.

9.13   Flanking position

One of the most important principles of defense is protecting one's weaknesses in order to prevent an attack. A flanking position specifically calls for identifying all weaknesses so as to respond aggressively to any possible risk of a flanking attack. A firm should know its strengths and weaknesses sooner and better than its rivals. Continually and honestly evaluating the areas of greatest vulnerability is a useful way to predict where a competitor is likely to attack. Whatever this weakness may be, the firm must correctly identify it and deploy the right resources to compensate for it. If not, this will be where the enemy gains a foothold and then brings all of its forces to bear. An astute commander doesn't wait for the enemy to attack. Instead he intelligently allocates defensive resources, studies the layout of the battle ground in order to identify the directions of possible attack, and deploys forces to these areas to deter an enemy advance.

When assuming a flanking position, the company can defend its territory by establishing outposts that serve to protect a weak market front. Also, the firm can gear up for a counterattack (Section 9.16), to be launched in case of invasion or intensification of competitive pressure by an aggressor.

Last, even with defensive strategies management must always make it a priority to optimize performance, rather than to maximize investments. This means, for example, that when the firm realizes that it can no longer effectively defend its position on all fronts and still achieve acceptable financial results, it has to carefully consider strategic retrenchment, as we'll discuss further on (Section 9.15).

9.14 Defensive maneuvers in response to an attack

In the previous sections we discussed what firms can do to deter attacks from challengers (preventive maneuvers, static defense, flanking position). If these behaviors are not successful deterrents, the defender is left to decide how to react to the attack. First and foremost, the firm under siege has to understand the underlying reasons for the aggression. In fact, the type of reaction depends on the objectives that may have triggered the offensive. Clearly, strategic reactions can differ depending on levels of resources and capabilities required, as well as inherent risks involved.

Before detailing the individual strategies, we must remember that maneuvers can differ widely depending on the firm's competitive positioning (leader, challenger, follower, or nicher) and the market growth rate (Figure 9.7).

Naturally, firms that enjoy a dominant position are more interested in defending their territory, and all the more so in a highly attractive

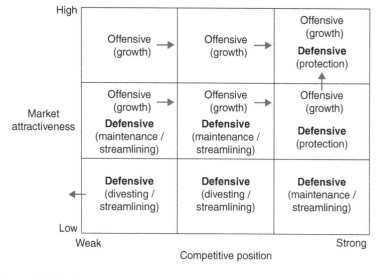

Figure 9.7 Market attractiveness and defensive strategies

market. At the same time, however, these firms have to invest more than others to curb the erosive forces at play in the competitive arena, such as new entries and aggressive challengers. Defending one's position is relatively simple in mature markets, but much riskier in rapidly expanding ones. A similar environment requires substantial resources, in numbers that rise *more* than proportionally to the share to defend,[7] placing the leader in a more precarious financial position. Some defensive strategies can be mentioned.

- **Strategic Compliance.** The first option in responding to an attack is to react by not reacting, or paradoxically, by downsizing marketing efforts. Accommodating the adversary may prove the most profitable course when there's a chance that the attack will trigger a rise in primary demand. This happens, in many cases, thanks to the attacker's efforts to educate the market via communication campaigns. Pfizer is following this rationale by choosing not to respond directly to attacks against Viagra by new entrants. However, with strategic compliance, the risk that defenders must avoid is that non-belligerent behavior is taken as a sign of weakness by the adversary, who could then ramp up the offensive (Catignon and Reibstein, 1999). To this end, the cooperative intent of such a response must be unequivocal.

We'll take up the theme of cooperation in more general terms in Section 9.19.

- **Strategic Withdrawal and Retreat.** A firm can also opt to respond to an attack by retrenching its positions, slackening its control of the market, or even abandoning the field altogether. This strategy is outlined in Section 9.15.
- **Counterattack.** In many cases, this is the only viable option for defending one's market or a specific client. This response can be implemented with the traditional marketing levers, as described in Sections 9.16 and 9.17.
- **Creative Mobile Defense.** When faced with an attack in the Position Game, more creative firms can dodge the blow instead of blocking it or counterattacking. Taking up our original metaphor, this is done by moving into a new competitive trajectory. By launching a counterattack, the firm aggressively utilizes traditional levers to defend the status quo. Instead, with a mobile defense the firm tests out less orthodox defensive methods, in light of the fact that the fundamental rule for achieving or maintaining an advantage over competitors is to control the conditions of the game. A creative reaction inspires the defender to rewrite the rules of play, quitting the Position Game and initiating a new Movement Game. We'll come back to this in Section 9.18.

9.15 Strategic withdrawal and retreat (abandonment)

Downsizing our market position may be the right option when:

- We no longer have *enough* of the *right* resources to compete in the new competitive scenario.
- The profit potential of the market is compromised, or the only way to improve profitability is to focus on one or a few customer targets.

This approach translates into strategically divesting from lines, brands, areas, or market segments that the firm deems expendable, or consolidating micro-segments that were previously differentiated (*counter-segmentation*). Defending by retrenching does not mean abandoning the market altogether, but rather refocusing on the most attractive products or businesses.

Put another way, when a firm implements a defensive retrenchment strategy, it needs to redraw the map of the market it serves, centering its activities entirely on enhancing the profitability and productivity of its investments. This was the approach that General Electric took when it abandoned the light bulb market, leaving an open field for a particularly aggressive rival: Philips. At the same time, Philips deserted the mobile phone market as part of its strategic retrenchment.

Figure 9.8 shows the results a company can achieve by redefining its strategy, shifting from a mass-market approach to serving only a few customer segments, or even a single one. As we can see, returns on sales and investments required to fund the maneuver in question vary widely from option to option, as does the productivity of these investments, which increases from 5:1 in the mass market strategy to 8:1 for the selective strategy.[8]

Figure 9.9 provides a useful example for verifying the expediency of retrenchment. On analyzing the income statement and performance indicators, we can see that three of the five product lines do not cover relative fixed costs, while two generate no return on marketing investments. Generally speaking, the firm's competitive position is on par with its competitors in a fairly unappealing market. Under the circumstances, the firm should consider either selective divestment or even more drastically, a strategic retreat, by opting to sell the business outright.

In order to assess the first option, we can model results from the following market scenarios:

• An increase in retail prices, as with the scenario illustrated in Figure 9.10, hypothetically by 8% and 15% in product lines A and B, and by 10% for C and E.

• A decrease in marketing investments, specifically calibrated for each of the different product lines.

Once again referring to Figure 9.10, the market reaction is clear. Product lines A and B lose 15–20% of their customers, and C and E fare even worse, with a 33–35% migration; in addition turnover drops from 18.3 to 16.9 million euros. Despite all these negative repercussions, performance indicators show that retrenchment is the right choice. All the product lines show a positive contribution, and return on sales jumps from −4.4% to 7.1%.

The strategic retreat option, clearly a more radical solution, means abandoning the market altogether. This decision is prompted by reduced market appeal and a weak competitive advantage (Figure 9.11).

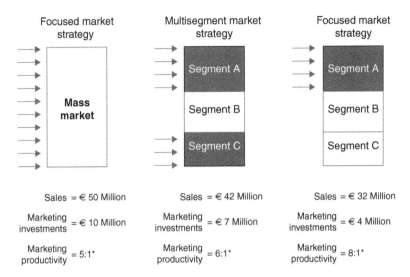

Figure 9.8   Retrenchment defense: downsizing the market we serve

Performance indicators	Pigments & silicone	Primary products	Special products	Basic colors	Improved colors	Overall
Market demand (000)	5,500	8,650	15,000	9,500	55,000	
Market share	18,2%	23.1%	13.3%	26.3%	9.1%	
Unit volume (000)	1,000	2,000	2,000	2,500	5,000	12,500
Unit price	€4.50	€2.80	€1.60	€.80	€.60	
Sales revenue (millions)	€4.5	€5.6	€3.2	€2.0	€.3.0	€18.3
Variable costs per unit	€3.50	€2.00	€1.30	€.70	€.54	
Unit margin	1.00	.80	30	.10	.06	
Total contribution (milions)	€1.00	€1.60	€.60	€.25	€.30	€3.75
Marketing investments (milions)	.20	.70	.50	.30	.45	2.15
Net marketing contribution (milions)	€80	€.90	€.10	€.05	−€.15	€1.60
Augmented costs (milions)	.40	.40	.20	.15	.20	1.35
General costs (milions)	.25	.40	.20	.10	.10	1.05
Net profit (milions)	€.15	€.10	€−.30	€.30	−€.45	−€.80
Return on sales (%)	3.3%	1.8%	−9.4%	−15%	−15.0%	−4.4%

Figure 9.9   Divest and retrench strategy: example 1

This translates into an equally weak competitive position and disappointing financial performance. In this case, rather than retrenching and refocusing the business, the firm may take the more radical option of divestment.

Performance indicators	Pigments & silicone	Primary products	Special products	Basic colors	Improved colors	Overall
Market demand (000)	5,500	8,650	15,000	9,500	55,000	
Market share	15,5%	19.8%	11.0%	17.1%	6.1%	
Unit volume (000)	852	1,713	1,650	1,625	3,355	12,500
Unit price	€4.95	€3.20	€1.90	€.98	€.75	
Sales revenue (millions)	€4.2	€5.5	€3.1	€1.6	€.2.5	€16.9
Variable costs per unit	€3.50	€2.00	€1.30	€.70	€.54	
Unit margin	1.45	1.20	60	.28	.21	
Total contribution (milions)	€1.24	€2.06	€.99	€.46	€.70	€5.45
Marketing investments (milions)	.20	.70	.45	.20	.30	1.85
Net marketing contribution (milions)	€1.04	€1.36	€.54	€.26	€.40	€3.60
Augmented costs (milions)	.40	.40	.20	.15	.20	1.35
General costs (milions)	.25	.40	.20	.10	.10	1.05
Net profit (milions)	€.39	€.56	€.14	€.01	€.10	€1.20
Return on sales (%)	9.3%	10.2%	−4.5%	.6%	4.0%	7.1%

Figure 9.10   Divest and retrench strategy: example 2

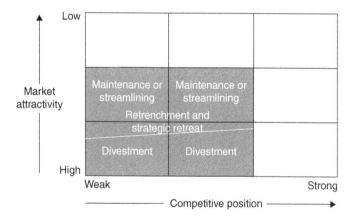

Figure 9.11   Divestment and strategic retreat

9.16   Orthodox options for counterattacks

To respond to the threat of attack, a firm can design a counter-offensive, especially if the following is true: it holds a prominent market position, the market is still highly attractive, and the attacker rebuffs every overture of cooperation. In these circumstances the strategies we outlined above, strategic compliance or entrenchment, would be ineffective or inefficient. A counterattack is a defensive maneuver adopted when loss of market share is so severe (quantitatively or qualitatively) as to require immediate and effective countermeasures.

Speed of reaction in the face of an attack is essential to prevent the morale, the exit barriers, and the commitment of the challenger from rising as it achieves initial success. *Aggression* necessarily goes hand-in-hand with this, because it puts the challenger in a more vulnerable position and undermines an otherwise successful strategy. In most cases, a counter offensive should be even *bigger* than the original attack; this sends a message to the aggressor (and any spectators) that the firm is fully *committed* to its positions. As General Patton used to say: *"A good plan, violently executed today, is better than a perfect plan next week."*

In any case, there is no guarantee that the final result won't be an *escalation* of the conflict with devastating results for every player. This, as we have often reiterated, is the underlying danger of the Position Game.

Having described the circumstances, the intensity, and the timing for a counterattack, now we'll discuss where and how to launch this maneuver. The first decision, in fact, is where to respond – that is, whether in the same market or segment as the attack, or in another market or segment of the rival.

Crossfire defense (or cross-parry): counterattacking in enemy territory. The counter offensive can be launched deep in the competitive territory of the adversary in the form of a *cross-parry*, which serves to thwart the attack. A well known example is Bic's counter-strike following Gillette's raid on the market of writing implements with its launch of Paper Mate pens. Bic responded with a rapid and effective counter offensive, not only by blocking the invasion of its market, but invading the razor market, introducing an innovative line of disposable razors and extending the offensive, attacking Gillette's most important geographic market: North America. When rival firms limit their reciprocal presence in respective markets to subdue competitive intensity, we refer to this as *mutual forbearance*, as we have discussed already. Destinies intertwine to reestablish the equilibrium upset by the actions of the aggressor.

Pincer defense (or encirclement): counterattacking on multiple fronts. Countermeasures can also take the form of what's known as a *pincer response* (Figure 9.12). The defender deflects the force of the attack at its source through multiple offensive/defensive moves that force the aggressor to dissipate its resources on several fronts, as we saw for the strategic offensive of encirclement (Section 9.8)

Retaliation: counterattacking in our own market. A memorable example of this kind of defensive reaction, which we detail in the next section, is Angelini vs Procter & Gamble. The latter launched the Pampers brand in

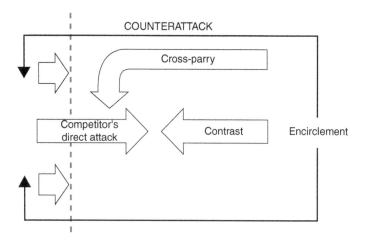

Figure 9.12 Counterattack maneuvers

Italy in a bid to usurp Angelini's leadership in the diaper sector. With its Lines brand, Angelini reacted using an opposition strategy. It expended every possible effort on multiple fronts, innovating and differentiating its product lines, increasing advertising investments, and growing its market driving ability. All this enhanced the effectiveness and creativity of the countermeasures it employed.

9.17 Retaliation and defensive strategies for a counterattack in our own market

A defensive reaction on home ground can take the form of *complementary* actions, differentiated according to customer type. So, these moves are (Roberts, 2005):

- defensive strategies aimed at keeping our key customers; and
- defensive strategies aimed at slowing the defection of our more susceptible customers.

In order to achieve each of these objectives we can use two different levers:

- enhancing our own strengths; or
- mitigating our attacker's strengths.

By intersecting these aspects we get four complementary options for defensive opposition, as illustrated in Figure 9.13 using data from Telstra (ex-Australian telecom monopoly). This template implicitly highlights the importance of knowing the home territory. This means knowing exactly what the different customer segments want, what they're willing to pay for it, and how they see the firm and the competition. It means knowing strengths and weaknesses. Last of all, it means knowing which customers are most valuable for the firm – in other words, what their (direct or indirect) impact is on long-term profitability. Only by cross-referencing this crucial data can we decide on the most logical actions for every box in the matrix.

In light of this, fundamental resources for building any defensive strategy are market research, information systems, and market driving ability. The most sophisticated firms construct ad hoc analyses and models to analytically identify the factors that shape customer preferences. Then they use this input to simulate the competitive scenarios that would result from the implementation of specific countermeasures.[9] Decision making support of this kind – *in the Position Game* – can be extremely useful in comparing and identifying the most effective and lucrative responses.

The final consideration in this overview of defensive strategies is a brief description of the canonical levers that can be used to implement defensive opposition strategies (again, for the Position Game).

Cutting prices. This lever is an inherently susceptible and dangerous one, as we've often reiterated. However, if the offensive is launched by a small and inexperienced firm, or one with a heavy cost structure, price cuts could effectively sideline this attacker. In other cases, a *selective price reduction* would be a viable option, as demonstrated by Telstra (Figure 9.13). Similarly, a firm could reduce margins on the product under siege and recoup resources by increasing prices on products with more rigid demand that are not offered by the adversary.

Escalating promotions and communication. Since communication costs are fixed, the besieged leader has the structure advantage of higher volumes, that is a lower per-unit cost for relative expenses. Telstra fully exploited this lever, as did Budweiser to defend its leadership position in the US beer market. For example, Budweiser is often the top spender on TV advertising during the Super Bowl event.

Enhancing the value proposition continuously. Innovation and continual improvement make a product a moving target for challengers, quickly canceling out the temporary advantage of the aggressor in the Position

Potential levers

		Enhancing one's own strengths	Mitigating attacker's strengths
Primary defensive objective	Retain key clients	Telstra exploited its greater financial resources and deeper customer knowledge to focus on higher value attributes, supporting initiatives with large-scale communications campaigns.	Telstra responded to the optus attack by cutting rates, but only for certain time periods/areas, depending on the customers the company wanted to retain.
	Slow migration of more vulnerable customers	Telstra leveraged patriotism and a sense of belonging to the national community, underscoring the company's national roots while implicitly reminding consumers that Optus was a foreign-owned firm.	Telstra launched a massive communication campaign to inform customers that the company was continuously striving to improve its services "Good, Better, Best"

Figure 9.13   Defensive tactics for a counterattack in our own market

Game (think at the quick sequence of iPad v.1, v.2, v.3 ...). We should keep in mind, though, that continuous improvement must never divert energy or attention from the more radical innovations that propel the firm toward a higher-impact Movement Game.

Introducing fighting brands. This defensive tactic, the occasional object of legal controversy (see below), involves introducing smaller brands or sub-brands ad hoc in response to an attack. By doing so, the firm avoids having to respond with its current brand or lead product. Fighting brands incur minimal marketing costs, and take a lower price positioning with respect to the brand being defended; such brands can be introduced for limited areas and time periods. An example of this strategy in action is when 3M launched a new brand, Highland, with extremely aggressive promotional policies, in order to respond to the price attack by LePage against Scotch. To maximize the defensive impact without resorting to price predators, 3M leveraged big distribution chains, offering special discounts to retailers who sold its products along with the competitor's. In no time, LePage disappeared from the shelves of the major chains. This defensive move was a huge success, but it was later deemed anti-competitive behavior in court, and 3M was levied an enormous fine for unfair use of its dominant market position.[10]

9.18 Creative mobile defense and market expansion

Creative defensive moves, generically speaking, are all the behaviors a firm may adopt in order to mitigate risks and surprises arising from changes that could radically transform the competitive context or increase market-dependency. As the competitive confrontation in the Position Game gradually intensifies, the first such maneuver is a *mobile defense*. "Mobile" refers to the fact that the firm is constantly on the lookout for a chance to engage in its arena/market, building up a reserve of resources and capabilities far from the combat zones. These can be called up in case of market emergencies. Specifically, this strategy requires two critical capabilities. The first is technological, both in terms of product and technical/production processes. The second involves market driving, which the firm needs in order to react freely and effectively to adversary action. The defensive depth guaranteed by technology allows the firm to expand its business in two directions:

a) enlarging the market; and
b) diversifying.

With market expansion, the firm shifts its attention from the current product to the generic needs this product satisfies, and comes up with new products that do the same. A case in point is when petroleum companies broadened their scope to encompass the much broader energy market. In order to do business in this new expanded arena, major players had to acquire new competencies in terms of technology, procurement, and commercialization. In fact, these companies extended their research to mining, nuclear energy, new technologies for energy production, and diversified their business into chemicals and petroleum refining.

Mobile defense, with its typical strategic depth, consists of creatively redefining the market in order to defend a firm's core businesses from environmental or competitive fallout. This type of defensive maneuver, therefore, pushes the firm toward the Movement Game.

Another direction for creatively contesting an external threat arising from changes in the competitive arena is *horizontal growth* in correlated markets. This move hinges on discovering lucrative combinations of related business areas. When firms capitalize on such combinations, the competitive confrontation moves to the level of *multipoint competition*. Here, achieving a competitive advantage lies in the ability to exploit potential synergies among various businesses. Let's say for instance that we've identified a key source of a competitor's advantage in synergies among some of its businesses (for example, a market presence in both communication networks and content). At this point we should defend our own position by expanding our portfolio in the same direction.

Sharing businesses in several markets can generate substantial advantages in terms of economies of scope or range of action. Such economies, by definition, enable firms to make more products in tandem while paying less than they would with separate production. Or, costs being equal, with this approach the customer can get more value for the money: new or integrated services, one-stop shopping and so on. Cost savings are possible thanks to shared assets and costs (e.g. know-how, shared distribution channels, brand image). Once a firm acquires these assets for one business, it can also apply them to other products with no (or low) added cost.

Horizonal market growth does have its limitations, however. The most common involve:

- diseconomies of sharing, including increased coordination costs, compromise costs (every business has to give something up), and costs of rigidity (it's more difficult to respond to competitors' moves or it becomes impossible to pull out of a market);
- diseconomies deriving from differentiating the offering by using conflicting distribution channels or disparate images;
- congestion of management activities due to assiduous use of information (which ties into the coordination costs mentioned above).

Mobile defense maneuvers generate new catalysts in order to create new markets. As we've said before, this in turn initiates a new Movement Game, a new orbital journey that motivates other firms to make imitation moves, thereby reverting back to a Position Game. We can see once again the fascinating circularity in the destiny of firms, which explains the nature of creative destruction in the Shumpeterian matrix, and forms the foundation of the *Competition Based View*. This means that businesspeople must pursue an ongoing quest that at its best is a source of social progress.

9.19 The middle ground between offensive and defensive maneuvers: cooperation and coexistence

When two or more companies (or groups) decide to coordinate their efforts to find shared solutions to a common problem, cooperative strategies are at work. Cooperation requires individual firms to work in sync, no easy task because in some cases there is no activity or formal authority to orchestrate these efforts. Cooperative maneuvers can involve competitors or buyers and sellers, and consist of joint action aimed at reducing risks and costs to firms. Relative strategies include:

- *Co-optation*, in internal executive bodies of the firm, with external public bodies (such as credit agencies or financial institutions, political lobbyists, or members of pressure groups, unions, etc.). Alliances with these organizations can help tone down hostile behavior or enable a firm to acquire new capabilities to interact with the public.
- *Coalition* of one or more industrial groups in order to pursue common goals over an established time horizon.

As regards this last point, collaboration can be *explicit* or *implicit*. *Implicit* cooperation refers to states of:

- Balanced competition.[11] Here no explicit agreements exist. This state corresponds to a strategy of peaceful coexistence because, in this context, every company tends to promote its sales without upsetting the preexisting balance of power;
- Tacit collaboration. Here the companies of a sector operate by common consent, and yet with no formal agreements in place, in order to eliminate more extreme expressions of competition. The clearest implications of this affect pricing, advertising, and product innovation; this competitive approach is typical of mature oligopolistic sectors.

When firms formalize agreements of collusion to regulate market competition, this is *explicit* cooperation. A consortium is the most prominent example of this type of agreement, established with the aim of:

- regulating the market, in terms of limiting competition (i.e. cartels). An example is OPEC, set up to control oil prices, or other cartels set up in the mining, steel, or chemicals industries.
- enhancing distribution efficiency, by establishing an agreement among firms/groups to exchange products, services, information, and know-how. Beyond distribution of material goods (as with commercial consortia), agreements can also cover services.
- maximizing research investments (in this case we refer to *co-opetition*). This consists of combining the financial efforts and know-how of two or more competitors in the initial development of an innovation, who then go on to commercialize respective products separately. The investments required today to perfect new technologies or prototypes force firms to find ways to share relative costs and risks of new commercial initiatives. One example of the myriad cases is the agreement between Toyota and the French group PSA to develop a city car that led to the production of the Toyota Aygo, the Citroen C1 and the Peugeot 107.
- optimizing infrastructural investments via co-opetition. A recent example is in the field of communications. Numerous cost-cutting contracts pertaining to infrastructure include the agreement between Vodafone and O2, a British mobile phone provider controlled by Telefonica. Since 2008 the two competitors have shared a number of antennas for digital transmissions, efficiently increasing reciprocal coverage.

Through cooperation, in general, the firm seeks to reinforce its performance and potentially shore up its leadership in a market, without undermining the performance or positions of its direct rivals. This type of orientation can be further divided into behaviors that can enhance the position of the firm and its rivals:[12]

- *without* the latter having to actively contribute to their own development (typical in cases where the firm can develop primary demand to such an extent as to generate positive repercussions for competitors);
- *only* if the latter contribute to their own development (typical with various types of cartels, consortia, or coalitions).

To conclude, cooperative strategies are common and even prominent in sectors where technology changes quickly and radically. The more sophisticated and interdependent technologies become, the less chance the individual firm has to possess the capabilities needed to develop and market a product quickly and with acceptable costs, without the contributions that other firms can offer. From this point of view, therefore, the proliferation of collaborative agreements we see is often a direct consequence of reciprocal dependence on other industrial sectors and other firms.[13]

10
The Final Frontier of Value

10.1 The value map

In the previous chapters we rediscovered an ancient truth: "You cannot step into the same river twice, because everything flows." Situations that have been apparently static for years sooner or later are destined to flow toward the only two possible outfalls of the Position Game: a new Movement Game (an environmental shock), or the implosion of the sector – that is, the state we call the final frontier of value. A sector reaching this state, after many competitive cycles of innovation and imitation, is like a train that after many runs reaches its final station: the end of the line.

Offensive and defensive strategies used in the Position Game may lead to a series of price and value maneuvers that push the market toward the final frontier in terms of profitability. In Chapter 8 we called these "competitive micro-cycles" smaller movements and Imitation Games within the Position Game.

To visually represent this situation, we illustrate the succession of competitive games through the value map (Figure 10.2) (not to be confused with the function of value discussed in Chapter 4).

This map shows price on the y-axis (i.e. the overall cost for the customer), and perceived benefits on the x-axis. These variables are the numerator and denominator of the value equation:

$$\text{Value} = \frac{\text{Perceived Benefits}}{\text{Price}}$$

By adopting a wider definition of value, we can argue that customers compile their set of purchase choices based on usefulness. This usefulness,

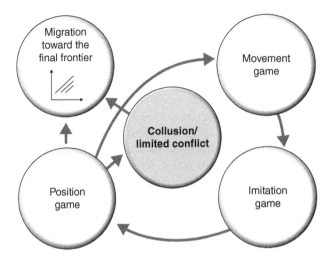

Figure 10.1   Evolutionary scenarios in the Competition Based View

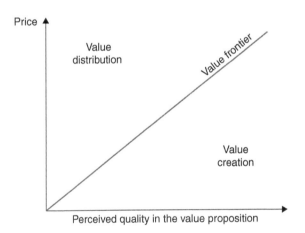

Figure 10.2   The value map

which represents the expected value for each known offer, is the result of a cognitive trade-off between:

(a) the level of satisfaction that the customer associates with the set of perceived benefits of the offering;
(b) the price, or rather, the cost-sacrifice associated with buying and enjoying these benefits, taking into consideration both monetary

(price paid, installation costs, management costs, etc.) and non-monetary components (seeking information, learning, etc.).

A value bisector thus divides the Cartesian diagram into two areas:

(a) The upper area defines the set of products or services offered under conditions that raise customer perceptions of negative value, because they are proposed at a higher price than the overall perceived benefits.
(b) The lower area, asymmetrical to the previous area, identifies all those offers that generate added value for the customer, offered at a lower price level than the benefits perceived.

Phase 1 – The Movement Game within the Position Game

The Movement Game, which begins with the launch of an innovative value proposition, occasionally generates a new market. If this is the case, and there are no rivals, the firm should position its offering along the value bisector, where customers pay for exactly the value they perceive. Initially we'll assume the firm's offering is positioned in the center of the Cartesian diagram (Figure 10.3): average quality and average price.

Phase 2 – Imitation Game within Position Game: early followers and indirect competition

The success of the innovative firm encourages competitors to "jump on the bandwagon," activating an Imitation Game. So as to prevent the competitive confrontation from deteriorating into a price war, first

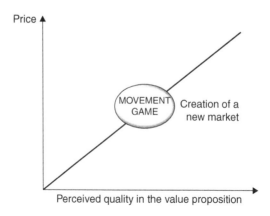

Figure 10.3 The creation of a new market

entrants generally try to differentiate their offer by maneuvering simultaneously on prices and benefits offered.

Figure 10.4 exemplifies this behavior, highlighting how some competitors can set themselves apart by proposing higher quality products at higher prices (upgrading strategy), while others redefine their offerings in a diametrically opposed direction, that is lower quality products at a lower price (downgrading). Still others maintain the same position as the innovator (parasitic imitation). In this way separate groups of strategic contenders are formed (A, B, and C in the figure), which exploit the opportunities of demand segmentation in order to compete indirectly with the innovator.

These firms, while serving different targets, offer equivalent value, in the sense that customers receive a level of quality exactly proportional to the price paid. This is expressed in the formula below:

$$\frac{Qb}{Pb} = \frac{Qa}{Pa} = \frac{Qc}{Pc}$$

Each offering in this ratio lies on the actual frontier of value, as we've defined it.

Phase 3 – The intensification of imitations: from indirect to direct competition

With the increase in the number of competitors, the situation described above evolves into a new form of direct competition. The objective

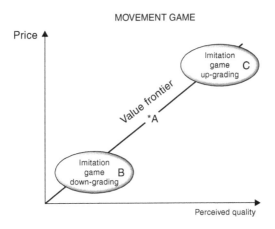

Figure 10.4 First stages of the Imitation Game: the indirect competition phase

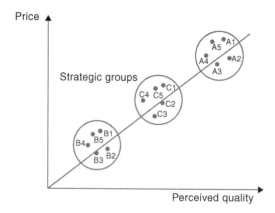

Figure 10.5 Continuous innovation: direct competition phase in strategic groups

now for firms is to positively differentiate themselves in the same strategic group, that is to say, in the eyes of the same target segment. As shown in Figure 10.5, for example, the maneuver of Competitor A2 aims to distinguish its value proposition in relation to direct competitors A1, A3, ..., A5.

Phase 4 – The Position Game and the maturity phase: extension and specialization maneuvers

The Position Game is a natural competitive development that begins with the Imitation Game and intensifies with market sharing strategies for establishing or defending positions conquered.

The Position Game may initially involve limited maneuvers directed at only one strategic group, as described in the context of the previous phase. Soon, however, fresh competitive maneuvers aim to serve broader customer segments, often timed when the first market slowdown occurs. Subsequently conflict will spread as firms seek to extend coverage of the value bisectors, namely by amplifying their product portfolios. In time, competitors will launch more and more lateral attacks to wedge themselves into the niches of an as yet untapped demand (Figure 10.6).

When the market is mature and demand remains relatively stable for several years (or even decades), two types of players tend to survive in the Position Game: generalist firms, namely those that have undertaken line extension maneuvers, and specialized firms focused on specific customers and their needs. The two groups can coexist at length without overlapping, although the generalist strategy is sustainable

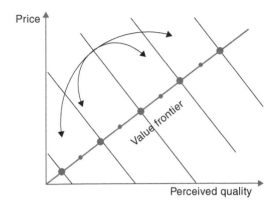

Figure 10.6   Extension and coverage of value bisector maneuvers

only by a limited number of firms (often three).[1] The competition, by contrast, tends to marginalize firms that position themselves in the middle of these two groupings: those not large enough to compete with the generalist giants and those not sufficiently specialized to "delight" a particular group of customers.

Generalist firms base their profitability on volume, by improving the efficiency and economies of scale they have achieved. Specialized firms, on the other hand, base their returns on very high margins thanks to unique and refined capabilities that satisfy, or even delight, narrow customer segments. The first have a market share of 10% to 40% or more; the latter may have shares well below 5%, but are essentially monopolistic in their niches. Empirical evidence shows that competitors with a share between 5% and 10% find themselves unable to leverage either volume or margins. As the Position Game intensifies, large generalist firms end up buying out these middle-sized enterprises. In fact, these companies would have done better to redefine their own mission, consider a strategic retreat (Section 9.12), and refocus on a precise target segment or niche market. Another option, financial resources permitting, would be acquiring or merging with another player, with the aim of growing rapidly and entering the exclusive club of generalist firms. The only alternative to these scenarios is a radical Movement Game to upset the current order of the sector.

Similarly, a specialized firm in this context should resist the temptation to grow too much, unless its goal is to move into a Movement Game. In the Position Game, the firm must stay focused on current customers, continuously innovating for them, concentrating on the brand, on customer experience and service, and on loyalty and strategic lock-in. In any case, fixed costs cannot and should not increase excessively, because this is the only way for firms to avoid the need for large volumes.

Phase 5 – The Position Game in a downslide: the price war

Since it may take a long time for a sector to reach its mature phase, sooner or later the cyclical nature of competition will lead to a downturn in demand, perhaps as a result of a new Movement Game. The hostilities, at this stage, move toward their climax.

The culmination of the competitive confrontation is manifested in all its violence when competitors implement maneuvers to increase value below the price–benefit equilibrium. In other words, they no longer position their offerings along the bisectors. In general, as we saw in Chapter 8, this means increasing the quality/price ratio, to the benefit of demand. As shown in Figure 10.7, this occurs when:

- low-end brands:
  (1) reduce price while maintaining quality (from B to B' in the figure); or
  (2) maintain the original price, developing higher quality products and services (e.g. the new Fiat 500);
- high-end brands:
  (1) increase the quality of their offer, but not the price; or
  (2) reduce the price while guaranteeing the same quality (from C to C' in the figure).

Increasing the quality/price ratio radicalizes the Position Game, projecting it toward the final frontier of value. When a competitor alters its value equation, it in fact generates a shadow in its own strategic grouping. All other contenders positioned in the vicinity are forced to imitate it, on pain of extinction. This will ultimately cause a migration toward the bottom of the current frontier of value: all competitors must align themselves to a new (higher) quality/price ratio, represented by segment B' in Figure 10.7. The example of the new Fiat 500 mentioned above abruptly placed the Mini in a competitive shadow, reducing its expected sales since 2008.

A price war is unleashed in a market when a firm realizes that it's become too difficult to enhance its value proposition any further by acting on the numerator alone (that is, benefits and quality, represented on the horizontal axis in Figure 10.8). In this case, the intensity

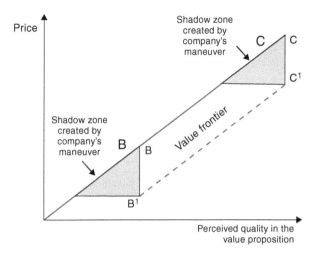

Figure 10.7 Maneuvers to increase the quality/price ratio: generating competitive shadows

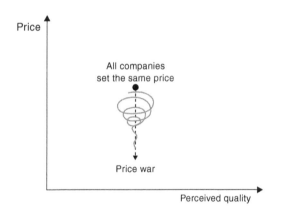

Figure 10.8 The price war: when perceived quality is no longer a success factor

of conflict rises rapidly, particularly if competitors with a more favorable cost structure use pricing as a weapon to win over greater market share.

This maneuver is always a dangerous one because of the ease and speed of a potential response. This violent move allows the initiating firm to achieve a profit margin only if it can develop sales while maintaining costs significantly below the cost of sales. In this respect, as

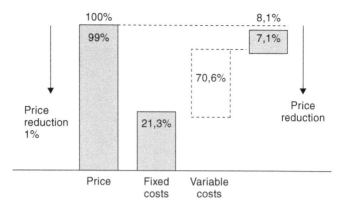

Figure 10.9 The effects of reducing retail price on profit

we can see in the generic example given in Figure 10.9, the decline of a single percentage point in price, without a reduction of costs and/or an increase in sales volume[2] (a realistic hypothesis should an opponent react immediately), will result in a drastic drop in profits (over 12% in the case illustrated).

Price wars, as mentioned above, are based on the assumption that significant market share can be gained by leveraging the advantages of the learning curve. In favorable market scenarios, when demand exceeds supply, the firm can sustain the decrease in profit caused by a price reduction. By doing so the firm exploits the elasticity of demand to grow its own sales and achieve the economies of scale and learning necessary to cut costs.

When, however, the market enters into a phase of economic downturn and production capacity decreases, the effects of a price war become dramatic. Marginal competitors, less equipped to sustain large losses, abandon the market. Even after this happens the remaining firms still find it difficult to increase prices to recover the losses incurred during the conflict. This is particularly true when customers do not show high brand loyalty or do not perceive the replacement costs they will incur to switch to other offers. In Chapter 8, for example, we already mentioned the case of a price war over online music: when Yahoo launched its new low-cost, unlimited access music service, the entire industry lost part of its value, with no winners. Apple, Warner Music, Napster, Real Networks, and Yahoo all saw their share values decrease.

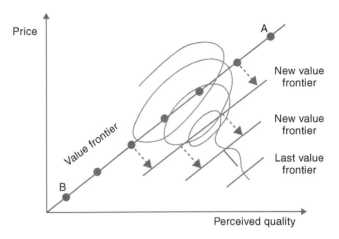

Figure 10.10 Moving toward the final frontier of value

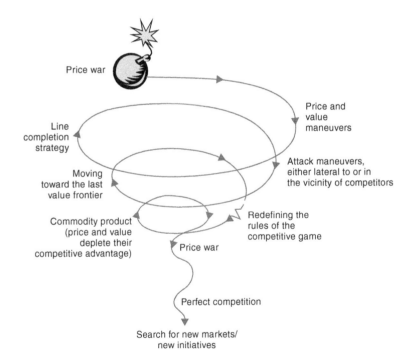

Figure 10.11 The spiral of competitive confrontation based on the price/value ratio

The disastrous consequences of a price war, therefore, serve as a warning for firms, which should seek other approaches to competitive confrontation before turning to this last resort.

Phase 6 – The final frontier of value[3]

Classical economists define "perfect competition" the final frontier of value. In this scenario, all rivals offer products equivalent in price and quality; no one has a specific competitive advantage and profits are nil. The price war has leveled marginal revenues and marginal costs; the two are now equal.

The evolution of the market toward the final frontier begins when firms pursue maneuvers to increase the quality/price ratio, sometimes acting on the numerator, sometimes on the denominator, sometimes on both by offering more for less. In this way, players upset the balance between benefits and sacrifices required from the customer – an equilibrium effectively summarized by the popular expression: "You get what you pay for." When competitive conflict in a sector escalates, we can say: "You get more than what you pay for." Thus, the sector is dramatically propelled toward the final frontier of value. The consequences are illustrated in Figure 10.10 above.

The result of these maneuvers is that the frontier of value will tend to move toward the right, forcing all competitors to match the new positions. These behaviors trigger a continued migration, pushing the new boundary further and further, until the market reaches the final frontier. At this point, all products are offered at more or less the same quality and price, to the maximum benefit of the customer.

Not all sectors evolve toward the final frontier in the same way or at the same speed. There is no doubt, however, that if the competitive situation does not attenuate confrontation (limited conflict), or does not move toward market regeneration (Movement Game), then the spiral toward the last frontier is unstoppable. This will become the black hole into which firms and industrial sectors will descend if they do not succeed in relaunching their destinies toward a new orbital position, to refer back to our simile in Chapter 1. By the same token this scenario can become the stimulus for excellent firms to find new ways to compete or new initiatives with which to pursue their mission through a new cycle of the Competition-Based View.

Notes

1 The Revolution in Competitive Games

1. Extant customer-centric theoretical contributions are myriad. Among others, noteworthy are: Srivastava, Shervani, Fahey (1998) and for the Italian school, Valdani and Busacca (1999).
2. Grant (1991 a e b); Barney (1991); Wernerfelt (1984); Penrose (1995); Rumelt (1984); Barney (1986); Jacobsen (1988); Teece, Pisano, and Shuen (1997); Peteraf (1993); Boschetti and Sobrero (1996); Sciarelli (1997); Ancarani (1999); Verona (1999).
3. According to analysts at the research firm "iSuppli", per unit production costs for PS3 at launch were estimated at approximately $800, which would result in a net loss of around $200 for every console sold. Naturally, these costs would plummet due to the effect of economies of experience; also, most of the profits are actually generated by subsequent sales of games and accessories.
4. Tushman and O'Reilly III (1997); Christensen (1997); Iansiti (1998).

2 The Movement Game: Breaking Down Orthodoxies

1. As Nardone observed (2003), "Winning without a fight also means having reached a level of strategic capability to generate in any adversary not only fear, but respect and admiration, to the point that they would not even dream of the idea of a confrontation. The aim is not to appear invincible, but as a model to be followed, not leveraging on power but on admiration" *Riding the Tiger*, ed. Ponte and Grazie, p. 17.
2. Valdani (2000).
3. Downes and Mui (1998).
4. Steinbeck (1962).
5. We recall here the timeless words of Schumpeter who described the capitalist process as "an organic process of transforming the industry, revolutionizing economic structures from within, relentlessly destroying the old and relentlessly creating the new" (Schumpeter, 1942). Figure 2.5 conveys precisely Schumpeter's idea of creative destruction.

3 The Maneuvers of the Movement Game

1. Sherman and Shultz (1998).
2. Drucker (1985).
3. Foster (1986); Afuah (2003).
4. Mahajan and Banga (2006).
5. Silverstein (2006).

6. Kumar (2006).
7. Kim and Mauborgne (2005).
8. Kim and Mauborgne (1999).
9. See the literature on the experience economy (Pino and Gilmore 1999), and experiential consumption (Castaldo and Botti 1999; Soscia I., 2001).
10. Bosshart (2006).
11. Kotler and Trias de Bes (2008).

4 The Barriers to Change

1. Sheth (1985).
2. Itami (1988).
3. Henderson and Cockburn (1994).
4. Verona (1999).
5. Teece, Pisano, and Shuen (1997).
6. Warglien (1990).
7. Iansiti and Clark (1994).
8. Eisenhardt and Brown (1998).
9. On the theme of customer barriers and adoption stimuli see also Arbore (2007).
10. Parasuraman (2000).
11. Rogers (1983); Moore (1995). Rogers' work was inspired by Ryan and Gross's (1943) classic study.
12. The tools proposed here focus on the evaluation of an innovation with reference to "barriers erected by customers" dealt with in this chapter. Assessment of the risk of the firm's portfolio of innovations, on the other hand, refers to the tool introduced at the conclusion of the previous chapter (Section 3.19).
13. Valdani, Ancarani, and Castaldo (2001).
14. "Smart Phones are Edging Out Other Gadgets," The Wall Street Journal, 24 March 2009
15. Valdani (2000).
16. See Brandengurger and Nalebuff (1996); Gomesasseres (1996); Segic (2001); Dussauge, Garrette B, and Mitchell (2000); Robbins and Finley (1998).
17. Simmel (1990).
18. Rafii and Kampas (2002). See also Christensen (1997).

5 Defense Strategies in the Movement Game

1. D'Aveni (2002).

6 The Imitation Game

1. Schnaars (1994).
2. See, among others, Shapiro and Varian (1999).
3. See among others: Hopkins, Kontnik, and Turnage (2003).

4. Lippman and Rumelt (1982); Rivkin (2000); Szulanki (1996); Ounjian and Carne (1987).
5. Levitt (2006).
6. Bikhchandani, Hirshleifer, and Welch (1992).
7. In the neoinstitutionalist vein, see DiMaggio and Powell (1983).
8. See, for example, Fligstein (1985 and 1991).
9. Porter (1979, p. 217). Cited in Lieberman and Asaba (2006).
10. Bernheim and Whinston (1990).
11. Empirical evidence for the efficacy of this strategy is scarce as we go to press.
12. Schneider et al. (1992).
13. Teece (1987).
14. Mansfield, Shwartz, and Wagner (1991).
15. Jacobson (1992).
16. Classification freely adapted from Schnaars (1994).
17. The classification is freely adapted from Hopkins et al. (2003).
18. Shapiro and Varian (1999).

7 Creating Barriers to Imitation

1. Porter and Robertson (1980).
2. Ibid.
3. Robinson and Fornell (1985).
4. Schmalensee (1982).
5. MacMillan (1983).
6. Mainkar, Lubatkin, and Schulze (2006).
7. Itami and Roehl (1987).
8. Salop (1986).
9. Tirole (1988).

8 The Position Game

1. The idea of three-dimensional representation of competitive dynamics is adapted from Cooper (1995).
2. Jackson (2007).
3. Vermeulen (2005).

9 Offensive and Defensive Maneuvers in the Position Game

1. Enthusiasts, please see Sun Tzu, (1963); Von Ghyczy, Von Octinger, and Bassford C., (2001); Pezzy (1990); Laurie (2001); Kotler and Achrol (1984); Clemons and Santamaria, (2002).
2. Sims, J. T. (1986), "Japanese Market Entry Strategy at Work: Komatsu vs. Caterpillar," *International Marketing Review*, Vol. 3, pp. 21–32.
3. This assertion does not exclude the possibility that a firm can outperform an incumbent. However, we emphasize the commitment and capabilities

that a firm must deploy to come out a winner in a head-on confrontation. In order to demonstrate the tactical primacy of defense, we can refer to the previous example with 2000 strong Army A facing Army B with 1000 soldiers on the battlefield. This time, thanks to B's greater defensive capabilities and fortification, we assume this army will suffer one casualty for every 15 shots fired by A, while A will suffer one casualty for every three shots fired by B. After the first volley, A's forces would drop to 1667 [= 2000 – (1000 × 1/3)], while B's would be reduced to 867 [= 1000 – (2000 × 1/15)]. After the second round, A would have 1378 soldiers and B 756. After the third volley, the soldiers on the field would number 1126 for A and 664 for B; after the fourth, 905 for A and 589 for B; after the fifth, 709 for A and 529 for B. The numerical superiority of A has already fallen from 2 to 1 to only 1.3 to 1. After the sixth round of fire the opposing forces would be approximately equal, while after the seventh the tide would turn in favor of B, which after the eighth round would actually have twice as many soldiers as A. The competitive game would see a total turnaround in favor of the defender, even though this army was the smaller one at the outset of the battle.

4. *"Igitur qui desiderat pacem, praeparet bellum"* – the original Latin of the famous words by Vegetius, from his *Epitoma Rei Militaris* (4th century).
5. Bertoli (1988).
6. Kotler and Achrol (1984).
7. Buzzell and Gale (1987).
8. Best (2000).
9. For an example of these models see Roberts, Nelson, and Morrison, Marketing Science, 24(1), 2005.
10. *LePage's, Inc. v. 3M*, 324 F.3d 141 (3rd Cir. 2003). In the end, LePage was awarded $68 million in damages.
11. Guatri (1974), p.39.
12. Porter (1980), p.92.
13. Vaccà (1985).

10 The Final Frontier of Value

1. Sheth and Sisodia (2002).
2. To calculate the necessary increase of volumes, see the formula in Chapter 9, Section 9.4.
3. D'Aveni (1994).

Bibliography

Abernathy W.J., Utterback J.M. (1978), "Patterns of industrial innovation", *Technology Review*, June–July, pp. 40–47.

Afuah A. (2003), *Innovation Management*, Oxford University Press, Oxford.

Ancarani F. (1999), *Concorrenza e analisi competitiva. Una prospettiva d'impresa*, Egea, Milano.

Arbore A. (2007), *Il mercato family per la banda larga. I driver e gli ostacoli all'adozione*, Egea, Milano.

Barney J. (1986), "Strategic factor markets: expectations, luck and business strategy", *Management Science*, 42.

Barney J. (1991), "Firm resources and sustained competitive advantage", *Journal of Management*, 17.

Bernheim B., Whinston M.D. (1990), "Multimarket Contact and Collusive Behavior", *Rand Journal of Economics*, 21(1), pp. 1–26.

Bertoli G. (1988), "Le manovre concorrenziali nei settori concentrati", in Vicari S. (a cura di), *Analisi della concorrenza e strategie concorrenziali*, Unicopli, Milano, cap. 8.

Best R.J. (2000), *Market-based Management*, Prentice Hall, Englewood Cliffs.

Bikhchandani, S., Hirshleifer, D., Welch, I. (1992), "A Theory of Fads, Fashion, Custom, and Cultural Change as Informational Cascades", *Journal of Political Economy*, 100 (5), pp. 992–1026.

Booz, Allen, Hamilton (1968), *Management of New Products*, Booz, Allen and Hamilton Inc., Chicago.

Boschetti C., Sobrero M. (1996), "Risorse e vantaggio competitivo. Ricorsi storici o nuove prospettive di analisi", *Economia e Politica Industriale*, n. 91.

Bosshart D. (2006), *Cheap: the Real Cost of the Global Trend for Bargains, Discounts & Customer Choice*, Kogan Page, London.

Brandengurger A.M., Nalebuff B.J. (1996), *Cooperation*, Currency Doubleday, New York.

Brown S.L., Eisenhardt K.M. (1998), *Competing on the Edge*, Harvard Business School Press, Boston.

Busacca B. (2000), *Il valore della marca tra postfordismo ed economia digitale. Accumulazione, ampliamento, attivazione*, Egea, Milano.

Buzzell R.D., Gale B.T. (1987), *The PIMS Principle*, The Free Press, New York.

Castaldo S., Botti S. (1999), "La dimensione emozionale dello shopping. Una ricerca esplorativa sul ruolo del punto di vendita", *Economia & Management*, n. 1, gennaio.

Castaldo S., Verona G. (1998), *Lo sviluppo di nuovi prodotti. Teoria e analisi empiriche in una prospettiva cognitiva*, Egea, Milano.

Charan R., Tichy N.M. (1998), *Every Business is a Growth Business Times*, Times Business, New York.

Christensen C.M. (1997), *The Innovation's Dilemma*, Harvard Business School Press, Boston (ed. it. *Il dilemma dell'innovatore*, FrancoAngeli, Milano, 2001).

Clark K.B., Fujimoto T. (1991), *Product Development Performance*, Harvard Business School Press, Boston.

Clemons E.K., Santamaria J.A. (2002), "Maneuver warfare: Can modern military strategy lead you to victory?", *Harvard Business Review*, April, 80 (4).

Cook V.J. (1983), "What should language teaching be about?", *ELT Journal*, 37(3), pp. 229–234.

Cook V.J. (1985), "The Net Present Value of Market Share", *Journal of Marketing*, 49 (3), pp. 49–63

Cook V.J. (2006), *Competing for Customers and Capital*, Thomson Learning, Mason.

Cooper R. (1995), *When Lean Enterprises collide*, Harvard Business School Press, Boston.

Costabile M. (2001), *Il capitale relazionale dell'impresa. Gestione delle relazioni e della customer loyalty*, McGraw Hill, Milano.

Coveney P., Highfield R. (1995), *Frontiers of Complexity*, Columbine, New York.

D'Aveni R.A. (1994), *Hypercompetition: Managing the Dynamics of Strategic Maneuvering*, The Free Press, New York.

D'Aveni R.A. (2002), "The empire strikes back: Counterrevolutionary strategies for industry leaders", *Harvard Business Review*, November.

Day G.S. (1984), *Strategic Marketing Planning*, West Publishing, St. Paul.

Day G.S., Schoemaker P.J.H. (2006), *Peripheral Vision: Detecting the Weak Signals That Will Make or Break Your Company*, Harvard Business School Press, Boston

Day G.S. (2007), "Is It Real? Can We Win? Is It Worth Doing? Managing Risk and Reward in an Innovation Portfolio", *Harvard Business Review*, December, pp. 110–120.

DiMaggio P.J., Powell W.W. (1983), "The Iron Cage Revisited: Institutional Isomorphism and Collective Rationality in Organizational Fields", *American Sociological Review*, 48(2), 147–160.

Downes L., Mui C. (1998), *Killer Application*, Harvard Business School Press, Boston.

Drucker P. (1985), *Innovation and Entrepreneurship: Practise and Principles*, Wiley New York.

Dussauge P., Garrette B., Mitchell W. (2000), "Learning from competing partners: Outcomes and durations of scale and link alliances in Europe, North America and Asia", *Strategic Management Journal*, 21, pp. 99–126.

Eisenhardt K.M., Brown S.B. (1998), "Time pacing: Competing in markets that won't stand still", *Harvard Business Review*, March–April, pp. 59–69.

Fine C. H. (1998), *Clockspeed: Winning Industry Control in The Age of Temporary Advantage*, Perseus Books, New York.

Fligstein N. (1985), "The Spread of the Multidivisional Form among Large Firms, 1919–1979", *American Sociological Review*, 50(3), pp. 377–391.

Fligstein N. (1991), "The Structural Transformation of American Industry: an Institutional Account of the Causes of Diversification in the Largest Firms, 1919–1979", in Powell W.W., DiMaggio P.J. (Eds), *The New Institutionalism in Organizational Analysis*. The University of Chicago Press, Chicago & London, pp. 311–336.

Foster R. (1986), *Innovation: The Attacker's Advantage*, Summit Books, New York.

Gambardella A. (1995), *Science and Innovation*, Oxford University Press, Oxford.

Gatignon H., Reibstein D.J., (1999), "Formulating Competitive Strategies" in *Wharton on Dynamic Competitive Strategies*, edited by George Day and David Reibstein, Wiley, New York.

Gomes–Casseres B. (1996), *The Alliance Revolution*, Harvard University Press, Cambridge.

Grant R.M. (1991a), *Contemporary Strategy Analysis. Concept, Techniques, Applications*, Blackwell, Oxford (ed. it. *L'analisi strategica per le decisioni aziendali*, Il Mulino, Bologna, 2006).

Grant R.M. (1991b), "The resource based theory of competitive advantage: Implications for strategy formulation", *California Management Review*, Spring, pp. 114–135.

Guatri L. (1974), *Il Marketing*, Giuffrè, Milano.

Henderson R., Cockburn I. (1994), "Measuring competence? Exploring firm effects in pharmaceutical research", *Strategic Management Journal*, 15, pp. 63–84.

Holland J. (1996), *Hidden Order*, Addison Wesley, Reading.

Hopkins D.M., Kontnik L.T., Turnage M.T. (2003), *Counterfeiting Exposed*, Wiley, New York.

Iansiti M. (1998), *Technology Integration*, Harvard Business School Press, Boston.

Iansiti M., Clark K. (1994), "Integration and dynamic capability: Evidence from product development in automobiles and mainframe computers", *Industrial and Corporate Change*, 3 (3), pp. 557–605.

Itami H. (1988), *Le risorse invisibili*, Isedi, Torino.

Itami H., Rohel T. (1987), *Mobilizing Invisible Assets*, Harvard University Press, Cambridge.

Jacobsen R. (1988), "The persistence of abnormal returns", *Strategic Management Journal*, 9, pp. 415–430.

Jacobson R. (1992), "The Austrian school of strategy", *Academy of Management Review*, 17(4), pp. 782–807.

Kauffman S. (1995), *At Home in the Universe*, Oxford University Press, New York (ed. it. *A casa nell'universo*, Editori Riuniti, Roma, 2001).

Kim W.C., Mauborgne R.A. (1999), "Creating new market space", *Harvard Business Review*, January–February.

Kim W.C., Mauborgne R.A. (2005), *Blue Ocean Strategy: How to Create Uncontested Market Space and Make Competition Irrelevant*, Harvard Business School Publishing, Boston (ed. it. *Strategia oceano blu: vincere senza competere*, Etas, Milano, 2005).

Kotler P. (1997), *Marketing Management: Analysis, Planning, Implementation, and Control*, 9th edn, Prentice Hall, Upper Saddle River.

Kotler P., Achrol R. (1984), "Marketing strategy and the science of war" in Lamb R.B. (ed.), *Competitive Strategic Management*, Prentice Hall, Englewood Cliffs.

Kotler P., Trias de Bes F. (2008), *Il Marketing laterale. Tecniche nuove per trovare idee rivoluzionarie*, Il Sole 24 ore, Milano.

Kumar N. (2006), "Strategies to Fight Low-cost Rivals", *Harvard Business Review*, December, pp. 104–112.

Laurie D. (2001), *From Battlefield to Boardroom*, Palgrave, New York.

Lele M.M. (1992), *Creating Strategic Leverage*, Wiley, New York.

Levitt S.D. (2006), "An Economist Sells Bagels: A Case Study in Profit Maximization", *NBER Working Papers*, *12152*, National Bureau of Economic Research Inc., Washington, DC.

Lieberman M.B., Asaba S. (2006), "Why Do Firms Imitate Each Other", *Academy of Management Review*, 31(2), pp. 366–385.

Lippman S., Rumelt R. (1982), "Uncertain Imitability: An Analysis of Interfirm Differences in Efficiency Under Competition", *Bell J. Economics*, 13 (1982), 418–453.

MacMillan I.C. (1983), "Preemptive strategies", *The Journal of Business Strategy*, 4 (2).

Mahajan V., Banga K. (2006), *Il mercato che cerchi: la soluzione 86%*, Egea, Milano

Mainkar A., Lubatkin M., Schulze W. (2006), "Towards a product proliferation of entry barriers", *Academy of Management Review*, 31(4), pp. 1062–1076.

Mansfield E., Shwartz M., Wagner S. (1991), "Imitation costs and patents: An empirical study", *Economic Journal*, December.

Moore G.A. (1995), *Inside the Tornado*, Harper Business, New York.

Nardone G., (2003), *Cavalcare la propria tigre*, Ponte alle Grazie, Milano.

Ounjian M.L., Carne E.B. (1987), "A study of the factors which affect technology transfer in a multilocational multibusiness unit corporation", *IEEE Transactions on Engineering Management*, 34 (3), pp. 194–201

Parasuraman A., Colby C.L. (2001), *Techno–ready Marketing*, The Free Press, New York (ed. it. *Techno–ready marketing*, Sperling & Kupfer, Milano, 2001).

Penrose E. (1959), *The Theory of the Growth of the Firm*, Wiley, London.

Peteraf M. (1993), "The cornerstones of competitive advantage: A resource-based view", *Strategic Management Journal*, vol.14.

Pezzy L.T. (1990), *Offensive Strategy*, Harper Business, New York.

Pine A.J., Gilmore J. (1999), *The Experience Economy*, Harvard Business School Press, Boston (ed. it. *L'economia delle esperienze*, Etas, Milano, 2000).

Porter M.E. (1979), "The Structure within Industries and Companies' Performance", *Review of Economics and Statistics*, 61 (2), pp. 214–227.

Porter M.E., Robertson T.S. (1980), *Competitive Strategy: Techniques for Analyzing Industries and Competitors*, The Free Press, New York (ed. it. *Il vantaggio competitivo*, Edizioni Comunità, Milano, 1987).

Porter M.E. (1980), *Competitive Strategy: Techniques for Analyzing Industries and Competitors*, The Free Press, New York.

Rafii F., Kampas P. J. (2002), "How to Identify Your Enemies Before They Destroy You", *Harvard Business Review*, 80 (11), November, pp. 115–123

Ryan B., Gross N.C. (1943), "The Diffusion of Hybrid Seed Corn in Two Iowa Communities", *Rural Sociology*, 8, pp. 15–24.

Rivkin, J.W. (2000), "Imitation of Complex Strategies", *Management Science*, 46(6), pp. 824–844.

Roberts J. H. (2005), "Defensive Marketing: How a Strong Incumbent can Protect its Position", *Harvard Business Review*, vol. 83, issue 11, November, pp. 150–157.

Roberts J. H, Nelson C. J., Morrison P.D. (2005). A Prelaunch Diffusion Model for Evaluating Market Defense Strategies, Marketing Science 24 (1), pp. 150–164.

Robbins H., Finley M. (1998), *Transcompetion*, McGraw-Hill, New York.

Robinson W.T., Fornell C. (1985), "Sources of market pioneer advantage in consumer industries", *The Journal of Marketing Research*, 22 (3), August.

Rogers E. (1983), *Diffusion of Innovations*, The Free Press, New York.

Rumelt R. (1984), "Towards a strategic theory of the firm", in Lamb R.B., *Competitive Strategic Management*, Prentice Hall, Englewood Cliffs.

Rust R.T., Zahorik A.J., Keiningham T. L. (1996), *Service Marketing*, HarperCollins, New York

Salop S. (1986), "Practices that credibility facilitate oligopoly coordination", in Stiglitz J.E., Mathewson G.F. (eds), *New Development in the Analysis of Market Structure*, The MIT Press, Cambridge.

Schmalensee R. (1982), "Product Differentiation Advantages of Pioneering Brands", *American Economic Review*, 72 (3), June.

Schnaars S.P. (1994), *Managing Imitation Strategies*, The Free Press, New York.

Schumpeter J.A. (1934), *The Theory of Economic Development*, Harvard University Press, Cambridge. (Ed. origin. in tedesco, 1912).

Sciarelli S. (1997), *Economia e gestione dell'impresa*, Cedam, Padova (2a ed. 1999).

Scott J. (1991), *Social Network Analysis: a Handbook*, Sage, New York.

Segic L. (2001), *Fast Alliances*, Wiley, New York.

Senders S.J. (1999), "Mimetic identification: Ethnic German repatriation in post cold-war", unpublished doctoral dissertation, Cornell University, Berlin.

Shapiro C., Varian H.R. (1999), *Information Rules*, Etas, Milano.

Sherman H., Shultz R. (1998), *Open Boundaries: Creating Business Innovation Through Complexity*, Perseus Books, New York.

Sheth J.M. (1985), *Winning Back Your Market*, Wiley, New York.

Sheth J.M., Ram O. (1987), *Bringing innovation to market*, Wiley, New York.

Sheth J.M., Sisodia R. (2002), *The Rule of Three: Surviving and Thriving in Competitive Markets*, The Free Press, New York.

Silverstein M. J. (2006), *Treasure Hunt: Inside the Mind of The New Consumer*, Portfolio, London (ed. it. *Caccia al tempo: il nuovo consumatore tra lusso e hard discount*, Etas, Milano, 2006).

Simmel G. (1990), *The Philosophy of Money*, Routledge, New York.

Sims J.T. (1986), "Japanese Market Entry Strategy at Work: Komatsu vs. Caterpillar", *International Marketing Review*, 3, pp. 21–32.

Soscia I. (2001), "L'experience economy", in Valdani E., Ancarani F., Castaldo S. (a cura di), *Convergenza*, Egea, Milano.

Starbucks Coffee Company (2007), *Company Fact Sheet*, available from www.stardbucks.com.

Steinbeck J. (1939), *The Grapes of Wrath*, Viking Press, New York.

Stuart E.J. (2007), "Reaching for value: Creating value through acquisitions", *Journal of Business Strategy*, 28 (6), pp. 40–41.

Sun Tzu (1963), *The Art of War*, translated by Samuel B. Griffith, Oxford University Press, Oxford, England. (Lavoro originale risalente al 500 a.C.).

Sun Tzu, Sun Pin (1999), *L'arte della guerra e i metodi militari*, Neri Pozza Editori, Vicenza.

Szulanski, G. (1996) "Exploring internal stickiness: Impediments to the transfer of best practice within the firm", *Strategic Management Journal*, 17 (10), pp. 27–43.

Teece D.J. (1987) "Profiting from technological innovation", in Teece D.J. (ed.), *The Competitive Challenge: Strategies For Industrial Innovation and Renewal*, Ballinger, Cambridge, MA.

Teece D.J., Pisano G., Shuen A. (1997), "Dynamic capabilities and strategic management", *Strategic Management Journal*, 18, pp. 509–533.

Tirole J. (1988), *The Theory of Industrial Organization*, The MIT Press, Cambridge.

Tushman M.L., Anderson P. (1986), "Technological discontinuities and organizational environment", *Administrative Science Quarterly*, 31 (3), pp. 439–465.

Tushman M.L., O'Really III C.A. (1997), *Winning Through Innovation: A Practical Guide to Leading Organizational Change and Renewal*, Harvard Business School Press, Boston.

Vaccà C. (1985), "L'economia d'impresa alla ricerca di una identità", *Economia e Politica Industriale*, n. 45.

Valdani E. (1986–1995), *Marketing strategico*, Etas, Milano.

Valdani E. (1989), *Pricing*, Etas, Milano.

Valdani E. (1991), *Marketing globale*, Egea, Milano.

Valdani E. (a cura di) (1995), "Marketing", in Aa.Vv., *Enciclopedia dell'impresa*, Utet, Torino.

Valdani E. (2000), *L'impresa proattiva*, McGraw–Hill, Milano.

Valdani E., Ancarani F., Castaldo S. (2001), *Convergenza. Nuove traiettorie per la competizione*, Milano, Egea.

Valdani E., Busacca B. (1999), "Customer Based View", in *Finanza Marketing e Produzione*, giugno.

Vermeulen F. (2005), "How acquisitions can revitalize companies", *MIT Sloan Management Review*, 46 (4).

Verona G. (1999), "A resource-based view of product development", *Academy of Management Review*, 24 (1), pp. 132–142.

Verona G., Ravasio O. (2003), "Unbundling dynamic capabilities: an exploratory study of continuous product innovation", *Industrial & Corporate Change*, 4.

Von Ghyczy T., von Octinger B., Bassford C. (2001), *Clausewitz on Strategy*, Wiley, New York.

Von Neumann J., Morgenstern O. (1944), *Theory of Games and Economic Behavior*, Princeton University Press, Princeton NJ.

Warglien M. (1990), *Innovazione e impresa evolutiva*, Cedam, Padova.

Wernerfelt B. (1984), "A resource-based view of the firm", *Strategic Management Journal*, 5.

Wieffels P. (2002), *The Class Companion*, Harper Business, New York.

Woodall T. (2004), "Why marketers don't market: rethinking offensive and defensive archetypes", *Journal of Marketing Management*, 20 (5/6), pp. 559–76.

Zook C., Allen J. (2001), *Profit from the Core*, Harvard Business School Press, Boston.

Index